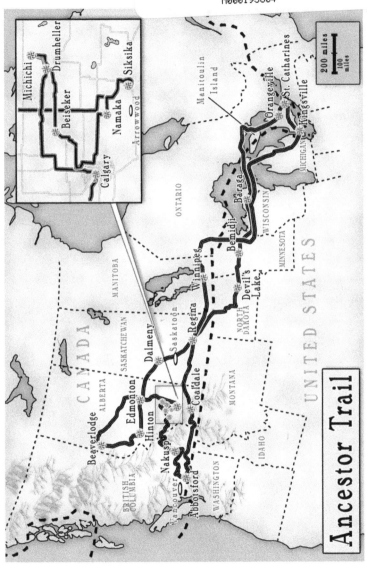

Michichi Drumheller

Beiseker

Michichi Namaka Siksika

Arrowwood

Calgary

200 miles
100 miles

Manitoulin
Island

Orangeville

St. Catharines

Kingsville

MICHIGAN

ONTARIO

Baraga

WISCONSIN

Bemidji

MINNESOTA

Winnipeg

MANITOBA

Devil's
Lake

Saskatoon

Dalmeny

Regina

NORTH
DAKOTA

CANADA

SASKATCHEWAN

Beaverlodge

Edmonton

ALBERTA

Coaldale

MONTANA

Hinton

UNITED STATES

Nakusp

IDAHO

Vancouver

Abbotsford

BRITISH
COLUMBIA

WASHINGTON

Ancestor Trail

John,
Trust the voice
of your heart to guide
you home.
Thanks.
Liz J.

≈ **A Memoir** ≈

CRASH LANDING
The Long Road Home

LIZ JANSEN

TRILLIUM WORDWORKS

Crash Landing is a work of nonfiction. Some names and identifying details have been changed.

For information about this title or to order other books and/or electronic media, contact the publisher:

Trillium Wordworks
Orangeville, Ontario, Canada
www.trilliumwordworks.com

ISBN: 978-1-987853-08-7

Cover photos:
Country Road: themacx
Author Photo: Jessie Steinberg

PROLOGUE

I'd seen the orange sign advising traffic that the 547 Bridge over Alberta's Bow River was out. No doubt the previous year's massive floods had damaged it as they swept through the valley. After a cursory glance, I assumed the warning applied to heavy trucks only and continued up the road. Motorcycles could get through where most vehicles couldn't. Two thousand miles from my Ontario home, I'd begun the fourth week of a twelve- to eighteen-month solo journey. At age sixty, I was on a quest to understand who I was before my culture *told* me who I was.

It turned out the sign applied to everyone. High waters had washed away an entire section of the bridge. I didn't want to backtrack all the way to the detour sign but didn't have many options. The roads in rural Alberta are set up in a grid as far as the eye can see. A side road I'd passed two and a half miles before the river might be a viable shortcut.

Township Road 205 led east out of the hamlet of Arrowwood, towards Blackfoot Crossing Historical Park, my destination for the day. As soon as I turned onto its loose, deep gravel I wavered and stopped. Some riders love the thrill of their motorcycle dancing under them on unstable surfaces. I'm not one of them, especially when I'm alone. Yet my training had prepared me to handle these conditions and my 1200cc Yamaha Super Ténéré was the right kind of motorcycle to take them on. If I came across this road in Central or South America, I'd have to manage it, so best put my fear aside and get on with it.

Standing on the foot pegs as I accelerated, I fixed my gaze far in the distance. No tire tracks interrupted the deep bed of golf ball-sized gravel. Although my trajectory averaged straight, at any moment I felt like I could be carried anywhere on—or off—that road. I prayed that my wheels would be on the right side of center if a farm vehicle careened toward me.

Every inch of the next eight miles terrified me beyond anything I'd experienced. It's normal for the front wheel to wobble as it seeks traction, and there's a technique to manage it when the wobble gets too wild: Speed up slightly to lift weight from the front end and stabilize the movement, then lean back to transfer weight to the rear of the motorcycle. As you decelerate to normal speed, resume the normal standing position. I had the first part down pat. The next step not so much. I refused to reduce the throttle, fearing the front tire would dig in again and throw me off. That meant that with every wobble correction, my speed increased. By the time the road turned ninety degrees to the right, eight miles later, I was going too fast to maneuver the corner and lost control. The handlebars slapped back and forth against the gas tank. My eyes instinctively looked around the bend to where I wanted to go and my motorcycle tried to follow and stay upright. In vain, I applied a combination of muscle and will to regain control, calling to the animal spirit accompanying me, "Jaguar, help me NOW!", but he'd already leapt to safety. The motorcycle careened over on its right side, bounced up and over, and with me still on it—my hands clenched around the handlebars and knees fused to the tank—

continued the skid on its left side. After crossing the full width of the road, we came to an abrupt stop down a small grade.

Miraculously, I jumped up from where I'd landed, brushed the dust off my riding gear, and surveyed the damage. Somehow, my motorcycle continued to run. Distorted engine guards had protected the engine, and my legs. Headlights, torn from their mounting, stared back at me, their wires trailing like roadkill guts. Misshapen handlebars rested at a curious angle. Chrome mounting brackets splayed skyward, the only remnants of a mirror and windscreen.

With my right hand, I reached over and hit the kill switch, turning off the engine. Standing in the ditch looking at the twisted wreckage, I knew my plans had changed. Moments ago, the companion I'd trusted with my life had given its life for me. I felt no anger or fear, only bewilderment about the turn of events. My incapacitated motorcycle and my own, now palpable, injuries gave me a new reality to work from. But my quest hadn't changed.

My left arm hung at my side. I could make small movements with my hand and forearm, but the slightest upper arm movement shot excruciating pain through my shoulder. My right thumb tried but could not respond to commands. I needed help.

A car and a large grain truck passed by in my peripheral vision. They'd driven over shards of windscreen and mirror strewn on the road but hadn't noticed me. I had come to rest below the grade and they mustn't have seen the crash. I needed to take charge, starting by making myself seen. That meant clambering up the side of the embankment to the road.

A plume approaching from the west signaled hope. I waved at the driver of the silver Ford F-150 pickup and found my Good Samaritan, Bill Cormier. A self-employed contractor on the way to a job, he pulled over to the far side of the road and hopped out. He couldn't figure out how a woman wearing a helmet and motorcycle gear had appeared in the middle of nowhere. Bill's day had just changed, too.

Hot and claustrophobic, I was desperate to get my helmet off. It had a modular chin piece, but my injured thumb couldn't undo the ratchet on the strap, nor could it work the button to flip the chin piece up. I instructed Bill to press the red button to release the chin guard, then pull the red tab to release the strap. Finally, he pulled it off my head. What a relief! Good gear had paid off.

Bill supported me down to where my bike lay. Under my guidance, he removed my tank bag and grabbed the few items in my pannier, including my laptop. Before leaving I wanted photos of the scene, but Bill didn't have a camera on his flip phone or know how to use my iPhone. Rather than try to explain, I asked him to steady me so I could take them. My right hand could hold the phone but not push the button, so I managed to press the button with my left fingers without moving my shoulder. Then I bid my motorcycle a quick farewell.

Bill had already pulled a U-turn, parked on the near side of the road, and opened the passenger door. The height of the bench seat presented a challenge because I couldn't grab anything to pull myself up. Somehow, between the two of us, we hefted me in, strapped on the seat belt, and got underway.

Bill outlined my options. He could take me to one of two small county hospitals, each twenty to thirty minutes away in different directions. Or, he could drive to a large teaching facility in Calgary, ninety minutes west. Calgary was the best and only option in my mind. I knew I had a complex shoulder injury and wanted the best trauma care possible. In a fortunate oversight, it didn't even occur to us to call an ambulance, which would have taken forever to arrive and then would have delivered me to one of the small hospitals.

We'd just abandoned a mangled motorcycle at the side of

the road. Someone might notice and call it in to local authorities, prompting them to search for the operator. Prudence dictated we notify the police, in this case the Royal Canadian Mounted Police (RCMP). Bill made that call, while on my phone I punched in the numbers for friends and family.

I didn't know the extent of the damage to my motorcycle yet, so wanted to get it to a shop in Calgary that I trusted. I also had a campsite set up fifteen miles south of the city, and I'd need to get that packed up. I'd used it as home base while I explored the area for two days, and paid for that night, expecting I would leave the area the next morning.

The only person in Calgary I could think to call for help was Paul Williams. I'd been trying to pin him down for an interview for several weeks for a client's newsletter. Ever since leaving a corporate human resources career in 2003 I'd freelanced, leading motorcycle tours and hosting motorcycle events. My work transitioned to consulting, writing, and counseling; then, designing webinars and training programs, all drawing from the symbolism and spiritual insights inspired by motorcycling.

When Paul and I learned we'd be at the same event in Nakusp, British Columbia, we'd agreed to talk there in person; however, those events have too many exciting distractions to be sitting down for business, and the interview never got done. But Paul knew I'd planned to head to the Calgary area after the event, so we agreed to meet there. That hadn't happened yet but soon would, thanks to the crash, minus the interview.

I also needed to notify my insurance company, but my adrenaline rush ended during that conversation and cut it short. An hour after the crash and still twenty minutes away from the hospital, I felt faint. Without warning, and still on the phone, I began babbling like a baby, completely incoherent. As much as I tried, I couldn't form a word.

Bill turned to me in alarm, not knowing what to do. I, too, was frightened, thinking I had a head injury.

The insurance rep kept his cool.

"Sounds like now's not a good time to talk. Call me tomorrow."

I laid my head against the headrest and took a few deep breaths. Thankfully, it passed, but I stopped making calls.

My email had caught Paul, preparing for a few days away, just in time. Bill waited with me in the Emergency Room until Paul could make the one-hour trip to the hospital. Here, I'd have my shattered shoulder rebuilt and begin my rehabilitation.

I'd crashed on August 27th, 2014, the date my maternal grandparents had married ninety-two years earlier. I was on the western border of the Siksika Nation (the community changed their name from Blackfoot reserve to Siksika Nation in the early 1990s), near the land where my father had spent much of his boyhood. Clearly, my ancestors and the land had stories I needed to hear. Two years would pass before I'd resume that trip. When I did, it was from an unexpected perspective, and with a clearer focus.

1

J uly 31st, 2016, my first day back on the motorcycle journey, got off to a shaky start. Because I planned to follow my grandparents' 1920s migration after they arrived in Western Canada as German-speaking Russian Mennonite refugees, I dubbed my route the Ancestor Trail. Day One would take me north from my home in Orangeville, Ontario, and up through the Bruce Peninsula. At Tobermory, its terminus, I'd take the two-hour ride on the MS Chi-Cheemaun ferry to Manitoulin Island. A campsite on the north side of the island, where I'd stayed before, would serve as my home for the night.

But two hours out of the garage, a crisis of confidence had me ready to turn around, return home, and scrap the whole idea. Although I travel a lot, getting out of the driveway is always hard. You're leaving the perceived known for the unknown. This time that inner resistance extended beyond the driveway.

It wasn't the physical or logistical part that had me anxious. I had a one-year-old Triumph Tiger named Trudy, the first bike I'd named, and we made a perfect match. She was the same sky-blue color as my Ténéré, the bike I'd crashed, and reminded me to dream big. Over the years, I'd taken care to select the fewest pieces of riding gear, clothing, and camping equipment that best suited my needs, added minimum bulk and weight, and worked in all kinds of weather. Even pared down, however, it added up. Packing was an art. The left pannier held my clothing and personal items; occupying the right were my heated jacket, spare gloves, footwear, tools, electronics, and a pair of two-pound barbells for shoulder exercises. My tent and sleeping bag got stuffed into a yellow dry bag strapped across the back rack. A blue dry bag, laid across the passenger seat, held camping and cooking utensils, and food. My cot, table, camp chair, and items I'd need during the day went into a yellow waterproof duffle that got placed on top of the two other bags, creating a comfy backrest. Two straps cinched down tight kept everything secure. A two-liter water reservoir, so I could sip while I rode, took up much of my waterproof tank bag but left room for incidentals like coins, hand sanitizer, and my camera. Even with a GPS, I like to have my bearings, so I folded a paper map to display the area I was riding through and slid it into the clear vinyl pocket on top of the tank bag.

My tailored black BMW riding suit was made of waterproof, abrasion-resistant textile, with impact-resistant armor (padding) at the back, shoulders, elbows, hips, and knees, and reflective strips on the arms and legs. The removable plum quilted liner was dressy enough to be worn as a casual jacket. Black BMW mid-calf waterproof and abrasion-resistant boots had extra reinforcement in the heels and shins. I had two pairs of gloves—for warm and cold weather—both BMW, black, and padded in the palms. A white Schuberth modular helmet protected my head. To increase the odds of other drivers noticing me, I wore a high-visibility mesh vest over my jacket. Underneath, merino socks, leggings, and a T-shirt helped keep me cool in the heat and warm in the cold. For coldest riding, an electric jacket and glove liners, which ran off Trudy's battery, fit under my jacket and gloves and kept me toasty.

This day it wasn't the riding that had me uneasy. True, it had taken nine months of recovery to get back on a motorcycle after the crash, then another month of patience, persistence, and courage to recharge my confidence to functional levels. What I questioned was whether I should even complete the interrupted trip.

Setting out on another solo motorcycle trip at age sixty-two didn't faze me. I'd started riding at sixteen, when I learned to ride my brothers' Honda Cub on my parents' fruit farm, and a motorcycle became my muse. Since then I'd logged many miles traversing Canada and the United States, most of them traveling solo in the past thirteen years. Every year, the exhilaration from riding intensified. It's like you think you can't love another person more than you do, yet as time goes on, that love deepens. So, too, it was for me with motorcycling.

Nothing matches the connection between Spirit and self that you feel when riding the open road. The endless blue sky permeates your being and dissolves any boundary between you and the elements. You can't help but smile as the wind caresses your face and delights you, dispelling all worries. The air informs you of subtle temperature changes as you dip into a valley or snake up a mountain. A drop in atmospheric pressure alerts you to an impending storm. Raindrops remind you that tears are part of life. The fragrant scent of lilacs or the sweet smells of fresh-cut summer hay invigorate every fiber of your being. Without effort beyond a slight twist of the throttle, you move through space and time, embraced by the energy of the land. You're free. Whole.

From the start, I knew with certainty that resuming my travels was right. But then, I'd also felt that confidence when taking the original trip—the one that had uprooted me from my known world. Now I had to manage my self-doubt to prevent it from eroding my conviction.

Since, again, I'd chosen to leave on the busiest weekend of the summer, I factored in an extra thirty minutes to reach the ferry. Still, the traffic I encountered on two-lane roads through farmland was heavier and slower than I anticipated. The lineup of cars, trailers, and RVs was too long and packed together to overtake.

Arriving at the dock in time for my reservation began to look doubtful. Heat, traffic, time pressure, and self-doubt injected stress into what was supposed to be an exciting and enjoyable day. Then along came another thing to worry about. I made a pit stop at a Tim Horton's donut shop to stretch my legs and use the restroom. My lower abdomen felt crampy and uneasy, and my urine looked cloudy. I panicked, convinced I had a bladder infection, a condition that had plagued me for years. I was taking prophylactic antibiotics but knew from experience the infection-causing organism could become resistant to specific medications, allowing the infection to return. My greater fear was that bladder infections can lead to a potentially life-threatening kidney infection if not treated in time. I worried about needing medical treatment while I traveled out of the country, knowing my insurance company would decline coverage because of a pre-existing condition. I'd only be traveling in the United States for a few days but didn't want things to flare up during that time. I also didn't want to ride when I felt unwell but hadn't expected to use my time buffer to deal with an illness this early in the trip.

When I'd started out two years ago, I'd also been taking medicine for a bladder infection. The symptoms had cleared several days into the trip, but I'd crashed soon after. Had I missed the message? It seemed like whenever I was ready to make a big step in this journey to find myself, I got knocked to the ground. Since the crash, I second-guessed myself about how to proceed on my life's journey. Was this illness another of those messages to wait longer before resuming my trip? Was I pushing myself too hard? Mind chatter ratcheted up my anxiety level beyond uncomfortable. The further I rode, as devastating as it felt, the more turning around seemed like the best idea.

Two long years of recovery, physical therapy, and sporadic feelings that life was on hold had passed since my crash. I'd done very little work in that time, focusing instead on healing. I'd so looked forward to getting back on the road.

How could this be happening?

Gary and Joanne, long-time friends I knew through riding, lived along my route about an hour south of the ferry. Before I committed to either continuing or turning around, I'd stop at their place and reassess my plans. They weren't expecting me, but as always welcomed me with open arms and hugs.

Ever compassionate, Joanne, a retired nurse, responded to my despair with a suggestion. "C'mon in and get cooled off. Then let me take you to the walk-in clinic. There's a doctor on call who can check you over."

I couldn't come up with a better idea, so I changed out of my riding gear and hopped into her car. As she drove, we chatted, and I tried to sort out my thoughts, bouncing my options off her.

To my surprise, my urine showed no signs of infection. That had never happened. Anytime I'd gone to the doctor with symptoms, I'd needed treatment. This time, an astute doctor treated me with empathy and kindness, reading the anxiety etched across my face. She offered compassion with wisdom. Physically, everything was fine. It was my fear that I needed to get under control.

The doctor's reassurance allayed my irrational thoughts and

fear-induced physical symptoms. Sure, I had a medical condition to watch, but my anxiety had blown it out of all proportion.

The ferry had long ago departed, but I rescheduled passage for the next day's early morning sailing. That gave me an evening to spend with friends and recharge my confidence.

THE SEEDS for this quest actually took root three years earlier, in 2013. That summer, I'd taken a six-week trip from my Orangeville home to the Pacific Northwest. I'd used it as an experiment to test the viability of living and working location-independent, traveling anywhere in the world, stopping wherever I wanted, for as long as I wanted.

A month before leaving, I'd found myself on The Four Winds website. Over the previous decade I'd researched many spiritual teachings, seeking a tradition that fit me. Those that resonated most came from the ancient wisdom taught by Dr. Alberto Villoldo. Educated as a medical anthropologist, psychologist, and shaman, he'd founded The Light Body School to train practitioners of Shamanic Energy Medicine. I'd devoured most of his books, finding the teachings simple, rational, and powerful. They held no dogma; rather, they espoused a way of living as one interconnected with all other life on earth, in harmony with the beings with whom we share it. I found the concepts grounded and practical, not "new-agey" or flaky.

In a stroke of serendipity, the first course in the program was being offered at the Stillwater Lodge in Park City, Utah, at the end of July. With my flexible itinerary, I could incorporate the course into my trip. I had nothing to lose, other than the cost of tuition.

Most attendees were staying in the lodge, but for budget reasons, and because I prefer to sleep outside, I pitched my tent at Jordanelle State Park, within walking distance of the lodge.

Light from floor to ceiling windows on two sides flooded the room in the lodge with a warm, calming glow. Our space overlooked the reservoir-turned-lake around which the park was built, and, further in the distance, the Rocky Mountains. As soon as I entered, I felt a strong sense of community, spiritual intimacy, and personal power. The evening fires under the stars awakened me. In all my years of attending the Mennonite Brethren (MB) Church of my youth, I had never felt anything so sacred. Here in Utah, with a group of strangers, I'd found the communion I sought.

I'd signed up for a three-day course aimed at people embarking on a journey of self-healing. However, we weren't yet through the first day when I understood I was there for another reason: I'd been called to study the five-day training designed for practitioners.

The Illumination process lies at the core of the Energy Medicine sessions. It's a technique to combust the heavy energy of emotional wounds and ancestral imprints, healing the wounds and freeing the energy for constructive use. It helps clear psychic and emotional memories that influence your thoughts, beliefs, and choices you carry without knowing it. During the sessions, the practitioner guides the client into a deep meditative, dream-like state. It's not unusual to feel physical sensations or connect with spirit or animal guides. For clarity, no plant medicine, used as a revered sacrament by shamans to induce spiritual awakening, was involved during this or any later sessions.

The practitioner begins with prayers to create a sacred, protected space. That's followed with skilled questioning and assessment to help the client articulate what burning issue she would like to receive guidance on. For my first practice session as a client, I sought an answer to two related, entrenched, and personal trouble spots: I wanted to know why I feared losing everything, and why I feared ostracism or even persecution if I exposed my true thoughts.

Imagine my shock when during the session, my maternal grandparents, Gerhard Reimer and Susa (Susanna) Koop, showed up in spirit form! It felt like being part of a Technicolor dream where I could interact with them. They were in their early sixties and looked like they'd come over after church, their black Vauxhall parked in the background. Gerhard wore a dark grey suit, white shirt, and tie, and held his fedora in his left hand. Susa's signature black hat topped her matching outfit—a wool, knee-length skirt with matching jacket fitted to her slender frame, a purse over her left arm, and black pumps.

Mennonite fundamentalist beliefs and Shamanism don't mix. In a Mennonite church, if I'd dared to ask, I would have learned that these practices came from the devil. But, thankfully, that wasn't the message Gerhard and Susa brought. They acknowledged my questions and let me know how grateful they felt that I was doing this introspective work—they had come to support me on my healing journey. They'd heard my questions and had no idea that the religious beliefs that had sustained them during years of terror in Russia had, thirty years later, created fear in me. They'd raised their children with the teachings that had been passed down to them and passed them on in the best way they knew.

When the practice session ended, I mentioned my experience to Chris, my teacher. She was not surprised.

"When we heal ourselves," she said, "we also heal those who have come before and those who have yet to come." I'd have plenty of opportunity to ponder her wisdom during the next six weeks of motorcycle travel.

That first course awakened my interest in understanding who I am. I felt a burning desire to peel back the layers of protection I had built to protect myself from getting hurt. The teachings might help me understand repetitive patterns I'd migrated to. Over-planning, then working too many hours in a day to honor my commitments plagued me. Achievements motivated me, even when they drew me beyond the scope of my priorities.

Learning to live and work from the road on that 2013 pilot trip challenged me more than I expected. To help pay for my meanderings, I'd pitched six travel stories to a national motorcycle magazine. I'd planned to leave lots of time open for reflection and contemplation, especially after completing my course, but commitments got in the way. A professional travel article takes time to research, photograph, and write. Before I knew it I was rushed, with little opportunity to sit back and relax.

I became frustrated seeing these familiar patterns emerge. Just because I looked as free as a bird didn't mean I wasn't pushing myself. I'd cram too many miles into a day and commit to unrealistic deadlines. The milieu had changed, but my engrained behavior hadn't. The setting wasn't the issue, and that's what I needed to understand. Irritation with myself for falling into old patterns transmuted into insights. For that reason, I deemed the 2013 trip a success.

The Shamanic Energy courses, the motorcycle journey, the constructive and counterproductive patterns I'd observed in myself, and the space to think all caused me to question how my culture and early teachings had shaped me. Why had I made the life choices that had gotten me to this point in life? How could I lead a more fulfilling life that answered the call of my spirit? What did that look like?

When my marriage ended in 2002, I'd become a resolute renter, living alone in apartments on country properties. After travels, I returned to "home base," as I had begun to refer to these Orangeville-area apartments, energized and inspired. I'd learned a lot about living and working from the road, enough to confirm I wanted to do more. I also wanted to continue my Energy Medicine studies.

The idea of a longer trip hatched after that exploratory excursion. Seeking ancestral history and Indigenous wisdom, I'd explore answers to the questions that had tumbled around in my mind, addressing my curiosity about how the experiences, beliefs, and teachings of my ancestors had shaped me.

Once you open up to new possibilities, the Universe sends more prompts. The teachings in the Energy Medicine training I'd begun came out of Peru. Nothing held me home, particularly if I could work from the road. I had no reason not to extend my trip and go all the way to South America. With a little luck, I'd study with the shamans in their home setting.

And so, what began as an idea for a quest by motorcycle to the U.S. Southwest grew into a plan for a twelve- to eighteen-month road trip through the Americas, beginning in 2014. With my Jaguar guide helping me track through the shadows and push my comfort zone, I'd have lots of time to explore life choices and patterns I'd been reluctant to face.

THERE COMES a point when you settle into the rhythm of the road, and in the three weeks leading up to my crash, I still hadn't found it. I tried to shake the unease, but something felt off. I'd not planned in too much detail for two reasons. The first was to stay open to destiny and the inevitable serendipity of solo motorcycle travel. The second was more banal: I was trying to break my pattern of over-committing and squeezing too much into a day. Breaking my word to someone else was unacceptable. Honoring my commitment to myself to prioritize and pace myself better seemed somehow less important.

Even though I'd scaled back and given myself plenty of leeway, I had fixed dates I was working with for the first three months on the road. First, I'd meet with and interview a Lakota author in South Dakota in early August. Later that month, I'd attend a Horizons Unlimited motorcycle travelers' gathering in British Columbia, where I'd give a presentation, and another in Yosemite in September. These events attracted the community of motorcyclists with whom I felt so at home. I looked forward to meeting friends who shared a zest for life and love of the road. After that, I could explore the Southwest before I'd have to head through Mexico and Central America, timing my travels with the seasons in the Southern Hemisphere.

By the end of the second week, I'd gone off track. The two days I'd expected to spend in South Dakota turned into five. To reach the Horizons Unlimited event in British Columbia in time, I'd have to go straight there. That meant back-tracking into Alberta for a travel article I'd committed to and to visit Dad's childhood farm. By walking the land, I'd hoped to get a sense of what his boyhood life had been like. I hadn't expected plans to unravel like this, at least not so soon.

Worse, I hadn't allowed enough time on that initial trip to explore my ancestral roots before leaving Canada. I'd placed the priority on exploring Indigenous wisdom. I thought understanding my relationship with the land would satisfy my craving for a closer connection with Spirit, something that hadn't happened through my Christian teachings. As it turned out, my crash, barely three weeks into that trip, set me on a completely different tack.

DURING MY TWO years of recovery, I'd had plenty of time to rethink my route. Initial planning for the 2016 Ancestor Trail route had me spending seven weeks on the road, meandering with purpose through Western Canada for six of them. The last week, I would come back to a retreat center in New York State's scenic and tranquil Hudson Valley. There I'd take the final course to complete my Energy Medicine Practitioner certificate, a fitting end to an epic journey. The course and the setting would create the perfect place to assimilate what I'd learned on the Ancestor Trail and the history I'd discovered during my recovery. South America didn't even come onto my radar.

I had two landmark dates: a Siksika Pow-wow in southern Alberta in August, and the Four Winds course in New York in mid-September. Everything between was flexible.

Both of my parental lines landed in Canada in the mid-1920s. My grandparents then migrated along different routes through Manitoba, Saskatchewan, and Alberta, before settling in the Niagara area of Ontario in the 1930s. There, the families, and my parents, met.

I intended to follow the Ancestor Trail from where they first settled to where they tried to reestablish their lives, again and again, until they made it. I wanted to walk the earth they had walked, trying to understand the lives of these penniless refugees in their twenties, fending for themselves in a new land. Those experiences, and those from the Russian homeland they fled under duress, had shaped me.

However, two weeks before my departure, in mid-July 2016, I realized a glaring omission in my route. I hadn't thought to visit Beaverlodge, the community in the Peace River district of northern Alberta where Dad had spent his first two years, and where his father had died. Dad had no recollection of these years and rarely talked of them. But this grandfather's blood ran through me. My DNA did not come from Dad's stepfather, whose name we carried and from whom his childhood memories originated. I *had* to include Beaverlodge on my route, but it meant adding 850 miles and scrapping the casual pace I'd envisioned. I had to get back down to southern Alberta in time for the Pow-wow and fit Beaverlodge in before that. I wouldn't miss either for anything. Yet, already I was falling back into the pattern of cramming too much into my schedule. It didn't escape me that the additional stress had contributed to physical symptoms, leading me to question the wisdom of taking this trip. It frustrated me, but what else could I do? At least I'd built in buffer time.

After that rough first day that ended at Gary and Joanne's home, I was back on the road early the next morning, headed for the ferry, physical and emotional strength renewed. I knew that Spirit journeyed with me, looking out for my best interests.

Traveling with me on my motorcycle was an entourage of unseen, energetic beings, their excitement matching mine. I pictured them with my mind's eye, as in a dream; they were in their late twenties, and I sensed their presence as vividly as if they were with me in person. My paternal and maternal grandparents Johann Klassen and Elizabeth Friesen, affectionately known as Liese (lee-za), and Gerhard Reimer and Susa Koop would stay with me for the duration of my travels. They sat behind me atop my yellow duffle, animated as they relived the old stories while I chauffeured. When they all got together to talk, especially when they got excited, they lapsed into *Plautdietsch*, the Low German language used for informal conversations, and I only understood the odd word. It was somewhat like a non-rider joining a conversation with a group of motorcyclists and not understanding the lingo. I had to remind them to please speak English.

More than a decade of introspection and learning had brought me to this point. My Shamanic Energy teachers had opened me to the experience of tapping into unseen energies that surround us. They'd always been available—I just hadn't been aware of them.

Johann, Dad's father, exuded a quiet strength. Tall with short dark hair, Johann wore the muscular physique of a farmer. He'd come into my consciousness mere weeks before I left, eager to go along on this mission.

Liese was the youngest of my grandparents. The shock of red hair that crowned her at birth forecast the fiery temperament that would become her ally and savior throughout her long life. She dealt with the prevailing superstition that her red hair, and mine, was a sign of the devil by calling it reddish brown. Yet she kept the hue into her nineties.

Susa was slight, fair, and willowy. She wore her waist-length medium brown hair in a *Schups*—a long braid, wrapped around the back of her head and kept in place with long hairpins. As the oldest grandchildren, my cousin Jude (Judy) and I, born two months apart to sisters, and more like sisters ourselves, reaped benefits, like overnight visits. We'd gape in awe when Susa let her hair loose to brush it and it would cascade down, almost to the floor.

True to form, Gerhard joked and talked rapidly, almost non-stop. When they had tea, he'd pour from his cup into his saucer and slurp from it like he always had. Susa would nudge him and giggle when he teased her. Johann and Liese contributed to the lively banter whenever they could get a word in. Johann had never met Gerhard and Susa in life, but here they were long-time friends, enjoying each other's company, bringing to light stories that had lain dormant for many years.

Besides my ancestors, four animal guides of my Energy Medicine practice came on board. Serpent—who brings renewal and teaches us how to shed behaviors and beliefs we've outgrown like she sheds her skin—curled up on the skid plate under the motor. Jaguar invites us to push our limits and boundaries and investigate the unknown. Jaguar, who represents the power of transformation and shows us how to leap into who we are becoming, sunned himself on the back luggage, behind my grandparents. Tiny Royal Hummingbird, keeper of ancestral wisdom and source of courage and guidance for epic trips, tucked into a crevice in the instrument panel. She teaches us how to trust the gentle calling we hear, and to trust we'll reach our destination, even if we must pass through tests and challenges. Eagle, who reminds us of our connection with Spirit, perched on either my front fender or shoulder. Eagle sees the finest details without losing track of the big picture and shows us how to avoid getting caught up in minutiae and old stories. He teaches us to spread our wings and soar over mountains we only dare to dream of. True to his nature, he'd often fly off, not wanting to miss an opportunity to glide the thermals.

Being sidelined by the crash had given me time to research my cultural history and the lives of my ancestors, while deepening my spiritual practice. My grandparents had extended the first overture of support for my reconciliation by appearing during my course in Utah three years before. Since then, they'd rarely been out of my mind. While Spirit was omnipresent, they and the four animal guides felt like a personal core team, available for support, guidance, and teaching. Other guides were also available; all I had to do was ask and listen. And to bring them on my motorcycle was sensational, like having someone along on the trip to share special experiences.

Many motorcyclists hang a gremlin bell—a small silver talisman—on the lowest part of their motorcycle to keep the road gremlins away. I'd had one on my Ténéré, but it had disappeared during the crash. That didn't compare to the powerhouse I carried now.

Thankfully, all these unseen beings didn't add physical weight to an already loaded bike. And I didn't have to pay an extra fare for my entourage. They'd come along simply as emotional and spiritual support, ready to pitch in when needed. I'd gotten off to a slow start on the Ancestor Trail, but now it was Day Two. I climbed onto Trudy, bowed my helmeted head in prayer, expressed gratitude for the journey, and prayed for safety. Then I started the ignition, released the clutch, and pulled away, waving good-bye to Gary and Joanne. Fueled by curiosity and a renewed passion for the quest, we headed to the ferry.

2

The dock was almost an hour's ride away, enough for the energy of dawn stirring the day awake to energize me as I rode north. Often booked solid during high season, the 143-vehicle capacity Chi-Cheemaun (Ojibwe term meaning *Big Canoe*), transports travelers between Ontario's Bruce Peninsula and Manitoulin Island. Knowing they can often shoehorn in one more motorcycle, I wasn't too concerned about waiting on standby. Sure enough, the attendant allowed another last-minute rider and me up the ramp and into the hold as the yawning hatch clanked shut.

Little communities form around designated motorcycle parking clusters, especially in odd-shaped areas too small for cars. Meeting and chatting with other riders made a delightful start to the voyage. Once I secured my bike and was comfortable it wasn't going to tip if the boat lurched, I headed for the top deck. There I could lounge and watch the world go by for the next two hours. Because I hadn't gotten as far as I expected yesterday, I planned to make up some distance today. I'd need my energy for a long day in the saddle. The Big Canoe shuddered as we set sail. Cautious optimism and excitement replaced yesterday's anxiety. We were off!

A two-hour boat ride and the familiar terrain I'd cross over the next seven weeks seemed tame compared to the journey my grandparents faced. What had they thought as they pitched and yawed to their new home? Emigration meant leaving behind the place their ancestors had called home for more than 100 years, as well as separation from their *Völklein*—a people with a distinctive linguistic, religious, and cultural-ethnic identity. But social and political events beyond their control had shattered their communities, so leave they did.

The water was as smooth as glass while we cruised past lighthouses on the rocky inland shore. Memories from the steamers that had brought my grandparents here had been agonizing. Gerhard and Susa had buried eight-month-old Ellie, their only child, the day before they got on the train. Shortly before leaving a year later, Johann and Liese's two-year-old Elizabeth and eight-month-old Anna had died from typhus. Both women spent the crossing in their third-class quarters, seasick. Over and above typical nausea, they must have been wracked with grief and guilt.

The stoic men handled it differently, sitting out on the deck. They, too, were heartsick and lonely, although neither missed a meal. Gerhard and Susa's oldest son, my Uncle Ernie, had inherited Gerhard's journal of those days. Twenty-four years old, he'd written, *And here I am, leaving the country of my birth behind, just married, buried my first child, going to a strange country with strange people, and a strange language. What could God possibly have in store for me now?*

Gerhard knew he could find solace in song, so he'd assemble whoever was available and they'd sing praises to God for delivering them from hell on earth.

Still in their youth, they'd already lived a lifetime. Malnourished and impoverished, they had little left to lose. In their home country, they'd seen serial atrocities, and had left friends and family in a volatile situation. They mistrusted authority. Their new land held hope and opportunity, yet could they trust it? Russia was once a land of opportunity, too.

To try and describe their last raw, terrifying, and grief-stricken years in Russia would never come close to their reality. Yet the energy of those experiences lived in me. On this trip, when I was almost the age where I could be grandmother to these courageous souls, I wanted to place myself in the shoes they had worn as young people. What political, religious, and societal forces shaped nations and peoples? And me?

THE CAPTAIN'S voice crackled over the loudspeaker, announcing we were about to dock. We'd reached port on the southern side of Manitoulin Island, a geological formation in the waters of northern Lake Huron. It was time to gather my things and return below deck to where my motorcycle awaited. Equally eager to get on the road were my grandparents and my animal guides. For the next hour, I'd be crossing the largest freshwater island in the world, home to seven First Nations communities. Oral Tradition says that when the Great Spirit created Manitoulin, it was so beautiful He called it home. You feel that spiritual energy as soon as your front wheel rolls off the ramp and touches the ground. It stays with you your entire visit.

I hoped to travel almost 500 miles on this day of the journey, so I didn't have a lot of time to stop, but even traveling across the island invigorated me. Underlying rock pushed through the thin layer of topsoil in many places, exposing millions of years of life to current elements. In other areas, hardwood forests graced the roadsides. Gentle curves in the road followed the contours of the terrain. Manitoulin's rugged topography and natural beauty emanated peacefulness and strength.

An intriguing single-lane swing bridge, the only way off Manitoulin's north side by road, crosses the convergence of Lake Huron's North Channel and Georgian Bay. Even if you have to wait your turn for oncoming traffic to pass, the surrounding picturesque waterways and land formations make the wait enjoyable, especially under the sunshine and blue skies that graced the day. Once across the bridge, thirty-two miles of curvaceous two-lane highway cut through red granite rock, forests, and small lakes, culminating at the Trans-Canada Highway (TCH), where I'd turn left and head west. As the name suggests, it connects the country from Atlantic to Pacific. While I'd try and stay on back roads as much as possible, sometimes the TCH was unavoidable.

Physically I felt strong, with only a lingering trepidation about the risk of health issues. At this early stage of my trip, I was interested in the most efficient and expedient way of getting to Dalmeny, Saskatchewan—Gerhard and Susa's first home in Canada and my first stop on the Ancestor Trail. When you're traveling great distances, saving sixty miles—as I could by going through northern Michigan, Wisconsin, Minnesota, and North Dakota—makes a difference. I'd travel in the States for the next three days until I crossed back into Canada.

A three-hour ride west on the TCH began along the North Channel, where intermittent stretches offer gorgeous views of sparkling water lapping at rocky shores. Years after they'd first arrived here, my grandparents had laughed in retrospect, but when they first came through on the train, they were pretty scared. Houses which looked modest but acceptable to me had shocked them. They'd lived in sprawling red brick homes and couldn't believe people lived in "wooden shacks." They wondered what kind of life awaited them in this country. Where would they live? Would they find work to earn a living? Mennonite immigrants had been obligated to promise to farm, so as not to take away jobs in the city, but how could they farm on this rocky, rugged land?

I could see how they'd think that, especially when they'd been told they were traveling to land similar to what they'd come from. But gratitude overcame trepidation once they reached the prairies, reminiscent of the Russian steppes of their home, albeit free of the scars of revolution and anarchy. They knew how to inhabit that land.

The TCH swung inland on the final leg to the international border. Canadians tend to have a laissez-faire attitude about the border, especially when you've always lived close to it, as I have. This time was different. It wasn't the security check or even health insurance that concerned me. If I got sick I could return to Canada. It was the recognition that the border was a symbolic threshold, a point of no return. This trip of self-discovery would take me to places within where I'd never dared to venture. Was I ready this time?

Crossing the border out of Russia had been a monumental experience for my grandparents. They were leaving the land of their ancestors for a promise of freedom. They had two choices: stay and face almost certain torture, starvation, and death, especially for the men, or take a chance on the unknown. A strange place halfway around the world was their best chance for survival. Riding across the border seemed a pittance by comparison.

"Carry on," said the border guard as he handed over my passport.

IT's unusual for me to describe scenery as boring, but that's the only description for the next 100 miles of road through

Michigan. The road engineer must have shot an arrow at the shortest distance between two points—exactly what I needed. Straight as that arrow, the road cut into the forest, creating a tunnel through the trees, parting only enough to allow the sun's rays to reach the road. Because this kind of monotony threatens the vigilance needed to spot animals and oncoming traffic, my strategy on this stretch of road became to go as fast as I could without attracting the sheriff, taking breaks at regular intervals to hydrate and stay alert, and remaining patient. Even my animal guides were subdued, sleeping as they basked in the afternoon sun. It gave me the opportunity to reflect on my grandparents' early years in Russia, before external events shattered their world.

All four were born at the turn of the last century, when Mennonite prosperity enjoyed an all-time high, especially in the Molochna, the largest and most prosperous Mennonite colony in Russia. Highly productive farms, plenty of food, industry, education, health care, and a fledgling arts program hallmarked this Golden Age. Peace ruled in the Empire, or so they thought, and Mennonites, who had created economic prosperity since they'd migrated from Prussia in the late 1700s and early 1800s, enjoyed the favor of Tsar Nicholas II. My grandparents spoke little of this irreplaceable time while they walked the earth.

In 1927, Gerhard's father, my great-grandfather Heinrich Reimer, had written his life story, a legacy that gave his family insights into a history that would otherwise have been buried with him. The overcrowded Molochna had purchased land and established five daughter settlements to address the Mennonites' growing problem of landless families. In the mid-1800s, the Reimers had been one of those landless families, which is how Heinrich and his second wife Margaretha Regehr ended up in the village of Neu-Schoensee, Sagradovka Colony. Gerhard was born there in 1900, the fourth of their six children, in addition to the five from Heinrich's first wife. That farm wasn't large enough to support a growing family. Land had, however, become available in the Molochna, his home colony, and he bought a farm in the village of Lichtfelde when Gerhard was seven. By then, Heinrich's first five children had moved out. Still, it was a challenge to pull up stakes and move 100 miles away. Margaretha, Sara, age ten, Mariechen, two, and six-year-old Abram took the train. Jacob, age fourteen, Gredel, twelve, and Gerhard went with Heinrich to help with the horses that pulled the wagons carrying all their earthly possessions.

Despite the difficulties in their life, the Reimers loved to sing. Frequently, someone would accompany them on the guitar. Sunday after church, they'd all go for a walk, singing the whole time.

Heinrich couldn't finish his education, but he vowed to do whatever was necessary so his children could graduate from a school of higher learning. By the time Gerhard started school, teachers taught all courses in Russian. They still spoke *Plautdietsch* at home and High German on Sundays at church. After high school, he qualified as a teacher and began work as a substitute.

Susa and her twin sister Anna were born in 1898 to Heinrich Koop and Sarah Klassen in the village of Alexanderkrone in the Molochna. Five days later, their mother, age twenty-six, died. Everyone thought the babies would die, too, so they left Sarah's grave open. Both lived into their late eighties. Heinrich already had three daughters—Tina, age six; Neta, four; and Sara, barely two. He couldn't manage two more babies, even with his parents, who lived next door, taking care of Sara. To help out, the Enns, his late wife's sister and her husband, who lived four miles away in the village of Rueckenau, offered to take one of the twins. The only condition was that whoever joined them would be considered part of their family. She could visit her father and sisters, but had to accept their home as hers. Heinrich was in a poor bargaining position. In the end, they sent one of their teenage sons with instructions to "pick one." He picked Susa.

Already as a newborn, she'd lost her mother and was separated from her father, twin sister, and three more siblings. The community pulled together to support a family in need, but it must have been a wrenching experience for everyone, with Susa at the epicenter. How had that affected her, and what of those experiences and perspectives lived in me?

The Enns were well off. Their sons were grown, and a baby girl in a houseful of boys was a novelty, so they treated her like royalty. Russian servants looked after everyday housekeeping chores. She didn't even have to do any dishes until she was eighteen, just before the Bolshevik Revolution broke out.

Susa's life with the Enns was good, although she really missed her sister Anna, and would try and meet up with her whenever possible, like at church or school. Not too many girls got to go to school, but Susa went to both primary and secondary school. Her aunt and uncle knew that she loved music, so when she turned ten, they took her on the train to Moscow and bought her a harmonium. Often people gathered in their home and she'd accompany them as they sang for hours. She had a natural ear for music and a sharp memory. The rare times she used sheet music, she read from *Ziffern* (a system of notation using numbers instead of notes to represent the musical scale) in whatever key best suited the singers' voices. It was Gerhard and Susa's shared love of music and singing that brought them together. Both sang in the Concordia Choir, a community group outside the church.

It was a wonderful time for these young people. Their lives seemed idyllic, with no idea how quickly and dramatically things would change. It's just as well we can't predict the future. I didn't foresee the crash that changed my life, and if I could have, I would have avoided it. But it had become the catalyst for reconnecting with my ancestors.

Two highways intersected ahead and I could see a gas station and rest area. I needed a break, and both Trudy and I needed to be refueled, while I also replenished my water reservoir. Then it was time to get back on the road.

What little I knew about Johann came mostly through Dad and stories Liese passed on. He was born in 1899 to Bernhard Klassen and Anna Toews in the village of Elisabethal in the Molochna. Bernhard farmed with his father and knew how to work with the earth and produce the best crops. From a young age, Johann worked with him, helping with the animals. When he got old enough, he'd hitch up the plow and walk behind the horses, up and down the fields, turning over the rich soil. He loved the smell of the fresh earth and pictured the crops that would grow from it that season. They always expected he'd take over the farm and raise his family in the home he'd grown up in.

Liese never complained, yet right from birth, she'd had to work hard just to survive.

Strong, determined, and not afraid to stand up for herself, no prescribed gender roles defined her. She did whatever needed doing at home or on their farm. That inherited attitude could explain my parents' nonchalant response when I began riding a motorcycle at age sixteen, when few women rode.

The Friesens, Liese's parents and grandparents, were landless, dirt poor. They lived on the outskirts of villages, on small lots designed for those with no property of their own. They couldn't vote in municipal matters, and Mennonite property owners looked down on them, treating them as second-class citizens, although not as lowly as the Russian peasants or Jews, and nowhere near the lowliness of the nomads who surrounded them. Her family sought a better life in another Molochna daughter colony, Neu-Samara in Samara province. She was born there in 1901, the eighth child of Johann Friesen and Katharina Schroeder. Two brothers and one sister died before she was born, leaving Helena, Katharine, Peter, and Jacob ahead of her in the pecking order.

Her father worked as a postman but was always restless, dreaming of a better life. By the time Liese was seven, she had two more sisters and Johann (Friesen) knew he had to find a way to earn more money. He decided that if he could own his own farm, he could provide better for his family. So, with another baby on the way, he packed up his family and moved to the Terek Settlement in the Eastern Caucasus near the Caspian Sea. Everyone who went there did so out of desperation, looking for a better life.

They had land, but it was a hard life. Drinking water was hard to find. Well water was so bitter and salty even the animals wouldn't drink it. Some villages found fresher water by digging deeper, up to 770 feet, but many of these wells had oil in them, making them unfit, too. No one could afford to hire help. Everyone had to pitch in and dig. Liese graduated from Grade Six to hard labor, digging irrigation canals.

The surrounding Nogais, a Turkish ethnic group, disputed the boundaries, insisting that some of the territory belonged to them. Thieves robbed their farms and took their horses. Villages hired Tatar watchmen who hired others for the night watch, but these men, and even officers of the law, weren't above bribery from thieves. Liese referred to the neighboring Chechens, a Caucasian ethnic group, as "a murderous bunch." Several times the Tatars invaded their home, but Liese, a 5'2" girl, defied them and sent them away empty-handed. Maybe they were afraid of her red hair.

I moved over a lane to avoid a deer carcass. I needed to focus on the road. Since mid-afternoon, I'd been looking for a place to camp. We'd passed several State Parks but I deemed them unsuitable. A narrow road into the forest provided access to unserviced and isolated campsites. I don't need the Ritz, but I didn't want something too remote.

My concern about finding a suitable campsite grew as daylight faded and fatigue crept in. I hadn't thought to pick up an accommodation guide, assuming I'd have my choice of camp-grounds. It was time to come in off the road for the day. Animals would soon emerge from these woods, compounding potential hazards. Out of desperation, I decided to head to the village of Baraga and the closest motel room.

On the way into town I rode past a giant statue of Bishop Frederic Baraga, a Slovenian Roman Catholic missionary, standing sentry on a bluff. Nicknamed the Snowshoe Priest, he served the area during the mid-1800s, traveling hundreds of miles each winter to minister to his constituents. Half a world away in Russia, my ancestors had been establishing their farms in the Molochna.

Relief flooded over me as I rounded the bend and Baraga State Park came into view. Lake Superior was so close its waves almost crashed onto the shoulder of the road. A handful of other campers made me feel comfortable but not cloistered. Plenty of serviced, flat, and shaded lots with a lakefront view were open. I could connect with Wi-Fi and check in with friends. After 500 miles, I'd found home for the night.

3

To a non-motorcyclist, riders look homogenous, based in part on the instant, tangible, heartfelt bond among them. But insiders draw distinctions based on the kind of motorcycle you ride and the type of riding you prefer. Over the past decade, I'd settled in with the adventure riding community, an ambiguous term for people who travel all over the world, frequently on a shoestring budget. We love to get out on the open road, often the one less traveled, for long distances.

The same was true of Mennonites. While they shared a common origin in the European Protestant Reformation of the 1500s, many subgroups had evolved in the centuries since then. The MB Church formed the spiritual and social hub for my grandparents, their children, and most of their grandchildren. Everyone knew each other, their family, extended family and each person's relationship to the other. I was born into this community but drifted away during my adolescence. Although it strained my relationship with my parents, it did not lead to estrangement.

I admired the strength of their community but felt out of place. However, moving away from the church left a gap. When a motorcycle entered my life at age sixteen, I'd found a new social group with others who shared my passion, but it would take decades to find the spiritual family where I felt at home. I wasn't going to join one merely for the sake of belonging. I'd wait for the right fit.

My motorcycle community has been the source of deep and enduring friendships, knowledge, and even shelter on my long journeys. Through an online home-sharing network, I'd arranged to spend the next night with Bob and Kari in Bemidji, Minnesota, 360 miles west of Baraga. That was a manageable distance, leaving me time to enjoy the scenery and stop for rest breaks so I wouldn't arrive exhausted. Other than exchanging emails and knowing they both rode motorcycles, I'd never met them.

Knowing the GPS wouldn't lead me to the rural address of their lakefront property, Bob had given me explicit directions. Everything went well until I arrived at their gravel road. I might not have worried had the grader not gone through that day, freeing stones from their packed base and leaving behind four inches of a soft, loose nightmare. Both of them ride off-road and wouldn't have thought twice about it. It hadn't occurred to them that I might.

Up until my crash, I'd had no qualms about taking off down a gravel road. I'd lived on one for years. Your motorcycle dances around on the loose surface and it can feel unnerving. But if you know what you're doing, have your bike set up properly, and do it wisely, it's lots of fun. Still, I hadn't regained the confidence to do it proficiently. Every time the bike shifted, I'd fight the urge to tense up and lock my hands on the handlebars with a death grip —one of the worst things you can do.

I had to get to Bob and Kari's house and I had to get over this fear. It's better to go at a brisk rate, but I couldn't make myself do that, especially with the passengers I had on board. Taking a deep breath, I stood on the footpegs and picked my way forward, swallowing hard, and accelerating as the road curved around and up a grade. Focused on my path, I missed their driveway. Not only did I go farther than necessary, I had to turn around on that surface. That's usually what happens when you operate from a place of fear: You end up making more work for yourself.

Their long driveway was also gravel, but the surface was packed and a breeze to navigate. A huge sigh of relief, tinged with pride for having made it, escaped me as I pulled up in front of the garage.

Like other times when meeting motorcyclists, the camaraderie was instant as we exchanged war stories about our respective travels. Strangers only minutes ago, Bob and Kari welcomed me into their garage and home.

My grandparents experienced this in their early days in Canada. Although the familiar Russian colony structure didn't exist, these émigrés tended to cluster in farming communities. No strangers existed amongst them, just as no strangers exist amongst motorcyclists. Those who had arrived in earlier migrations provided familiarity, welcoming one another into their homes and offering food and shelter. New arrivals who had not yet gotten their footing found comfort and support. Such is the joy that arises from knowing and finding your people.

As much as I'd handled the ride into Bob and Kari's, it had unnerved me, especially when I thought ahead to my ride out. Going down the grade and around the corner required more skill than coming up, and I feared I couldn't do it with my loaded bike. I had the technical skills but less risk tolerance than in my pre-crash days. Knowing it would weigh on my mind all night, I took control of the fear and asked Bob if he'd ride Trudy, my beloved Triumph, out in the morning. Without a second thought, he said yes.

One of the big lessons I took away from the crash was to ask for help. Once upon a time I'd never have asked someone to ride my bike through a rough spot, seeing it as a sign of weakness, or worrying what others might think. No longer. Why risk my safety to save my pride? I was a skilled rider who knew and respected her limits.

My grandparents must have encountered the same thing when they started out in this country. Industrious and self-supporting in Russia, they'd arrived, impoverished, in a foreign culture that spoke an unfamiliar language. They depended on strangers for shelter and work. They had to ask for help or they wouldn't get by. For them, approaching someone was even harder because of their broken English and different way of life.

With the worry of how I'd get my bike to the road out of the way, I could relax and enjoy my stay. I'd arrived late in the day and dinner was almost ready. While it cooked, we sat in the screened-in porch off their living room, overlooking the yard as it sloped down to the lake. Elevated and surrounded by forest, it felt like a tree house.

Deep in one of my bags was a journal Susa had written during her first years in Canada. Faded penciled entries filled pages browned with age, their edges brittle and crumbling. Written in *Sütterlin-Schrift* (an ornate Old German script), I hoped one of her nieces I'd visit later in the trip could interpret it. As my new friends and I shared family histories around the dinner table, I brought it out, forgetting I'd tucked old sheet music into its pages.

Fragile pages written using *Ziffern* held the hymns Gerhard and Susa had sung in four-part harmony for comfort, gratitude, and peace. They'd brought this German tradition and book with them from Russia. Susa maintained it was easier to follow *Ziffern* than notes, and her fingers would fly across the keyboard as she played. I couldn't make head or tail of it.

Kari could. Her heritage was Norwegian—not Mennonite or

even German. But she had a master's degree in music composition and a black seven-foot Yamaha grand piano in the living room. We couldn't read the German lyrics, but she could play the melody.

I had no memory of hearing these songs as a child, though I would have listened as Susa played them. Somewhere in my being, I'd heard them many times and carried them with me. Closing my eyes, I envisioned young Gerhard and Susa in their Russian village, pouring their hearts out to God in song.

Unbeknownst to Bob and Kari, Gerhard and Susa beamed with excitement to hear songs that had once sustained them. They loved that I wanted to hear them and honor their tradition. Connecting with Bob and Kari had come about through our shared love of riding. In a stroke of serendipity, they'd also provided a poignant connection to my Mennonite roots. I slept peacefully, lulled to sleep by the hymns of my ancestors.

The next morning Bob suited up and rode my bike out to the main road with ease while I followed in his pickup truck. Once there, we swapped vehicles and continued into town. I couldn't neglect to stop and show my passengers the eighteen-foot statue of the town's most famous son, iconic lumberjack Paul Bunyan. Beside him stood a ten-foot statue of his trusty companion, a blue ox called Babe. After the requisite photos, we parted ways, Bob back to his home in the woods, and me to places unknown.

Riding across the plains is tedious and boring for some riders, but traveling on any road outside of urban areas exhilarates me. This day, the fourth of my trip, my trajectory was northwest towards North Dakota. I didn't know where I'd stop that night but wanted to cover 300 miles, unaware of an impending storm.

We cruised west in perfect weather, with the sun high in the sky, although I knew how fast things could change. The flat terrain offers nothing to slow the prevailing west winds once they decide to pick up force. We'd traveled under 200 miles, less distance than I wanted, but prudence and intuition advised me to find a campsite for the night.

It's always nice to camp by water and the only nearby large body of water, Devil's Lake, was coming into range. If I didn't stop there, I might have to go too far down the road before I found something suitable. I pulled into the Tourist Information office to ask about camping facilities. After talking with the rep, I decided to try Woodland Resort, a nearby fishing facility.

Woodland was nothing like the fishing camps my husband had taken me to early in our marriage. In those days, we'd get together with his family and rent a basic cottage. To fish, we'd troll the lake in an aluminum boat powered by a nine-horse-power motor. Woodland Resort, on the other hand, was an upper-end destination based on fishing, with a family atmosphere. Lodging ranged from short-term suites to cabins and mobile homes, many of which housed people who'd made this their vacation home. It also had a lovely wooded campground.

My tent had become my cozy little home. Although tissue paper-thin, the walls separated me from the elements and other people. I could have gotten by with less real estate but had chosen a three-person tent for the extra floor space and head-room. My virtual passengers took up no space, but I required comfort in my home and mobile office. Trudy had no problem handling the negligible extra bulk and weight.

By now I had my routine down pat, and set-up and take-down required only a few minutes. I'd lay out my ground sheet, then erect my tent on top of it. Next, I'd assemble my lightweight cot, unroll and inflate my foam mattress, and throw my sleeping bag on top. A small table placed beside my head served as a nightstand. On the other side of the table, I placed my clothing and personal items, stored in two removable bags which fit into my panniers. When not in use, my collapsible chair stayed under the tent fly.

My riding gear got folded and stacked beside my feet. Even if it rained, I could assemble and disassemble my "home" and keep things, except my tent, relatively dry.

I'd no sooner set up than a man came along and pointed out I'd camped in a low spot.

"I'd move your tent. We're supposed to get heavy rain."

I thanked him, sighed, and grudgingly packed up, leaving my tent assembled. It's the last thing you want to do after a day of riding, but it's preferable to waking up in a few inches of water. By the time I hauled everything up the lane a few spots and settled into my new surroundings, the wind had picked up. Dark clouds threatened to block out the sunshine.

I had to get out from the trees to get a good perspective on the weather. When I did, it was obvious a ferocious storm was brewing, and I needed to find shelter. The closest haven was the sturdy looking building housing the restrooms and showers. That's where I went, battening down my tent as best I could on the way by. I was powerless to save it should the wind decide to take it.

Joining others at the shower house, we watched the storm develop. Huddled around a weather radio, we strained to hear over the howling wind. The gusts at ground level that bent branches and sent loose objects skittering didn't compare to what was happening above us. Black clouds whistled over the trees and swirled around the lake, gathering momentum. The radio reported the first tornado sightings, across from us on the south side of the lake. On the eastern shore, two confirmed twisters touched down.

Luckily, the storm moved on as quickly as it had appeared, sparing the resort. The winds had died down, but hung around.

Nearby residents reported damage from heavy rain and strong winds. My little tent held fast.

The storm that uprooted my ancestors took decades to form. When those black, no, communist red, clouds burst, they set off a chain of devastation that would reverberate for years. Civil war, anarchy, terrorists, famine, drought, and hyperinflation touched down like tornadoes, invoking terror and confusion. Tornadoes, however, wreak havoc and then dissipate. The storms in Russia landed and stayed. Just when it appeared they might let up, they'd morph into another destructive form. While Mennonite culture and beliefs attracted the worst treatment, all Russians suffered. No longer was anything about my ancestors' way of life familiar to them, except their faith.

4

I awoke in my Devil's Lake campsite well rested, grateful, and energized. Confident. I'd made it through three days in the U.S. without letting my health fears get the best of me. Yesterday's winds hung around, but hardly any rain had fallen, and the weather ahead looked clear.

Today, I'd cross the border back into Canada, staying with another new friend from my motorcycle community whom I had connected with through Facebook. Dianne lived in Regina, Saskatchewan, and reading that I would pass through, had invited me to spend the night. I looked forward to meeting her and the others she'd invited over for the evening, grateful for my welcoming community.

It didn't take long to pack and load the bike. Now on Day Five, I was getting into the routine. I didn't rush in the mornings. After meditating, shoulder exercises, and catching up on email and the news, I'd savor the breakfast I'd purchased the day before—usually tea, goat cheese, and an avocado. I'd pull onto the road between nine and ten. Seldom during the trip did I eat prepared foods or stop in restaurants. It was more nourishing and budget-friendly to buy groceries at the local market.

Besides, I enjoyed the camaraderie of neighborhood shops and campsite meals with fellow campers.

I'd escaped the worst of last night's wild storm. Once I left the shelter of the trees at the resort and the town, I was greeted by the lingering prairie winds bringing clearer air, which would likely buffet me the whole day. I'd stopped earlier than anticipated the day before, and so had 500 miles to go to reach Regina.

THE STORM that had battered me after my crash two years earlier had taken longer to pass over. The first month pitched me into a different time and space.

"Your shoulder's *smooshed*," said the orthopedic technician, breezing into my Emergency Room cubicle. "*Smooshed!*" She'd seen the x-ray, but I'd have to wait for the doctor to give me an official report.

In any case, it didn't sound good. I'd also torn a ligament in my right thumb from the impact of the handlebar during the sudden stop. Other than that, I had only a minor friction burn on my left hip, the outcome of my base layers rubbing against my skin as I slid down the road. My gear was scuffed but intact after having done an exceptional job of protecting me.

Translated into literal terms, *smooshed* described a complex fracture of the head of the humerus, the ball of the ball-and-socket shoulder joint. Below that, the neck of the humerus was severed, separating the upper humerus from the bone shaft. I'd also incurred significant soft tissue damage to the muscles, tendons, and ligaments that held my shoulder together and allowed it to function. Surgery was my only option.

Fortunately, a hospital bed was available, and I was admitted late in the day of the crash to wait for an operating room opening. Within twenty-eight hours of landing in the ditch, my shoulder bones and soft tissue were pieced and stitched back together, held in place by thirteen pins and a plate.

The surgeon advised me I likely wouldn't ever regain full strength and mobility. I'd heard that before when I'd broken my other shoulder during an off-road riding course in May 2008. That injury wasn't as complex, but I'd regained most of my range of motion, albeit after almost two years of treatment. I was optimistic for a full recovery this time, too.

My home for the next six days was a private room looking towards the Rocky Mountain foothills in the distance. Even though it was late August, snow still clung to protected crevices.

I thought I was in control, but in retrospect, everything was a blur. My sister Mary and friend Ellen offered to come and stay with me, but I said no. Travel was expensive; I expected to sleep most of the time, and nothing they could do would change anything. I'd need the help once I got home.

I fought against a sense of failure. I'd lost control of my motorcycle and crashed, completely of my own doing. I couldn't get mired down in those thoughts, though. What had happened was in the past, and I needed to focus on getting through the day. It was a perspective I'd grown up with. For both my grandparents and parents, on the farm, self-pity was scorned. It served no purpose; too much work needed doing, and you'd only lose ground if you didn't get at it.

The ongoing support from Paul, my adventure-riding friend from Calgary I'd met the week before at the Horizons Unlimited event in British Columbia, was invaluable. "You had 50,000 miles on that bike in two years! Not too many people ride that kind of bike, that much, or in those conditions. You've got nothing to hang your head about."

It was a bit unnerving asking a guy I barely knew to go and pack up my campsite. I'd left it in pretty good shape but couldn't remember what personal items or habits hung on display inside my tent. Yet it was like I'd known him forever. There's a familiarity, trust, and comfort when asking for help from someone in your community. Besides, I had no choice. Now was not the time for pride or modesty. It had to get done; he was ready and willing to do it and knew exactly what to do.

By the time Paul could get to my bike, two and a half hours east of his home, the RCMP had towed it to their impound. He arranged to get it moved to Blackfoot Motorsports, a large motorcycle shop in Calgary. After disassembling my campsite, forty-five minutes south of the hospital, he brought in my personal things and took the rest back to the home he shared with his mother, Charlotte.

I couldn't think of anyone else in town I knew, and was 2,000 miles from home, so he was my one visitor. That was fine with me. I didn't feel like talking with anyone. I had to get my mind around what had happened and what I was going to do. Although this was a setback, I envisioned I'd only be off a motorcycle until spring. How I'd resume the quest was still a mystery.

I tried not to worry about finances. I'd planned to travel for the next twelve to eighteen months, but I'd also planned to work from my virtual office. I was six years wiser than when I'd broken my right shoulder. That time I'd hobbled back to full-time work almost immediately, and my first motorcycle ride was three months to the day from my flight over the handlebars. I learned in retrospect that not taking the time early on to allow my body to heal had prolonged my recovery. Now, I'd sustained a much more complex injury. I vowed to listen to my intuition, and to balance pushing myself with giving myself permission and time to heal.

Charlotte, Paul's mom, invited me to stay with them for as long as necessary. It would allow me to see my Alberta surgeon who'd reconstructed my shoulder for my first follow-up visit before he transferred me to a colleague in Ontario. So, after six days in hospital, I moved in. I was so grateful for that time of respite before returning to Ontario for a long winter. I didn't feel like having visitors or answering questions. It was enough to have the support of friends and family from home via email and phone. I also didn't have a lot of energy, and my body and soul needed rest.

In spite of plenty of time for thinking, I intentionally kept myself from overanalyzing the unexpected turn of events. Besides knowing it was pointless, my muddled mind needed rest, too. Almost immediately I recognized this was not a detour. This bumpy road was part of the main journey, just not how I'd planned it.

My shoulder was quite painful, unless I didn't move. But immobilizing it was the worst thing I could do, so I was vigilant about going through my exercises to prevent it from stiffening up. The rest of the time, I kept my arm propped up on pillows, wore a sling for comfort often, at first, and slept in a recliner. My right thumb injury made fastening buttons and grasping zipper pulls a chore. It took forever to get dressed, but then I didn't have to meet any deadlines. Every day I walked at least once, even in the unseasonal storm that covered the ground in snow.

Charlotte mothered me, made sure I was comfortable and well-fed, and shuttled me around for errands. Paul cooked, too, and drove me to my follow-up doctor's appointment. On the way, we stopped at Blackfoot Motorsports where my motorcycle awaited assessment. I circled it where it stood, upright on the center stand, sobered by the extensive damage. I'd been on it when the carnage had happened and was astounded at how lucky I'd been. I was far better off than my motorcycle. No doubt the insurance company would write it off. With reverence and gratitude, I removed the logos from the gas tank to keep as talismans and bade it good-bye.

Both Charlotte and Paul had plans that would take them away from home while I was there. Charlotte was going to Scotland for a hiking trip and Paul was marshaling a professional road cycling race. For the few days their schedule away overlapped, Paul enlisted the help of friends Dave and his wife Allison, also riders, to visit and take me to physiotherapy. I was fortunate to start almost immediately at WinSport Medicine Clinic at Canada Olympic Park. There, I had access to top therapists who work with elite athletes and, in this case, one broken rider.

Convalescing in Calgary gave me time to begin learning about the rich history of the Indigenous Peoples who'd lived in what is now southern Alberta. The permanent Blackfoot Gallery in the downtown Glenbow Museum was too hard to get to. Instead, Allison suggested we go to Fort Macleod, two hours south of Calgary. I could rest while she drove. The Piikani reserve is nearby and the land is the traditional territory of the Piikani Nation of the Blackfoot Confederacy.

That visit was pivotal. It was then that I met Quinton Crow Shoe, member of the Piikani Nation (Quinton refers to his community as Northern Piikani Blackfoot). I explained to him my quest, how I was seeking to understand how the experiences of my ancestors and the energy of the land they walked lived in me. I told him I thought that understanding Indigenous wisdom would help me understand my relationship with the earth, and thereby myself. And how I'd crashed on the border of the Siksika Nation. Quinton listened quietly, interjecting occasional questions, then told me to contact him once I got home. That meeting would change the course of my inner journey, although I wouldn't realize the implications for two years.

Now, on the resumption of that trip, I'd survived a powerful storm and was riding across the plains towards Regina in heavy winds, not unusual on the wide-open landscape. Managing a motorcycle in them, however, hastens the onset of physical and mental fatigue, and I knew I'd have to pace myself, stay hydrated, and take regular rests. I'd sailed along for almost ninety minutes and it was time for a break. After refueling, I went over to a picnic table under some nearby trees and lay on the bench seat. It didn't seem nearly so blustery here, but I knew the winds would return as soon as we got on the open road. I lay there watching the clouds shapeshift across the sky.

Managing the motorcycle was an adventure for me but I pictured Gerhard, Susa, Johann, and Liese enjoying it like they would a carnival ride. Their loose clothing flapped wildly. What little hair Gerhard had wafted backwards in thin strands, while Susa's *Schups* held tight. Johann and Liese's short hair blew away from their faces, flattened against their heads. Each wore a big smile. They loved this ride to what was once the promised new land.

By midday, we approached the border back into Canada. The legendary winds had stood up to their reputation and had buffeted us for hundreds of miles. Traveling long stretches, I usually give my arms a break by briefly letting go of the handlebar, one arm at a time. Not a chance that was possible this time. I had to hang on to Trudy as we leaned against the wind. With gratitude and admiration, Trudy's stability took care of us.

My grandparents had felt the same kinds of winds across the Russian steppes, albeit not on the back of a motorcycle. It wasn't hard to imagine we were riding across the Molochna, except instead of vast wheat fields, thousands of acres of tall corn and sunflowers surrounded us. As we passed, they swayed in the breeze, nodding their heads in greeting. What my grandparents had never noticed were the winds of change—the gales that had turned their world upside down and left wounds that would take generations to heal. What had I not noticed before my crash?

The storms in Russia wreaked havoc and destruction on the Mennonite colonies with greater ferocity than anything I'd experienced. My ancestors had no way of knowing how powerful and pervasive those turbulent currents had become, how long they'd last, or what the aftermath would ask of them.

Crossing the Canada-United States border at remote locations is usually quick and straightforward. My grandparents never got used to that. Terror branded the first border crossings they'd known, on their exodus from Russia. Crewmen would wedge 1,300 people into 50 boxcars for the three-day train ride. A two cubic-foot box held their food—dried *Zwieback* (two buns fused together, made from yeast, flour, butter, and milk), watermelon cookies, a teapot, cooked milk, and roasted and milled wheat that comprised substitute coffee.

Were it not such a sad and anxious time, they could have enjoyed the scenery as the train clickety-clacked across landscapes they'd never seen. Occasionally Russian soldiers would board and ratchet up their fear. They'd inspect papers, looking for irregularities, and search for contraband such as cash or journals. If the soldiers found anything to make them suspicious, even a sideways glance, they wouldn't hesitate to lay charges and throw that person, usually a man, off the train. The chance of seeing him again was nil. No stop was as terrifying as the checkpoint at the fabled Red Gate, the border between Russia and Latvia—the gate to freedom. As soon as they'd cleared it, the tattered refugees broke into a spontaneous hymn of praise: *Nun danket alle Gott* (Now Thank We All Our God).

At the Latvian coast, they'd board the steamer that would take them to Southampton, England. Standing along the railing, they bid farewell to the continent their ancestors had called home for centuries.

In a recorded 1977 interview with a Brock University researcher studying the evolution of Mennonite culture in Niagara, Gerhard described the impromptu eruption of song as their steamer edged away from the dock: "With our heart and mouth in our hands, we sang praises to God. I think the music still sounds over Libau." Once in Southampton, England, they cleared another medical check and lice inspection, had their clothes fumigated, and boarded the ship to Canada.

I pulled up to the single booth at the border, handed over my passport and answered the Customs Officer's cursory questions. Satisfied with my answers, she handed back my passport and sent me on my way.

Winds don't know borders, and the gales continued in Canada as they had in the United States. Now, back in my home country, those winds stirred up thoughts of what had led up to the trip that precipitated my crash.

Since I'd left my marriage and corporate career in 2003, I'd done many adventuresome things. I'd found deep meaning in my work within the motorcycle industry. I was recognized as a leader, especially among women riders. I'd helped organize international conferences and delivered workshops and retreats. I'd discovered a love of writing, freelanced, and published *Women, Motorcycles and the Road to Empowerment*. Yet I sensed I was capable of so much more. It was like I'd wandered in the wilderness for ten years.

I'd begun to design my business through activities like webinars, client sessions, and writing that I could do from anywhere. It didn't add up to a lot of revenue, but it helped. My bank account was by no means a bottomless pit, and since leaving a regular corporate paycheck I'd had to refine my financial prudence. Miraculously, and with the help of an astute financial advisor, a fellow rider, my savings had supplemented my meager earnings and provided for what I needed. I loved everything I was doing and was free to do whatever I wanted. What more could I ask for?

Always thinking I was on the verge of making a break-through, I was afraid to stop and slow down lest I lose momentum. In the months leading up to the trip where I crashed, I wrote four to five blogs a week, ran online courses, hosted webinars, and saw individual clients. I pushed to publish *Life Lessons from Motorcycles*, my second book, before I left. I started to learn Spanish. I picked up a variety of writing contracts that would help me through my trip.

I loved each pursuit, but together they took a lot of energy. Adding trip planning took even more. To be even more productive, I became relentless with self-discipline. For a short time, it worked, but it was never sustainable.

Blogging and webinars are often used as marketing tools and offered free to clients. I was spending an extraordinary amount of time on them and getting great feedback, but little of it led to revenue generation. The time and energy I invested was out of proportion to the return, and reflected the lack of worth I placed on myself.

I also created an auspicious new initiative: an online conference titled *Power of the Road,* scheduled for early April, four months before departure. I'd participated in similar events on themes of self-help, writing, and publishing, but nothing similar existed in the motorcycle world. I'd lined up twenty-four leaders and role models from across Canada, the United States, and Europe who would share what they'd learned about themselves through motorcycling and describe how it had changed their lives. It was meaningful, doable from anywhere in the world with internet access, leveraged my time and energy resources, and generated revenue. It was a ton of work, but I could plan my time and prepare the pre-recorded sessions anywhere. Never one to shy away from work, once I made a commitment, I'd pull out every stop to see it through, so I poured great energy into it.

At the same time, I was arranging my life to be away for at least a year. People often prepare for years for trips like this, while a few go on the spur of the moment. I had about seven months to prepare. Seriously, what was there to do? I didn't need to quit a job. I didn't have to sell a property and wasn't committed to a lease. The only things holding me back were my self-fabricated limitations.

Other than my precious cat Measha, I had no reason to stay anchored in place. My parents, both in their late eighties, still lived independently, two hours away. Leaving them tugged at my heart, but it wasn't a reason not to go; I could always fly home if the need arose. I had a great motorcycle that would take me the distance. When was I going to do it if I didn't do it now?

It was an exciting way to celebrate turning sixty—heading out for places unknown, with no time limit, on a journey of self-discovery. I knew it would turn into something monumental, not necessarily life-changing.

As I'd done when I walked away from the perception of stable employment, I targeted an August 1st departure. That would allow me to set a comfortable pace and get to the Siksika Pow-wow on time.

To say my schedule was full was an understatement. And then it got fuller. My parents decided to move and needed me to lend a hand. Two years earlier they'd relocated to a townhouse from their farm and home for fifty-five years. However, Mom's dementia was progressing, and they'd decided on an apartment complex where they could get care when the time came.

Meanwhile, I was preoccupied with making sure the *Power of the Road* conference got off without a hitch. Wading into unknown technological territory, technical glitches, and computer crashes heightened my anxiety. At the same time, I wanted to help my parents with what was a monumental undertaking for them. Health and circumstances can change quickly at any age, but when you're almost ninety, those chances increase. I wanted to spend as much time with them as possible.

As my sixtieth birthday approached in early May, self-pity crept in. I felt like a failure in love and business, and wondered what it was about life that I wasn't getting. I fought the mind chatter that told me I was running away because I hadn't achieved what I thought I'd worked for. I wanted to rise above what I perceived as a life of mediocrity. I wasn't exactly sure what transcendence would look like, but I hoped to find answers on this trip.

I celebrated my birthday week by attending another of the Shamanic Energy Medicine courses in my program. Held in an idyllic setting in New York State's Hudson Valley, it was a lovely eight-hour ride away. The people I met, studied, and connected with during this program had become another community. It was a perfect way to prepare for my quest.

I loved my country carriage house but it didn't make sense to pay rent and upkeep while I wasn't there, so I gave my notice. With the kind of quest I was on, I didn't even know if I'd come back. Maybe I'd settle somewhere else in the world.

I began to purge what was already a simple lifestyle. I'd lived and worked there for seven years, and as much as I tried to avoid purchasing unnecessary stuff, stuff has a way of accumulating. Objects carry little meaning for me, other than the function and convenience they add. When I do buy something, I look for high-quality items, which may cost more but last longer and don't end up in the landfill. I went through closets deciding what to bring, what to store, and what to divest. It didn't make sense to pay for storage for things I rarely used, so I either gave them away or donated them to a thrift shop. I sold a few pieces of gently used motorcycle gear and equipment to eager new riders.

My landlords had been kind and considerate throughout my tenancy. Knowing my intentions, we agreed I'd leave the furniture I wanted to keep in place and store personal items in the garage, in plastic boxes they provided. That way they could use the living quarters as a guesthouse. If and when I returned, I could have it back if I wanted. They weren't going to rent to anyone else. My friend and cat-lover Jane would take Measha for as long as needed.

My 1200cc Yamaha Super Ténéré's weight and high center of gravity and seat made me consider replacing it with something smaller. After talking to many people who'd traveled the roads I was still dreaming of, and weighing my options, I decided to keep it. After 50,000 miles together in two years of riding, it was familiar and comfortable, and I could look after basic maintenance. It had an excellent reputation for reliability and wasn't likely to break down and leave me stranded or rack up an exorbitant repair bill. I loved its aggressive look. Its large aluminum panniers held a lot of gear and kept it dry. Its sky-blue color reminded me to dream big.

My versatile, waterproof, and highly protective riding gear was in good shape and didn't need replacing. The only piece of camping equipment I needed was a tent. To prepare for the challenging roads I'd encounter, I sharpened my skills at an off-road riding school at nearby SMART Adventures, run by world-class trainer Clinton Smout.

By mid-July, I was down to the smallest collection of things I wanted to keep. I'd even sold my car. It didn't make sense to store it. With my motorcycle as my only transportation, it became a utility vehicle. In one day, I'd ferried items to the Re-Store and the hazardous waste depot, taken my sacred drum to a friend's for safekeeping, and returned ten freshly butchered chickens I'd stored in my refrigerator to another friend.

Seeing the pile of stuff I got rid of made me never want to

buy anything new again. Raw materials, manufacturing, shipping, packaging, and storing all use energy and generate waste. So often that stuff ends up in the landfill where, with luck, it will decompose in a century. I'd become increasingly environmentally aware and knew that's not how I wanted to treat Mother Earth, my home.

THE CITY of Regina appeared on the horizon. After getting blown around for the entire day, the cityscape was a welcome sight. The GPS and the ease with which I was able to use it to navigate a city I'd visited only once would have fascinated my grandfathers. They got around in Russia by horse or horse-drawn carriage, following well-traveled dirt roads between villages. Once they left to come to Canada, train engineers and boat captains got them where they needed to go.

It was lovely to meet Dianne in person and receive her warm welcome. I'd asked her to keep her eyes open for a sheepskin I could put on my seat to cushion long days in the saddle. She hadn't found any, but she soon had me at the local dealer where she'd sussed out alternatives. They weren't suitable for my needs, but another friend brought over an unused new sheepskin. It was too large for Trudy but a perfect fit for Dianne's Harley. I cut a piece off the hide Laura had used and it was a perfect fit. Everyone was happy. A wonderful evening of camaraderie and exchanging stories like old friends evoked the joy of community. My ancestors, too, knew that they could count on refuge, comfort, and strength in their community.

The next morning, Dianne rode with me to the edge of town and wished me well before turning back and heading to work. The scene reminded me of a Western movie, except we were on iron steeds. The road welcomed me with temperatures in the mid-seventies, a slight breeze, sunshine and fields of gold and green under blue skies.

We rode north on the Louis Riel Trail, a four-lane divided highway, headed for Saskatoon. Johann and Liese had traveled further west from Regina, but Gerhard and Susa had crossed this prairie land ninety years ago on their way to their first Canadian home.

What would my grandfathers have thought to see the John Deere combine in the field we were passing, cutting swaths across the waist-high grain, devouring a section of crops in no time. They'd done all that with horses, simple equipment, and back-breaking labor. It had been hard for them to believe how their land of peace and plenty changed so fast. They'd be minding their own business and then see the bandits coming up over the horizon and have to run for cover.

It had also been hard for the Mennonites to see how the systemic inequities in Russia, which gave them their comfortable way of life, left others in poverty and desperation. They worked hard, worshipped God, and minded their own business. They'd earned their lifestyle. God would protect them. But the system that kept them insulated in their colonies also kept them from understanding the plight of other Russian citizens and recognizing the escalating tensions. I'd grown up thinking hard work, discipline, and accomplishments would make me happy, and while they gave me a comfortable lifestyle, there was a whole part of life I'd missed seeing.

It's easy to see the warning signs and red flags when you look back, but not so easy when you're in the thick of it. I'd stayed in my marriage and career long after those roles no longer fit, unaware that my inattention and lack of action were robbing me of energy.

I needed to heed my own warning signs of fatigue and pull over for a rest. I wasn't sure where the next rest stop was, but I knew there'd be something not too far up the road. My gear is comfortable when riding but it sure feels good to stop, remove my helmet and gloves, sometimes my boots, and peel off my jacket for a few minutes.

A grove of trees ahead, an oasis, looked like a good place to pull over. I flicked my right turn signal on and moved off the main road, onto the parking area. It felt good to stretch my legs, then lie on the grass, breathe deeply, and close my eyes, taking in the energy in a way I couldn't while I was riding.

Less than a month before arriving here in 1924, Gerhard and Susa had been parents to a beautiful little girl. They were Soviet citizens, and lived in a large colony our forefathers had established 110 years earlier. They'd sung in the Concordia Choir. Seven years before that, Gerhard had qualified as a teacher and begun work. They laughed, played, and sang. They worshipped. State officials held the Mennonites in esteem, and the Tsar upheld their negotiated privileges, rewarding their loyalty.

Almost overnight they'd lost most material things and become peasants, having to beg for food at times. Gerhard had said two classes of people remained after the Revolution—poor and poorer. They'd pled with God to spare them and their country from one pestilence after another, including the human one. He'd grown angry with the people he called Russkies (roo-skis) and what they'd done. You couldn't trust them. The only thing they couldn't take from the Mennonites were their souls, although they tried.

I could have stayed on the grass for hours, but we were getting close to Dalmeny, the first landmark on the Ancestor Trail, and I was eager to get there. Jacket, helmet, and gloves went back on, in that order, and we were off.

As we approached Saskatoon, the Lois Riel Trail joined in with the Yellowhead Highway, a northern branch of the Trans-Canada Highway system. Although it was a few minutes past noon and traffic was light, I had to watch the road. Getting through the city on the freeway was a breeze and we were soon back out in the open country, close to where Gerhard and Susa got off the train so many years ago. We were all eager to get out and see where their new life in Canada had started. Thanks to their strengths, my own life began very differently.

5

I arrived on earth on May 9th, 1954: Mother's Day. When the nurses returned me to Mom after bathing me, a pink bow clung to a few strands of fiery red hair, forming a spout on top of my head. The cultural training had begun: Girls wear pink, even with red hair.

Mom put her nursing career on hold. Dad worked as a millwright helper at General Motors in St. Catharines, Ontario. After work, he looked after the five-acre farm where his twice-widowed mother Liese and three of his sisters still lived. The General Motors job was wearing on him, though. He once said of his work at GM, "On a nice spring day, I was going crazy in there. I didn't like that inside smell."

My second year was a landmark one for my family. On April 10th, 1956, two weeks after the arrival of my brother John, Dad walked away from stable, well-paying work. He'd decided to follow his heart into the uncertainty of farming. We moved to a raggedy twenty-acre fruit farm, bought for $30,000 with a $7,000 down payment. The only equipment was a small cultivator tractor that Dad said looked like a spider and "wasn't worth a pinch of salt." The previous owner was not an experienced farmer and had planted the wrong type of trees for the market. The farm's biggest asset was its rich soil—seven feet of well-drained, fertile and sandy loam, ideal for growing fruit.

In spite of its bedraggled appearance, the setting was beautiful. The land dropped into a ravine on three sides, shored with towering maple, oak, and walnut trees, and bounded by a meandering creek. It was paradise and the source of limitless childhood adventures.

Also on the farm was a ramshackle abode we called the "help house." Modifications to what was once a chicken coop made it fit for humans. The Dutch family who rented it had small children who played in our sandbox and taught me to speak Dutch, my third language, after German and English.

We lived in a two-story box, built in 1905 and clad in pale yellow stucco with green wooden trim. A porcelain sink, exposed plumbing, cracked green linoleum, and plank shelves formed the kitchen. Ten years would pass until Mom and Dad could afford to replace the sink and have cupboards with doors built.

The dining room, with its south-facing bay window and window seat, was the most exciting space. You could enter it from the kitchen through a swinging door, or pocket doors from the living room. My brothers and I would throw them open and chase each other in circles until someone got hurt or angry.

Wooden stairs with a windowed landing tucked in the middle of the house led to a tiny upstairs hallway. Seven doorways opened into four bedrooms, two with closets, a bathroom with a clawfoot tub, a linen closet, and a walk-up attic. Until I was four, John, Robert, and I each had our own bedroom. When Mark arrived, Robert got bumped out of the crib and moved in with John. Mark would follow into what became the boys' room, when Susan was born. By the time Mary came along, the house was out of rooms, so Mom and Dad moved a twin bed into the baby's room for Susan. Mary and Susan shared first the room, then a double bed when Mary outgrew the crib. I always had a room to myself.

Spooky and full of intrigue, the attic was stifling in summer but a favorite winter haunt. A small dormer window and single bulb hanging from the rafters lit the dark, dusty space, but the light was never strong enough to reach the corners. Insulation poked through the unfinished wooden floor, but only shingled planks separated the sloped ceilings from the elements. Wary, we had to protect our heads from protruding roofing nails. Boxes of treasures held things like miniature china tea sets and Mom's wedding dress. Others contained costumes in waiting—high-heeled shoes, dresses, and hats.

Doors from the kitchen on the north side of the house led to a dank basement. Half of it housed a cold cellar and our laundry room with a wringer washer that drained into two cement laundry tubs. For more than a decade, smells of bleach and dirty diapers wafted from soaking pails. A gigantic coal furnace, dubbed the Octopus, took up much of the dingy space that ran the length of the south side. Every year a big truck would pull up on the lawn and thrust a chute through the small window. Coal would tumble into the storage bin, stirring up a cloud of black soot. On cold mornings I'd watch, fascinated, as Dad opened the furnace door and shoveled more coal onto the embers. Like magic, the heat returned.

Without equipment for spraying, cultivation, and harvest, Dad's first order of business was to buy a small Ford tractor. Most work was done by hand or with borrowed equipment. Rusty, a big workhorse, came from the neighbors to help with the tilling. Sometimes Dad would let me and John ride on Rusty's back as he trudged back and forth across the field. Dad muscled the plow into submission to create straight furrows.

John and I shrieked and laughed from our lofty perch, invigorated by the smell of fresh earth.

The first year at the farm was the most difficult financially. Mom wasn't working as a nurse and Dad had us, as well as his mother and sisters, to support. A heavy frost at blossom time decimated what little potential grew on those trees. The gross income from the farm was a mere $3,600, but my parents resolved to make it work. It felt like home and they had every intention of becoming farmers and raising their family there.

Thus began a pattern where Dad would supplement the farm income by finding other winter work. By his own admission, pride kept him from seeking employment at General Motors. It didn't, however, keep him from visiting the local employment agency to see what else was available. As fate would have it, Columbus McKinnon, where he'd established himself as a capable and hard-working fire-welder during WWII, was desperate for someone with his skills. He started the next day, doing piecework. He was well compensated, but the extreme heat made the work too hard to sustain. They wanted him to stay but he wanted to farm, so he turned them down. I was too young to remember that, but something must have stuck with me. Dad followed his heart, with input from his head, even though he could make much more money and rely on stable employment at the factory.

In 1957, my parents rented acreage a mile north of the homestead that ended in a bluff above a narrow stony beach along Lake Ontario. That land bore strawberries, sweet cherries under which poison ivy thrived, and pears. It also gave me my first paid job—picking strawberries. We could keep what we earned but we had to buy some of our clothes. Geese eat weeds but not strawberries, so farmers fenced them in the berry patch. As long as we gave them space, peace reigned. But those geese would get nasty and try to bite us if we got too close, so they'd get relocated to a temporary enclosure during the harvest. After a hard day's work, Dad would round us up and herd us down the rickety stairs to go swimming in the lake. We loved that! We worked hard, yet always had lots of time to play, ride our bikes, go for hikes around the ravine, and splash in the creek.

Even though everyone lived close to the edge of poverty, the farmers in the area supported each other as best they could. They'd loan equipment, exchange marketing board scuttlebutt, and share best practices. Resources and information readily available today, like which fertilizer to use, or when and what to spray, were passed along through the informal farming grapevine. For struggling families, that community provided moral support, if nothing else.

Somehow Mom and Dad managed to pay off the bills at the end of each year. The next day Dad would walk into the bank for another line of credit. He'd always receive it.

As much as they enjoyed fruit farming and the lifestyle, Dad's heart remained with the vast grain farms in the prairies where he'd grown up. He talked to Mom about venturing west but she'd have nothing to do with it. "Write me," she'd say when he suggested moving. She, too, had worked hard to follow her heart into a nursing career and had put it on hold to raise a family. Once I was old enough to help with my siblings, she was close enough to a hospital that working part-time was possible, even as she helped on the farm.

Dad admitted that if he had it to do over, he'd never buy a fruit farm. Grain farmers used machines to do most of the work while fruit farming was labor intensive, and the greatest hardship was getting dependable workers. Every day Dad would drive his blue pickup to the St. Catharines market, which he called the slave market. Here a squadron of men—and the occasional woman—down on their luck gathered every morning, hoping someone would hire them for the day. This wasn't where they thought they'd end up, either. Few had farming skills or experience. Many had alcohol dependencies and reliability issues. The odd time he'd strike gold, like teenage brothers Ian and Alex MacDonald. They pleaded for a job and he couldn't turn them down. It was a wise decision—they worked for him for years.

But it isn't just the human resource factor that causes challenges to fruit farming. Nature presents uncontrollable variables and frequent worry for farmers. Too much or too little rain, or rain at the wrong time, can affect the size, texture, and sweetness of the fruit. Heat, cold, and wind play havoc with a bumper crop, damage trees, and affect future yields. Hail can wipe out fruit that's been painstakingly tended from pruning to blossom to harvest. Disease, insects, and birds love to feed on juicy fruit, too, so keeping them at bay was a constant and sometimes futile undertaking. Our lifestyle was tied to the cycles and caprices of nature, and to cultivating a healthy relationship with the earth so we could coax the most from it. Yet it was also separate from us, a raw material Dad worked with to make a living.

In spite of the risks, Dad craved the fresh air. "There's just something about spending your day outside. Even fruit farming beats working at General Motors." Little wonder I love the outdoors and the freedom I have found riding my motorcycle.

Dad loved to hold us on his lap and read us stories. As the first child, I had perks. Like for my second Christmas, Mom and Dad gifted me with *The How and Why Program of Child Mental Development*. The series of seven books dealt with topics like Nature and Heroes, both mythic and historical. Other volumes held stories, including my favorite, *The Little Steam Engine That Could*. Books on travel, knowledge, and *The Rainbow Dictionary*, an illustrated alphabet, completed the set.

By far the most worn of the series was the *Stepping Stones* book. It held fascinating stories from the Old and New Testament of the Bible. There was always a moral to the plot, but none of the fire and brimstone rhetoric that would later frighten me.

Particularly meaningful was this poem, an introduction to a kind of spirituality I didn't hear at church.

> *Sometimes when morning*
> *Lights the sky*
> *And gladness fills the air,*
> *I feel like telling*
> *Things to God,*
> *He seems so very near.*
>
> *Sometimes when flowers*
> *Are in bloom,*
> *And birds are singing clear,*
> *I feel like singing*
> *Things to God,*
> *He must be very near.*
>
> *Sometimes when trees*
> *Are standing tall,*
> *With branches in the air,*
> *I feel like saying*
> *Things to God,*
> *I know He must be near.*
>
> *Sometimes when work*
> *And play are done,*
> *And evening stars appear,*
> *I feel like whispering*
> *Things to God;*
> *He is so very near.*

Dad and Mom tried to protect us kids from adult worries. But it wasn't hard to feel their stress or see that they had to work hard to make ends meet. Around the time I was six, I found Mom sitting on the steps going up to the bedrooms, head in hands, crying. I never knew what prompted it, but I remember her angst. Dad would hold his cap by the brim while he scratched his head, trying to sort out what felt like big problems. Something was always breaking down at the worst time. Or the weather was threatening to damage the crop. If it wasn't either of those, the demand or the price set by the marketing board affected his ability to make a profit. Their tension would make me get knotted up inside. What was going to happen to us, I'd wonder? I wanted to make my parents happy.

But I didn't feel poor. Then again, I didn't know anything different, such as what it was like to have a store-bought dress. Mom sewed all my clothes, never fancy but always new. When I started school, I had two new dresses from the same pattern, made with different fabric and trim. As soon as I got old enough, I started sewing my own.

Bride dolls topped every little girl's Christmas list one year. Convinced Santa could bring my one wish, I tore downstairs on Christmas morning to see what he'd left under the tree. I stared at my bride doll, swallowing tears, unsure what to say. My parents couldn't afford the real thing, so Mom had made a bride dress from scraps of white satin and lace and put it on my doll Cathy. She was so proud of her creation and I knew she'd put great effort into it. I tried hard to conceal my disappointment. I didn't want to hurt their feelings, but it wasn't the real thing. A few years later, the same thing happened when I got a Suzette doll instead of the Barbie I'd asked for. I learned to protect their feelings at the expense of my own. They had enough to worry about without me adding to it. I was already taking on the role of rescuer and it was disempowering me.

Early on, Dad and Mom established family traditions to teach us etiquette, manners, and piety. Mom limited the use of her full set of Cornflower cut glassware and Paragon bone china dishes from wedding gifts to Sunday dinners after church. Everyday dishes came out of Tide laundry soap boxes. I loved digging through the granules to feel if we'd gotten a plate, bowl, or cup and saucer, and guessing what pretty hue it was. Meals were a colorful time, if not for the food or my three raucous brothers, then for the dishes.

"Devotions" started every day. Dad would get out his Bible and *Our Daily Bread*, a "non-denominational" booklet. He'd read the day's script, the corresponding Bible verses, and wrap it up with a prayer. For us kids, it was an exercise in endurance rather than enlightenment, but it was important to him and Mom. However, my disenchantment became so entrenched, that years later when my soul cried for a spiritual connection, I didn't even consider looking to the Bible and shunned fundamentalist teachings.

Mennonites across North America baked every Saturday. Mom started early—bread, pies, and *Zwieback*, best eaten warm, slathered with butter. Dinner was sausages and noodles. In the afternoon, we listened to *Back to the Bible Hour* from Lincoln, Nebraska, which still airs. It was an evangelical fire and brimstone program that Mom seemed to take comfort in. No doubt those airwaves played a role in scaring the dickens out of me.

We didn't let our lack of toys slow down our entertainment. Brothers John, Robert, and I played "church" on the steps leading to the second floor. The second and third steps were the choir loft. Usually, John took the roles of both minister and choir director and conducted the service in German. We didn't have the vocabulary to pull off a coherent church service, so when we got stuck, we made up words that sounded like German to us.

Our sandbox sat on the east side of the lawn with a view of

the orchards. I played with my back to the house, facing the trees and orchards in front of me. Even as a child, I didn't want to feel hemmed in. The sandbox sat midway between a gnarled sweet cherry tree and a tall black walnut. Around the corner, another cherry tree basked in the southern exposure while an old climbing rose bush clung to the side of the house. Cardinals loved to nest there, their red feathers a match for the flowers. But even the thorns couldn't keep the cat away, and we learned the realities of life early.

Every spring a profusion of delicate white petals would appear on those cherry trees. At the same time, a bed of shy lily of the valley unfolded under the walnut tree. The appearance of blossoms meant spring had arrived and I could spend more time outside.

Family and church topped my parents' priorities, which included keeping the Mennonite culture, traditions, and German language alive. Living out in the country, our life revolved around farm, church, and family gatherings until we went to elementary school.

Sunday morning and evening, we'd pile into the car and Dad would drive us eight miles to Vineland MB Church. I enjoyed Sunday School and singing, but the morning and evening sermons went on forever. At least when they interjected German, it added interest. Embracing and jesting with Gerhard and Susa made the day. They lived thirty minutes away, but they still farmed and so had little time to socialize. We'd see them at birthdays and special events, but we knew they'd be at church every Sunday.

I loved the women's Christmas Candlelight Service. Dressed in white gowns and carrying a single lit candle, they'd assemble at the back of the darkened church. Singing, they'd proceed down the aisle then take their places in the choir loft. It was super exciting when Mom walked by. The singing would sound like one choir, but as each woman passed, you could distinguish her voice, and then the next. The candlelight illuminated each face and mesmerized me. A choir of angels.

I also looked forward to the annual church picnics. Most often they took place at Queenston Heights, a historic park on the bank of the Niagara River. We'd enter contests, including the popular three-legged race or the wheelbarrow race. After, we'd have a huge picnic lunch under the canopy. Since it was on a Sunday, we didn't have to go to church that day.

Fun and laughter also rang from family gatherings in Gerhard and Susa's red brick two-story farmhouse, trimmed with faded white gingerbread. Out back stood a high wooden barn with empty horse stalls and a hayloft. The expansive yard meant lots of room for grandchildren to run and play. We'd take turns pushing each other on the red swing hung between two giant pine trees. We sang grace in four-part harmony, and after our meal we all sang our hearts out to hymns in German and English. Wherever you found Gerhard, you'd find good-natured teasing, laughter, and singing.

Visits to Mom's and Dad's aunts, uncles, and cousins introduced us to the different "clans." The Reimers (Gerhard's family) and the Koops (Susa's family) had the tightest bonds. Most often the gatherings involved Susa's siblings and their families. Mom used to take us to the midwife home that Susa's older sisters, Mom's *Tante* (Aunt) Sara and *Tante* Tina Koop, ran in Vineland. *Tante* Sara was the nurse, *Tante* Tina the support staff. We also visited the farm of Susa's brother, Mom's Uncle Jake Koop, up on the hill where they raised chickens. Jake was the youngest of a large family, so although his children were Mom's cousins, they were closer in age to me.

A common Mennonite *Völklein* custom involves dissecting your family tree to learn who you're related to. Often you learn you have links to most people in the room, either through birth or marriage, or both. We knew that, by default, we belonged to Gerhard and Susa's and our parents' large community. "Oh," people would say, "you're Ben and Margaret's daughter!"

The atmosphere was fun but less demonstrative when we got together with Dad's kin. Only Liese attended the MB Church and hers was in St. Catharines. There was no family singing like we enjoyed with the Reimers. The Jansens lived in poverty, and Liese worked as a housekeeper, making her way around town on the city transit. Neither of my grandmothers ever drove a car or wore pants, but I thought it was pretty cool when Liese took me on the bus to go shopping, even before she gave me the stick of Wrigley's Doublemint gum.

At age seven, I understood little about my ancestors and kin. I knew that as German Mennonites in Russia they'd gone through perilous times and that they'd come to Canada by boat. I knew Susa's mother had died five days after giving birth to Susa and Anna, and that an older married aunt with teenage boys raised her. I spoke fluent German and we honored traditions like lighting candles on the Christmas tree. Never did we see ourselves as anything but proud Canadians.

In 1960 I started elementary school, walking a mile and a half to get there. My path followed a road allowance through a gully, across Fischer's strawberry fields and through their peach orchards, past a few shacks housing farmhands and their families. Once across the township road, we passed smaller family farms with better houses. Jane Bakker was the daughter of one of the immigrant families at Fischer's. She was two years older than I and my parents thought she qualified as a good walking companion. They didn't know she had a proclivity for tall tales. The worst one told of a phenomenon that could happen at any moment. A cloud could come down and pick me up, then take me halfway up to the sky and drop me. The only way to avoid it was through vigilance. If I saw a cloud descending, I'd lie in the ditch where it couldn't attach to me. This story wasn't far off the rapture story I'd heard in church. For years, I'd glance at the sky to make sure nothing was coming to get me.

In spring, we'd detour through Fischer's greenhouses where the pungent scent from row upon row of red, pink, and white carnation beds filled the air. We always bought one or two plants for Mom for Mother's Day.

At school, a door to a new world opened and I met non-Mennonite kids. Our class of thirty held four other Mennonites, two Indigenous children, and a mix of white faces and backgrounds. I gravitated to friends based on affection, not religion or ethnicity. My parents commented on the beliefs of my classmates and whether their parents drank and smoked, but they never chose or denied me my friends. Most of the families farmed, worked on farms, or worked in factories and had small plots of land. In this, we all had much in common.

Still, as schoolkids, we ostracized and made fun of anyone who was different. Indigenous kids, poor kids, or those who spoke with an accent or stuttered got targeted. We called them demeaning names or crossed our fingers when they came near us so we wouldn't "catch their fleas." My family never taught me to respond to others with meanness, nor would they have tolerated that behavior. But unconsciously, I yearned for acceptance from the dominant culture, which ostracized anyone perceived as different or weak. I never considered how that must have hurt those we targeted. I didn't understand that we were equals in the eyes of Spirit, sharing space on this earth and interconnected, even if we came from different backgrounds or had different needs.

Dad referred to my first teacher, Mrs. Elizabeth Simpson, as Sarge because she was a taskmaster. She also smoked, but she was still a good teacher. He didn't dislike people because they smoked, but it was a mark against them spiritually. We didn't identify adults by their jobs or titles so much as by their religion and whether they smoked and drank. He didn't mention that Johann, who died from a respiratory disease, had smoked, though it's probably why smoking carried such an emotional charge.

I was smart, hard-working, and righteous. No one else measured up, especially if their beliefs differed from ours. Most of the parents attended the United or Anglican (Episcopalian) Church, which meant they likely smoked and drank. Dad said the Roman Catholic Church was a cult. I didn't get it. What made Mennonites right and everyone else wrong? I never got an answer that made sense.

With so much exposure to English, German became passé. In an attempt to keep the language of our ancestors alive, area churches started a German school. Every Saturday, a parent would drive Jude, John, and me to the basement of a local MB church. There we'd speak, color, read, and sing in German. It's where I saw my first dead body. Jude and I wandered into the sanctuary at recess to find an open coffin staged for an afternoon service. No one expected the wide eyes of curious children to find it.

Although I never balked at going to church, it was the ancillary activities I loved most. Stories from both the Old and New Testament of the Bible transfixed me. Like short Zaccheus sitting up in the tree so he could glimpse at Jesus as he walked by. Or miracle stories, like the loaves and fishes that multiplied like magic. The stories of Adam and Eve, Abraham, Moses in the desert enchanted me. I pictured myself in the scenes of the shepherd stories of David. But in those formative years, a deep unconscious fear took root. With nothing to stop it, it spread like a weed, creating doubt and eroding confidence.

Mom was a great one for holding onto childhood mementos, returning them to us when she and Dad moved from the farm.

One such treasure was a Junior Note Book, its green cover faded with age. It held a Sunday School Bible-alphabet project I'd done when I was seven. Each letter had a page, and the letter prompted a caption, corroborated by an excerpt of scripture. A rudimentary crayoned drawing illustrated the story. The collection exemplified how ingrained the fire and brimstone teaching was:

C is for the coming of the Enemies. Jesus and his disciples sit at the table set for the Last Supper. *Rise, let us be going, behold he is at hand that will betray me.*

F is for the fiery furnace. Two girls, one with orange hair like mine, stand inside a furnace. It looks like the Octopus in the basement of our farmhouse. They stand on burning coals, backs to the open door. *There is no other God but the true God.*

O is for Only a Few Men, referring to the belief that only a few people will make it through heaven's gate. Angels playing trumpets at the rapture filled the sky. *The hand of the Lord has saved us.*

Mennonites embraced a literal interpretation of the Bible, and a seven-year-old doesn't understand the difference between myth and reality. These illustrations came from the mind of a little girl who should have been carefree and joyous. It didn't occur to me that other ways of living or belief systems existed. As an adult, I realized the teachings came from a place of deep love in adults who wanted the best for me. They were doing as well as they could, passing on what they'd been taught, as they understood it. However, unknowingly, they were as afraid as I was and were passing on their fears. I had to put many years and much space between the teachings and me to see it.

When I was seven, I didn't know any of this. I knew about baby brothers, three of them, parents working hard, and tough times. I had a devoted dad who read us bedtime stories. I played in the sandbox and climbed trees in the yard. I adored my cousins, aunts and uncles, and grandparents. I knew about protecting my parents' feelings. I knew Jesus loved me. I knew how important it was to tell the truth, not steal, and be obedient. But I was beginning to feel bound. Fearful. An outsider.

As idyllic as life seemed, something was stirring at an unconscious level, a sense that I was being shaped into someone my spirit wasn't at home with. That's when my migraines started. Unknowingly, I'd started down a path that would lead me away from my culture, searching for roles that matched my heart.

My crash had dismantled the familiar. I'd left my itinerary loose so I could be open to serendipity and whatever the road delivered. It delivered me to an Alberta ditch and stripped away roles I'd held close to my heart. No longer was I a sixty-year-old woman on an adventure, flying across the country on her motorcycle. My motorcycle, my spiritual teacher since the age of sixteen, was gone. I'd lost the independence I cherished. For the first time, I'd needed to have body parts reassembled and work to regain mobility. Wounded pride undermined my reputation as a role model and proficient rider.

Confident I'd made the best decisions for myself in preparing and planning for this journey, including my choice of motorcycle, I gave thoughts of defeat little airtime. Other people's opinions didn't concern me. The adventure I'd envisioned had taken a dramatic twist, yet I knew the crash and its sequel belonged to the same journey I'd set out on. I couldn't work for a while, not even writing. What was Spirit asking of me?

With protective layers pared away and time on my hands,

maybe I'd be able to see who I was before I was *told* who I was. My Hummingbird guide reminded me to expect tests and challenges en route to my destination. Ultimately, the crash had laid the groundwork for an extended period of introspection and researching my roots. Even though it had ended my trip, my heart wasn't ready to leave Calgary and go back to Ontario, or wherever home was. All that awaited me there was loneliness and emptiness. I could have lived anywhere at that point and was grateful for the offers of accommodation I received. Jane would keep my cat Measha for as long as necessary.

In the end, I decided to return to Orangeville, to the familiar. A small group of friends lived there, and my family was only two hours away. My short-term priority was to heal and get back on the road. I had a wonderful family physician, Alex Caldwell, whom I trusted to manage my care. Alex and his wife Christine were also good friends and motorcycle riders, so I knew he would understand my desire to get back on the road as soon as possible.

Reluctantly, I called my former landlords to tell them what had happened and to confirm my place was still available, as they'd promised. In the five weeks I'd been gone, they'd changed their minds and I couldn't return. I could, however, keep my things there until I found another place. They offered no explanation, but it didn't matter. I was homeless.

My grandparents must have felt the same way once they left Russia. They had no place to call home. While they knew a handful of people in their new destinations, for the most part they had to depend on the kindness of strangers. Going back was not an option.

By comparison, my situation was tame, yet I felt adrift. I'd parted ways with my car, my motorcycle, and now my home, each one a major facet of my identity. I had to smile, even while shaking my head. This was exactly what I'd asked for—to understand who I am behind the roles and identities I'd come to treasure. Alex and Christine came to the rescue, offering me a small cabin on their property while I searched for a place of my own.

My friend Barbara and sister Mary offered to fly out and bring me back, but aside from the expense, I didn't want to travel by air. I guarded my reconstructed shoulder like a grizzly guards her young. I couldn't endure the jostling and, even with help, I didn't know how I'd summon the energy to lug my riding gear and camping equipment through that maze.

When Barbara offered to drive out to retrieve me after her vacation, I accepted. We'd have a fun road trip. It would give me a gradual re-entry and we could go at our own pace. She pulled into Charlotte and Paul's driveway two-and-a-half weeks after I'd arrived there.

Barbara, who'd never seen the Rocky Mountains, dreamed of going to Banff. Conveniently, Charlotte and Paul lived a mere hour away, so before heading east, we went further west. As much as it added time and distance to our trip, I knew years would pass before I'd see those mountains again. A week earlier, Paul had taken me on a mountainous back road route to visit mutual friends in Canmore and I was happy to return to the mountains' powerful energy. Peruvian shamans in the tradition I studied believe that when we return to the spirit world, our wisdom returns to the mountains. Mountains exude majesty, strength, and grace. There's something immensely comforting about being cradled by these magnificent forms.

Barbara was content with a quick view and a few photos before returning to the car for the drive home. Her Subaru Tribeca was as comfortable as I could have wished for. I got in and reclined the seat while she bolstered me with feather pillows she'd brought along to elevate my arm and keep me comfortable. We kept a cooler in the trunk for food and ice packs, essentials for the trip back.

I had two orders of business to look after on our way out of Alberta. The first was to return to the crash site and offer a gift of gratitude to Spirit for saving my life. I wanted to recognize the spirits of place and honor the earth that had softened my landing.

Once there, I thought I'd have no trouble identifying the bike's landing spot, but it took a bit of searching through the tall grass. It was Barbara who found the bits of motorcycle debris and a small spot of oil. I'd actually made it around the corner and further down the road than I thought. I was impressed! If fear hadn't taken over I could have recovered that wobble. How might my life have been different if, as a girl, I hadn't feared voicing my true feelings? What would my path have looked like if I'd ridden right through those early wobbles?

On the advice of my shamanic teacher, I'd created a despacho, or prayer bundle, as an offering of gratitude. I'd carefully selected symbolic elements and sacred plants, wrapped them in decorative paper, and bound it together with colorful ribbon. The only offering tucked into the despacho that wasn't biodegradable was one of the logos I'd taken off my motorcycle tank, but it had to be part of the offering. After a brief ceremony, I stood by while Barbara used a garden spade to dig a shallow hole. Reverently, she placed the bundle in the hole and covered it with earth. I closed the ceremony with a final prayer of gratitude. On her way back to the car, Barbara picked up a single piece of golf ball-sized gravel and placed it in my hand. It would become an integral part of my Mesa, my medicine bundle. Barbara didn't practice the same traditions as I did, but we shared a respect for the wisdom of the earth. She was also German and understood my Germanic roots.

The second place I wanted to stop was Blackfoot Crossing

Historical Park, the historic and cultural interpretive center I was headed for the day I crashed. I hadn't made it then and wasn't successful on my second attempt either. We got there safely, but the General Manager, the man I needed to speak with, had gone home by the time we arrived. I accepted the message from Spirit that learning about Blackfoot culture was not part of my path right now.

As much as I kept my pain meds topped up, the ride back to southern Ontario was long and torturous. Spending uninterrupted time with a close friend I rarely see eased the discomfort. While she drove, I settled into my nest of feather pillows, basking in the sunshine and gazing at the big blue sky, dozing on and off. Harvest was still in full swing across the endless prairies, filling the air with a cornucopia of rich scents. After three days of driving due east, the flat land gave way to the Canadian Shield of northern Ontario. Elevation changes, lakes, and forests resplendent in autumn foliage welcomed us.

And then we were back in Orangeville at Alex and Christine's place on the outskirts of town. Alex had arrived home following knee replacement surgery and his overall health was failing. It was an unsettling time for them, too, yet they were kind enough to offer me respite.

Barbara and Christine unloaded the car and stowed my things in the cabin. In a way, I was still living as I had on the road, from the things I'd packed for the trip. I'd given most of my other clothes away before I left less than two months earlier. As much as I wanted to snuggle into the otherwise comfortable, cozy bed, my shoulder hurt too much to let me lie horizontal. After one sleepless night, Christine hauled in a reclining deck chair for me to sleep in.

Being disabled and having nowhere to go conjures up an odd feeling. It wasn't how I expected my life would go. When I'd fractured my other shoulder in 2008, it had taken almost two years and many hours of therapy and exercises to recover. This current injury was much more complex and my recoverability uncertain. Mentally, I was still reeling from having my trip ended. It didn't make sense to make plans or long-term commitments, as I didn't have a clue what to do or how I'd manage physically or financially. It was beyond frustrating to lose my independence and know that even with aggressive therapy I had to wait for healing to take its time. I wanted to be doing something "productive." It was hard to imagine things would get better, although I was certain they would. I just didn't know how. I did know I had to focus my energy on healing, and other answers would come to me when I was ready.

I didn't dwell on it because I couldn't change what had happened. The facts were that my trip was over for the time being, my shoulder was now mending from a complex fracture, I had no place to call my own, and little means of supporting myself. Everything had changed. Not unlike how things had evolved for my grandparents. They couldn't allow themselves to be consumed by their years of hardships. They had to focus on surviving.

Getting dressed and undressed was an awkward chore. Without full use of both arms, mundane tasks like cooking, grocery shopping, and laundry took ten times longer than usual. I had to think everything through. In Calgary, away from my familiar surroundings, anything out of the ordinary had seemed temporary. Now that I was back, the reality, with its inherent uncertainty, was different. My grandparents had learned to live with unpredictability; acknowledging mine as temporary helped me cope.

With so many variables at play, deciding next steps was a challenge. My shoulder would take at least six months to heal. Without knowing how I'd be after that, I didn't want to commit financially or emotionally to a car or an apartment. I didn't even feel like driving. Winter was around the corner, and I decided to experiment with going carless for the season. When spring rolled around I'd be back on a motorcycle, I reasoned. I can give up a car, I thought, but please God, don't ask me to give up my motorcycle for good!

No car meant I'd have to find a convenient place to live. It was already the end of September and the likelihood of finding a place for the beginning of October seemed slim. Then, while chauffeuring me to physiotherapy one day, Christine stopped in a desirable neighborhood to ask some women walking on the sidewalk if they knew of any places for rent. One recalled a For Rent sign around the corner. We checked it out on the way back from therapy and it became my new address a few days later. I'd bunked at Alex and Christine's almost exactly two weeks.

The new place was on the second floor of an old Victorian home above a hair salon, right on Broadway, the town's main street. It was within walking distance to downtown, grocery stores, and physiotherapy. Local transit and Rapid Transit connections to Toronto were within a block. A two-minute walk took me to a car rental agency. I didn't have to sign a lease. Stately maples planted in horse and buggy days, before my grandparents were born, shaded the yard. A tall carving of a soaring eagle graced the sidewalk entrance, greeting me on this next leg of my journey. Eagle could see the big picture, even if I could not. Every day he would remind me not to get caught up in the minutiae of the moment. For the time being, it was perfect.

I'd hired movers, but while my personal things were in storage boxes in my former garage, dishes, books, pictures, and furniture still needed to be packed. I could only supervise. Again, I had to rely on friends, and I felt like an inconvenience. No one likes packing, least of all when it's not your own, at least that's how I felt. I'd divested myself of a lot, but what remained still needed to be done in a short time. Christine was a godsend, helping me pack and clean the new place, on top of her other personal responsibilities, including caring for Alex. I was relieved to be in my own space, even if it wasn't yet familiar, just as my grandparents must have felt when they finally had their own places. After living out of motorcycle bags for over two months, I unpacked.

Jane, who'd been prepared to host Measha for my entire journey, brought her home once I was settled. Measha's a dear pet but she isn't a replacement for meaningful human companionship. I was lonely as I sat in the living room, surrounded by boxes of contents that also needed a place to stay. Throughout my trip and recovery, I'd been with so many people that the solitude felt strange. But then *everything* felt strange.

I still had a few writing contracts to fill which would help generate revenue until I had a better idea of what I was going to do. Then, abruptly, my most lucrative contract ended. Initially discouraged, I concluded that Spirit was helping me honor my commitment to heal. There'd be other work when I was ready. Whether I wanted to or not, I was being forced to slow down and not fall back into old patterns of working too much, rushing too often. It was another of those tests Hummingbird was adept at navigating through.

It was arduous for me to ask for help. I was the one who helped others, not the person who needed it! Activities I'd taken for granted I could do—getting groceries, doing laundry, cleaning—now depended on assistance. I didn't want to be a bother to anyone and couldn't believe how much I'd taken my independence for granted, or how fragile it actually was. Having to ask for help was deeply humbling.

After my crash, I thought I was near rock bottom. However, like my grandparents, I had more trials coming my way. I also had expert ancestral guides to teach me how to navigate roads not highlighted on my map.

As the darkness of a cold winter descended, I plunged into uncertainty, but I wasn't going to let it overwhelm me or detract from my healing. Although the external path had been halted, my internal journey continued apace.

I didn't know how long it would take me to recover or when I'd be resuming my trip. I knew South America was no longer on my map, not because I was afraid to go there, but because I was clear it wasn't part of this mission. I had other work to do. In fact, that work was so significant I'd received a gift of stillness to do it in. This was a major shift, telling me to do things differently, and for someone who loved to be on the move, hard to understand, let alone accept. For people whose ancestors who had lived in one spot for generations and were forced out through no choice of their own, movement had been their path to a new way of being.

The next months were the loneliest and most alien of my life. I was so grateful for the friends who stopped by over the next weeks and months to help with cleaning, unpacking, decorating, and for company. I tried to establish some routine. My ex-husband Daniel and other friends helped a lot, giving me rides for physiotherapy and groceries. I had nowhere else to go.

Occasionally, well-intentioned people would promise to stop by for a visit or to help and would either not show up or cancel. I'm sure they didn't realize how much I looked forward to those interactions, or how disheartening it was to be let down, or how I needed help with routine activities. Lifting the mattress to tuck in the bottom sheet, for instance, was laborious, especially because the room was small, with little space to maneuver. It was a good lesson for me for when I got back on my feet and was in a better position to extend compassion to others. My grandparents were always quick to help those in need. They never forgot what it was like, and how much the kindness of others had meant to them when they needed it.

Although I no longer needed prescription pain medication, my shoulder discomfort still prevented me from lying in bed at night. I made do in a portable lounge chair, bolstered with pillows, often with a cat on my lap.

But that winter Measha got sick with urinary crystals. The vet said the condition is often caused by stress, especially in female cats. In the past few months, she'd moved in with Jane and Jane's cat, adapted well to life there, then I'd been injured. Now she was in another new place. She recovered, although it took a few weeks. It seemed we both needed time to heal.

From my second-floor vantage point overlooking Broadway Street, I could sit in my outdoor lounge chair, in relative comfort, cozy in front of the electric fireplace, and watch the snow fall and the world go by. As the calendar flipped into January, I had no more answers than when I'd set out on my quest. Lots of questions tumbled around in my head though.

No personal growth was going to happen as long as I continued as I had for all my life. My tendency for overwork and over-commitment was a pattern I'd used for decades. Even though the relationship and career changes I'd made at forty-eight seemed radical, I hadn't changed the underlying patterns. Sure, I'd changed how I used them, but I had to go deeper than that. Those patterns had kept me in safe mode during the years my spirit was sleeping. Even when I began to recognize they were smothering me, I still played it safe. I wasn't challenging myself or stepping into my power.

Fear had called the shots from inside that safe behavior. Fear of not making the most of my life. Fear of not accomplishing what I was here to do. Fear of running out of time. Fear of living my life out alone. Fear of not having enough money.

Fear alerts us to imminent danger so we can take evasive

action. It triggers the flight or fight response to save us from annihilation. That's useful and healthy when we're threatened by an intruder or learning new skills that involve physical risk—like riding a motorcycle, or downhill skiing, or even riding a bicycle. Or when we're threatened by terrorists, like my grandparents had been.

That little identity inside of us generates another kind of fear when it perceives a threat to its existence. It clings to roles and titles and is threatened by change. It listens to the myriad voices that tell us how we should behave, to worry about what others think of us, and what will happen if we don't conform. This fear constricts and confines.

Our subconscious reacts to danger without differentiating between real or perceived threats. We're unaware of generational beliefs that influence us from before we're born. They shape our beliefs, our behaviors, and influence our choices on relationships, and careers. I'd known that for a long time. Now I was ready to expose those roles and address the limiting beliefs that had prevented me from expressing my power and creativity.

Staying with the familiar, like I'd done for so many years, even when it's uncomfortable, can be seductive. It appears less risky than trying something new, but always my soul felt restless. I was always busy doing interesting and even meaningful things, but busyness can camouflage emptiness and frustration —and it's way overrated in our culture. Something had to give. Although I didn't see it at the time, like my Serpent guide, I was preparing to shed a skin I'd outgrown and make way for the new.

In the early months following the crash, I thought I had no map. I thought about the Hummingbird, who fearlessly navigates through seemingly insurmountable tests and challenges without a map. But I'd never navigated this kind of physical or spiritual terrain and had no idea what direction to set my compass for. Then I realized I did, even if I had to prospect for it. My grandparents had maneuvered through much more difficult times with no experience. The strengths that had been handed down through generations, long before the trouble arrived, had been their saviors. Cultural and religious practices lived in them, assets waiting to be used. Those same strengths lived in me, annealed by my grandparents' experiences since the Bolshevik Revolution.

Strengths also have a shadow side, though, provoked by fear or perceived threats. It was Jaguar work, exploring those places I'd been reluctant to look into. They needed to be exposed, too, to get the full picture of how I'd evolved. Owning shadows is humbling and painful work. It would take time, something I now had plenty of.

I couldn't get out and ride to clear my head, but I could walk. Both Susa and Mom walked miles every day. I walked a lot even in winter. When my head wouldn't clear, I kept walking. I couldn't think my way out of where I was or see an exit. I knew I had to recover my shoulder mobility, and to ease healing, I had to let my body and spirit rest.

My grandparents felt the closest connection to God through their singing, whether it was expressing gratitude or joy, or seeking solace in times of need. It was a big part of worship services, funerals, weddings, family get-togethers, and celebrations like Easter and Christmas. It was an opening to the Divine, and listening to those songs was an ideal way for me to get into their headspace. As Christmas approached, I downloaded their favorite carols, in German wherever possible, and the hymns we sang at their funeral services. As I walked, I sang my heart out to songs like *Blessed Assurance, How Great Thou Art, Stille Nacht* (Silent Night), *The Lord's My Shepherd,* and the anchor hymn —*Nun danket alle Gott* (Now Thank We All Our God), which burst from the refugees as they cleared the Red Gate. It would bring tears as I heard them singing with me, and felt their joy, angst, and sanctity.

Once, an elderly woman out with her dog startled me. She'd been sitting on a path-side bench overlooking the lake and had heard me coming. I didn't notice her until I rounded the corner.

"Please keep singing," she said, smiling, her voice tinged with emotion.

"I intend to," I said.

7

Right from the start, when I'd stood in that Alberta ditch before the dust had settled, teetering over the wreckage of the motorcycle that had given its life for me, I'd accepted the crash as a course correction. I never felt anger. Who would I be angry at and why? I had brought this on myself. I'd vowed to focus on physical healing. The questions I'd had when I set out remained unanswered. Instead of finding solutions through movement, I'd be searching in stillness.

Once they were clear of Russia, Gerhard and Susa, and Johann and Liese knew they couldn't focus energy on the past. They needed their reserves to survive the present. Out of necessity, they lived mindfully, one day at a time, with gratitude. Feeling sorry for themselves would be pointless. Dwelling on how hard life had been, how little they had, or the challenge of their early years in Canada, didn't serve them.

Understanding that didn't make it any easier. It was as hard as getting down those arduous gravel roads.

My overwhelming sensation during the months following my crash was one of blindness. Not physical blindness—my eyesight, with glasses, was acute. I thought I knew where I was going, but I'd ended up in an unfamiliar setting. My familiar points of reference were gone. If I tried to think about anything other than the immediate, my mind shut down. Like reduced mobility was part of my physical healing, so too I needed stillness to heal my emotional and spiritual self.

I felt stuck. Now I know why. Under a calm facade, emotional and spiritual healing was already in progress, mirrored by the winter season evolving outside my window. Although it looked white and desolate, with trees devoid of leaves and a blanket of snow carpeting the ground, seeds of new life germinated in the earth. Trees rested in preparation for bursting into leaf in spring, taking their strength from roots that had absorbed nutrients in warmer months. Hummingbird was teaching me about stillness in motion.

During this healing process, I questioned my value. Since leaving a six-figure income in the corporate world, I'd earned a small fraction of that. I didn't know how to make a living by following my heart. Dad had modeled this all my life, but there were many tough years when he didn't know how he'd get through, even though he always did. Unlike him, I flitted from one thing to the next. As if I wasn't bashed up enough, I was being brutally hard on myself emotionally. Why couldn't I get traction doing the work that I believed was Spirit-led? Then again, who said I wasn't? My mind was trying to rule my heart, rather than working with it. And I was operating from a place of fear and scarcity.

Over time, I began to view self-worth in a different way. I didn't have to prove my worthiness through income. My worthiness was a given, not something I had to earn. I knew from reader feedback that my work had touched lives and inspired people. Though I couldn't know what ripple effect that was having, maybe I was in exactly the right place for me at the time.

A sense of the surreal pervaded my days. My soul was the

same, but the outer layers had changed. It was hard to get my head around the fact that this had happened to me. I helped others. I didn't need help from them. Although I may have appeared vulnerable, I still felt independent. I doubt people I met during that early post-crash period, like my new landlord, saw the same person I saw, but it didn't bother me. I'd expected to be in South America by the winter, not laid up in Orangeville, having to ask for help, living in a small apartment on a noisy street, and walking for therapy four days a week, doing my exercises three times a day.

My grandparents lost a comfortable lifestyle in Russia through none of their own doing. Even if they had seen it coming, what could they have done? In times of peace and plenty, you never expect to end up in a civil war or a famine. Mom never expected to end up in long-term care with dementia. I never expected to get divorced. Or crash my motorcycle.

In spite of being in unfamiliar territory, I loved myself more than ever. I was proud of my independence and ability to take care of myself. I loved engaging in work I found meaningful and energizing, while having the freedom to do it on my terms. The work could be done from anywhere, so I could travel and still have a career.

I loved my involvement with the international motorcycle community and the opportunities and places it had led me to, and especially the people I'd met. I loved being on the road with my motorcycle and the rich encounters I experienced with an eclectic mix of people, including non-riders. Whether it was meeting friends I seldom saw in person, attending a gathering of riders, or spontaneous meetings I'd have along the way, I thrived on it.

I loved that I could make up my mind and had grown to make decisions on my own, rather than based on what other people would think of me or what they thought I should do. I was pragmatic, could prioritize, see the big picture, and make wise, rational decisions most of the time. Those attributes allowed me a lot of freedom. Even if the revenue stream was meager, I had a lifestyle many told me they dreamt of, although few would be willing to make the changes that lifestyle required. I still felt different than everyone and most of the time that was okay.

I was proud that I'd followed my spirit, even if I hadn't tapped into my power. I hadn't caved in and gone back to a job. That may have been easier, but I already knew it would suck the life out of me. A job is the right thing for those who are called to it, but it was not meant for me now.

Yet I didn't know where I was going. I didn't know who my community was, or where to find it. I was lonely. Along with the skin I'd shed, I'd been stripped of my identity, at least the familiar one I'd given myself, and stopped in my tracks.

The first motorcycle show in Toronto happens in early January and a friend invited me along. This is a crowd and community I'm familiar and comfortable with. I've worked in the shows in various roles for many years and received industry awards. This time I felt like a stranger amongst my own people. Everyone was walking around in black leather and patches, in a biker costume, playing the role. I was an observer of a bizarre subculture. Still, I felt the tug of being in that world. One good thing was that even though I was still not able to reach forward to grab the handlebars with both hands, I could browse through the new models and try them on. I always knew with certainty I'd return to riding.

My grandparents had felt different, too. Everything about this strange land made them feel out of place, especially having to depend on the mercy of strangers. How do you assimilate into a culture that's foreign to you when you were discouraged from assimilating into the culture of the country you lived in? And whom could they trust? In Russia, for good reasons, they'd grown to distrust anyone that was not Mennonite. They certainly could not trust those in authority. They'd grown up under the Tsar and experienced a collapse of an entrenched way of life. They were still leery of extending too much trust in the Canadian culture, especially when they didn't have full command of English. Not only were the customs and the language different, many people resented the *Russlanders* and had tried to keep them out of Canada.

As hard as it was, I appreciated the time alone and the nourishment it was giving me. I'd become conscious of defending myself from others who tried to give me encouraging, albeit often irrelevant advice. I needed to figure this out for myself, with Spirit's guidance. To do that, I needed to be alone, find my voice, and listen to it.

After my crash, I'd begun meeting monthly with Oriah Mountain Dreamer, a wise woman and transformative spiritual teacher. Oriah saw my journey from a bigger picture perspective, with a different lens than I looked through. Through my work with her, my Shamanic Energy Medicine courses, and subsequent reflection, I understood the need to surrender my expectations and my emotional attachment to them. I committed myself to releasing this pattern. Through my fears, I realized I was trying to force the fruit to blossom in winter when I should be allowing it time in darkness to germinate. Surrender is an active process—a dance of letting go and moving forward—that takes time and practice. Letting go of old ways of thinking frees up space for new, more constructive and creative ways of being. I gave myself time. What else could I do? This was a major course correction and until I could sort it out, I wasn't going anywhere.

At the end of January, I caught myself setting goals for the year. There needs to be some tension to move me forward, but old patterns of thinking and behavior had edged in. I threw out my lists. How, I asked myself, do I know what's right for me? What if what Spirit has in store for me is that much better? I'm standing in my own way! Instead, I prayed for guidance and asked to recognize and be open to the answers.

Even though I'd done a lot of decluttering when I got ready to go away, I went deeper. I got rid of anything I didn't use. I didn't want it any more. Anything with a negative emotional charge I'd hung onto went out. So, during this time of stillness, it wasn't as if I had nothing to do. I had the *Life Lessons from Motorcycles* books to publish for starters. They sat right there in front of me. Why would I want to start something else when I had unfinished business in front of me?

I began reading voraciously—books by Indigenous authors and other books about Mennonite culture and history. With the latter, I was still reading as an observer without realizing how it lived in me. In my journal, I wrote, "I am NOT a Mennonite." I concluded I was born into a Mennonite family for certain lessons I needed in this lifetime. Being born into that community had been the best way to learn them.

At the end of February, 2015 I had an appointment with the Toronto surgeon overseeing my care. After five months of intensive therapy, the range of motion in my shoulder was still pretty limited. He said I was nearing maximum recovery and gave me the go-ahead to ride. However, he added that the pins and plates installed to align and stabilize my shoulder for healing might be impeding my movement and removing them could increase mobility. I wasn't ready to give in and opt for more surgery yet, so we agreed I'd continue therapy. I didn't want to be off the bike another season, so he concurred that if I eventually did decide on surgery, I wouldn't lose any ground by waiting until after riding season.

March came in like a lion and didn't let up. It started with Alex's passing, a mournful and sobering time. He and Christine were dear friends who'd let me stay in the cabin on their property when I returned to Orangeville after my crash and had nowhere to call home. They'd given me the same kind of shelter and moral support my grandparents had needed to accept during their early years in Canada.

A few days later, I had to go to the bank to deposit a foreign currency check. While waiting in line, an elderly gentleman in a navy blue puffy winter jacket engaged me in social banter, waiving his spot in the queue for me. He pulled his bank book out of an inner pocket and asked, "Would you like some money? $500? $1,000?"

Shocked, I could tell he was serious.

"Thank you very much sir, but I can't take your money. You keep it and spend it on yourself."

Part of me wondered if this wasn't Spirit responding to my prayers. If that was the case, I didn't want to turn it away, but I couldn't take money from this old man. I suspected the lesson lay elsewhere.

"I've got more money than I'll ever spend," he said, his eyes welling with tears. "My wife is at home with dementia. I look after her twenty-four hours a day. I have no one to spend it on."

It was all I could do to hold back my tears, and I was grateful to be called to the wicket.

As I was leaving, he stood at the counter in the midst of his transaction. I put my hand on his shoulder in a passing gesture of friendship.

"Are you sure you don't want some money?" he said, in case I'd reconsidered. He had no idea how much money had been on my mind lately. I was certain if I'd accepted, he'd have withdrawn the cash and given it to me right there.

"No thank you, sir."

He smiled sadly. "All I really wanted was a hug." Time stopped. No one else existed in the bank at that moment except him and me. I recognized loneliness. I gave him a great big hug and my best wishes.

He'd delivered a lesson about abundance. I had no reason for financial fears. I had enough, and money would come to me when I needed it. What a profound way of conveying a message. You never know when angels will appear or who they'll be.

Three weeks later, my eighty-six-year-old uncle Ernie, Gerhard and Susa's eldest son, joined them in the afterlife. In robust health until shortly before his death, he'd recently given up riding his 1984 Honda Gold Wing. I wasn't riding yet and besides it was too cold and wet for motorcycling, so I rented a car to attend his service.

His funeral took place in the MB Church of my youth, two hours from where I lived. Except for the gymnasium, the church looked the same as it had fifty-five years ago. The insides had been gutted to adapt to changing times and customs. I wondered if the traditional roots had been damaged in the renovations.

Funerals are key rituals amongst Mennonites. Even though the culture has changed, it's a chance for the community, many of whom are dispersed, to come together. As such, it was heartwarming to reconnect with extended family I hadn't seen in decades. Faces had aged, but the blood bonds were timeless.

The hymns had not changed at all. After all this time, I still knew the words by heart. It was not surprising to sing *Great is Thy Faithfulness*, one of Gerhard's favorites and sung at his service, too. Written in 1923, when Russian Mennonites prepared to leave, it brought great comfort, especially with its association with nature:

Great is Thy faithfulness, O God my Father,

There is no shadow of turning with Thee;
Thou changest not, Thy compassions, they
    fail not;
As Thou hast been Thou forever wilt be.

Great is Thy faithfulness! Great is Thy
    faithfulness!
Morning by morning new mercies I see;
All I have needed Thy hand hath provided.
Great is Thy faithfulness, Lord unto me!

Summer and winter and springtime and
    harvest,
Sun, moon, and stars in their courses above
Join with all nature in manifold witness
To Thy great faithfulness, mercy, and love.

Pardon for sin and a peace that endureth,
Thine own dear presence to cheer and
    to guide,
Strength for today, and bright hope for
    tomorrow,
Blessings all mine, with ten thousand beside!

While that hymn reassured me, others evoked anxiety and helped me understand some of the teachings that had led me to feel unworthy and powerless.

O, the wonder of it all! The wonder of it all!
Just to think that God loves me.

Why *wouldn't* God love me? I'd been taught it was because I was a worthless sinner. Now things are so much clearer.

Trust and obey, for there's no other way
To be happy in Jesus, but to trust and obey.

In other words, do as you're told and don't question.

Channels only, blessed Master,
But with all Thy wondrous pow'r
Flowing through us, Thou canst use us
Every day and every hour.

Master? Aside from the convoluted English, who had I, as an eight-year-old, imagined God to be?

As I thought about the lyrics and what they'd meant to my grandparents, I looked at the words in a new light. *Trust and Obey* spoke to having faith and following Divine guidance and intuition. Wasn't that what had kept them alive?

Channels Only can be translated to reflect our interconnectedness with Spirit and all life on earth.

I realized that each person connects with Spirit in his or her own way. The particulars are merely different paths to arriving at the same end result.

WINTER WAS MELTING AWAY, but not yet gone. I still had limited function in my shoulder, but I was ready to buy a motorcycle, confident that I'd be riding it soon.

Almost home from a two-mile walk to the pharmacy, I made a quick decision to stop at the grocery store across the road from my place to pick up some almonds. Sometimes, I walked down to the parking lot entrance and took the driveway, but on days without snow or ice, I took a shortcut down a slight grassy embankment, saving a few steps. It wasn't icy, but the ground was damp from melted snow. In one quick move, my left foot slid on mud, then regained traction as I lost my balance and fell. The loud snap was my ankle breaking. My foot dangled from my leg as I sat on the hillside, stunned. *This can't have happened.* I wanted to turn back the clock for less than a minute and walk around.

There I sat, getting a wet bum, bracing my ankle with both hands to protect me from the searing pain. Immobilized and alone on a low-traffic lane behind the store, I waited for someone to come along. An elderly man drove by and another elderly woman hobbled to her parked car.

"Call an ambulance. I've broken my ankle!" I hollered.

The woman looked at me like I had two heads. "I don't have a cell phone. Someone will be along soon," she said, smiling and chirping sweetly as she drove off.

I screamed at the man to try and get his attention before he, too, left. I'm not sure who notified a store employee, but finally two of them came out to investigate the fuss. Then they had to go back into the store to call the ambulance.

At my request, one of the employees went across the street to ask my landlady, who ran the salon downstairs, to get my cell phone. When he returned, I called Daniel to meet me at the hospital.

X-rays confirmed what I already knew. I'd broken both the tibia and fibula. I'd need surgery and hardware on both sides to stabilize it.

Now I was utterly adrift. I couldn't use crutches because my shoulder wasn't strong enough, so I was relegated to a wheelchair. My apartment was on the second floor of an old house, accessed via a curved staircase. How was I going to manage? As soon as I thought I was starting to see a little further down the metaphorical road, I was reduced to one step at a time. Best get on with it, I knew. Giving my body the care and time it needed to heal was my best option in the long term.

A friend who lived forty-five minutes away took me to her place to await surgery, scheduled for five days later. She'd also keep me after for as long as I needed. Jane took Measha again. I was so grateful, yet all I wanted was my own home. That was out of the question. Getting up the stairs would be a nightmare, and I couldn't get out on my own in an emergency.

This was a horrible time, one I had a great deal of trouble accepting with grace. I now depended on help for everything. At least before, I could walk, but now I had to have assistance with showering, laundry, groceries, cooking, and out-of-town doctor's appointments. Everywhere I went, someone had to lug a wheelchair, and help me in and out of the car.

You disappear when you're in a wheelchair. I'd felt compassion for people in them but had no idea what it felt like. At one point as I sat in my wheelchair pushed by Daniel, getting advice from a health care practitioner who addressed him, I felt like screaming. "Don't assume he's my husband! Talk to ME! Ask ME about my living arrangements, not the person who's pushing the wheelchair I'm in."

Not being able to reach the credit card machine to complete transactions frustrated me. Getting groceries and trying to reach for anything above a sitting shoulder level was out of the question.

Christine, whose husband Alex had died a month earlier, invited me to stay with her. At least I'd be back in Orangeville. I hesitated because it was such a topsy-turvy time for her. She insisted, but before accepting, I consulted with one of her close friends. The friend told me to go. It would be good for both of us. And at least I wouldn't have to navigate stairs.

Then Christine decided to go away for ten days. It was good for her, but it left me alone again, fresh from surgery, in a wheelchair, with a large cast on my foot and a bummed-up shoulder.

The internet wasn't even connected. Clearly, I needed quiet time. All I could do was cede to it.

Mere weeks earlier, I'd been filled with anticipation of getting back on the road. I'd planned to attend several events—the Horizons Unlimited gathering in Virginia, my friend Trent's fiftieth birthday party in Georgia, a BMW motorcycle rally in Ontario, and a going away party for friends who were setting off to travel around the Americas. I couldn't get to any of them.

I was totally perplexed and timid about doing anything. I couldn't understand why, just as I got ready to start out again after my shoulder injury, I had been knocked back on my ass—literally! What was I missing? What were the lessons I had yet to learn? Was I trying to take off in the wrong direction?

I'd crashed, brushed myself off, gotten up, and gotten slammed again. For months I'd been seeking guidance on how to proceed. I'd worked hard to learn the art of surrender.

I had my answer. The message was this: Don't go anywhere. The way was sitting down. I could have resisted, but that seemed pointless. That was wasting energy I needed for healing. The best thing for me was to sit.

The symbolism of two left-sided fractures, both requiring hardware to stabilize the bones so they could heal, was striking. From an energetic perspective, the left side represents feminine energy; the right is masculine. Feminine energy denotes "being." Receptivity. Male energy is "doing." Action. As with all nature, energy always seeks balance. My preponderance for moving, achieving, and earning, masculine energetic aspects, had not given my feminine side a chance for nourishment or expression. Feminine energy loves times of stillness and reflection, exactly what I'd been given to bring things back into balance.

Often, I would joke that I could tell the naysayers who claimed how dangerous motorcycling is that you can break a limb while walking.

I'd tried to keep up with writing and blogging. Now I took an official break. I didn't feel sorry for myself or angry. I just couldn't figure out what was going on. I didn't want to be a burden on anyone, but I needed help, and I had to ask for it. The sense of disconnection with who I was resurfaced. I didn't recognize this person who was dependent on others, who couldn't come and go as she pleased.

I *could* identify with that woman out riding her motorcycle across the country, camping, and setting her own course. As free as a bird. I could do what I wanted, when I wanted, and go wherever I wanted.

My mind wouldn't let me write at Christine's. I couldn't figure out structure, content, or focus on a topic. Instead, I practiced enjoying the pause, the peacefulness. Pauses are a necessary part of life. We pause between breaths. There's a pause between each heartbeat. Nature pauses in winter. I needed a pause in my life, even if it was enforced.

Finally, on April 27th, a month after snapping my ankle, I had to get home. I could get up the stairs on my butt, and around most of my place in the wheelchair. It wouldn't fit in the bathroom, but I could get it to the door and then a hop, a pivot, and two more hops got me to the toilet.

Back at my own table, with my foot elevated, life started to come back. Encouragement from unexpected sources—emails from readers, kind words and visits from friends, buoyed me. They did not know how much of a difference their thoughts and words made to me.

The real bonus was when someone would offer to take me out. It was awful being stuck inside, but I knew it was a pain to help me out, lug my wheelchair down the stairs, into the car, to whatever our destination, then repeat the whole thing to get me back. But it brightened up my whole day. A core group of friends, to whom I'm eternally grateful, gave me rides to therapy and brought in home-cooked meals. It was tremendously humbling. Only once when I asked for help was I turned down, and I tried not to take it personally.

I'd always thought I was compassionate and empathetic, but until I'd lost my mobility, I really didn't appreciate how it feels to be disabled. Visiting those who can't get out on their own, for any reason, is good, but taking them outside in the fresh air, country air if possible, makes such a difference for them. No one likes to be cooped up inside all the time. Immobility gave me a whole new level of empathy for people who have lost their independence or mobility, temporarily or permanently. I hadn't appreciated how desolate it feels. Intentions and words are great, but it's often the small gestures that mean so much. Like when I stayed overnight with my brother Robert and he tied a long string to the ceiling fan and light so I could operate it without getting up.

I'd never experienced that degree of loneliness or the ease of slipping into obscurity. Intentionally, I seldom posted to social networking sites, although during this time I kept an eye on what others did. It was surreal to watch the world go on around me, without me. Stepping back also made me see how absurd many of the posts were and how easy it was for people, myself included, to get caught up in emotional issues based on our limited perspective, and to draw the wrong conclusion without having the full picture, letting our emotions run amok over incomplete facts.

My orange fiberglass cast came off on May 7th, two days before my sixty-second birthday, and was replaced by an air cast —the best birthday present ever. I could begin weight-bearing. Hallelujah! Neither casts had been covered by health insurance, but for some unexplained reason, both were given to me without charge, a gift of at least $300. Another gift from Spirit.

Thankfully, the air cast was temporary, and even though it

felt like I'd be wearing it forever, I knew that in time my ankle would make a full recovery. Then I could get around on my own. My shoulder mobility, however, was still not considered functional.

On May 22nd I was still weaning off my air cast but hadn't tried getting my foot into a shoe or boot. With a little bit of tugging and twisting, my motorcycle boot went on. I had my eye on a test ride at the end of the month and wouldn't go unless I could wear full protective gear. That boot gave my ankle good support and pumped in an infusion of new energy. The first step I took to cross my living room will stay in my mind forever. I was so grateful to be back on my feet again. To this day, I'm thankful for each step.

Two days after that, Measha came home, another sign that my life was returning to the one I knew. The next night, I abandoned the wheelchair for night duty and hobbled to the bathroom instead. My need to hop ended. Three days later I walked the large block to physiotherapy, although I needed a ride home. The energy and new growth of spring filled the air. I was back on my feet!

Finally, on May 30th, I rode a motorcycle for the first time since my crash. For years, BMW Motorrad had hosted a women's only demo day in Orangeville—an opportunity for women to try out the new models and network. Since its inception, I'd coordinated the day and scheduled rides, but thinking I'd be in South America, I'd advised BMW I wouldn't be available that year.

Now, I was there, but in a different capacity. Their staff was terrific when I asked if I could test a motorcycle in the parking lot where the event was being held. While most of the models had been taken out on a ride, an F800ST remained behind. I'd try it. How hard could it be?

My left foot does a lot more than I'd realized. To put my right leg over the seat, I had to place all my weight on the left. It was still pretty tentative and sore. Then I had to apply muscle to lift the bike off its side stand. That was out of the question. Humbly, I asked Steve, the promotions manager, to help.

I'm recognized in the motorcycle world. I've traveled all over the continent, organized events, been involved in the industry, and written extensively about motorcycle-related topics. This same person now needed help to get on a motorcycle and was scared to ride. But I was also determined! I had the strength and resilience of my ancestors to fuel me. Steve was completely supportive, although I'm sure he could sense my anxiety. He'd crashed before and knew what it felt like to get back on a motorcycle again for the first time, and how important that first ride was.

The pavement was wet from recent rains and I was frightened beyond belief. Gingerly, I shifted into first gear, twisted the throttle just a little, and released the clutch. I moved at a snail's pace and couldn't stop smiling. On the second lap, I got it into second gear and kept it there for a victory lap before handing it back, unscathed. Getting off was another challenge requiring help. I'd done it though, even if only for a few minutes. I was back in the saddle! *This* was the person I knew! Even though more inner work awaited, I'd be doing it from familiar ground.

Less than two months later, after much deliberation, I bought Trudy, a brand-new Triumph Tiger! She was the right fit and had all the attributes I wanted. On top of that, the symbolism of the word *Triumph* spoke to my heart, and the Tiger model reminded me of my Jaguar animal guide. Trudy was the same style of motorcycle as the Ténéré I'd crashed, except smaller, lower, and lighter, and the same sky-blue color—a reminder to keep dreaming.

No one could have prepared me for how life-altering the past year had been. The physical crash was merely the catalyst. At first, I assumed I'd take six to eight months to recover, get a new bike and be on my way again. I even called it a detour, but that was an initial misperception. It wasn't what I planned. I was beginning to see that easier, more scenic roads could take me to my destination with a lot less angst, and more peace of heart and mind. The route I'd taken looked radically different than the one I'd planned. What I'd hoped to learn by traveling the Americas, I'd started to learn from home—like letting go of old ways that once worked but now needed to make way for the new. Or releasing perceived control of the outcome. Patience. Waiting. Listening. Learning to ask for help. Engaging with the power and strength of community. Following my heart. Heeding my intuition.

My apartment, which was only ever meant to be temporary, had started to wear on me. I dreaded another move but staying was worse. The noise from the street and the cacophony of hair salon sounds and smells made it impossible to focus on writing. It was hot, and I didn't want to buy an air conditioner. The landlady didn't respond to maintenance issues. I felt unsafe. Measha couldn't go outside. And the only place to park Trudy was on a busy street.

At the end of September, a year after my crash, I'd bumped into a well-connected friend. On a whim, I asked if she knew anyone with an apartment to rent. Four days later, I had my new place—a walkout in a house that backed onto a ravine, on a quiet court. My doors opened into a wooded area of tall cedars, nourished by a lively stream. The garage had space for my motorcycle. Had I not needed to give two months' notice where I was, I could have moved in that day. I'd be away for most of October so we targeted mid-November for the move.

I'd committed to three more intensive Energy Medicine courses that month. The first half of October I'd be in the picturesque Catskill Mountains in New York State, a good day's ride with Trudy. When I returned, I'd fly to Joshua Tree, California, for the third course. Ever since that first course in Utah, I'd hungered for the wisdom of these ancient teachings, which helped me understand that, energetically, I carried the experiences of my ancestors. Each course took me deeper into understanding and recognizing how the stories and beliefs that had been passed down from one generation to the next had influenced my thoughts, beliefs, and life choices. It was exactly what my quest was about.

The introspection from my courses and the motorcycle riding dovetailed nicely. I still didn't know where my Road was leading although I sensed the general direction, subject to change of course. I recognized my job was to keep moving forward, even if the action called for was non-action. My mission was to take one step at a time, knowing it was leading me in the right direction.

Then it was home for another winter of hibernation, introspection, and research.

THE LOCATION OF MY CRASH, at the border of the Siksika reserve, was not a fluke. I couldn't explain it, although I knew it was part of my journey. In my first conversation with him, Quinton Crow Shoe had suggested I may have been stopped on my quest because I hadn't prepared spiritually for delving into Indigenous cultures. It's not unlike riding a motorcycle: You're not ready to ride until you've taken a course to understand how to do it properly. You're not ready for advanced courses until you've mastered the basics. He advised me to go to any First Nation's reserve when I got home, offer a gift of tobacco, ask to speak with an Elder, explain my quest, and ask for a blessing and protection. My path would become clearer after that.

That had been reassuring. I was conscious of being an outsider probing into cultures very different than mine, where I had not established relationships and the people I approached had no grounds for trust or openness. In my favor, I knew Spirit was guiding me on a spiritual quest. Quinton had understood and given me a starting point.

Once settled in my own place after the crash, I drove two hours to the nearest reserve, looking for the Band Office. The receptionist directed me to another location where I could find Elders. The place was closed up tighter than a drum. On the way off the reserve, I stumbled over the Tourism Office. The representative listened and deduced that the Elders were preparing for that weekend's Mid-Winter Celebrations. She empathized and asked me to wait while she called an Elder who might be available. No one answered, but she gave me the Elder's phone number and told me to try her in a week, after the festivities.

When I finally reached the Elder, we chatted for more than an hour. But my spiritual questions were off-limits. She asked me what rituals and ceremonies my people used to connect with Spirit. Rites like communion and baptism had acted as a wedge breaching the thin veil between God's love and wrath. Embracing them meant buying into something I couldn't accept, yet I hadn't wanted to offend my parents by turning away.

"Go back to your blood," she said. "Don't look for answers in another culture."

"That's too painful," I said, surprising myself, adding "and they don't consider earth-based spirituality."

I'd never even admitted the pain to myself. For most of my life, I'd shielded myself from opening up my heart to who I was. I didn't know whom I'd find. Convinced she didn't understand my quest, I tried another approach. She wasn't having any of my excuses.

"Find yourself through your people. That will be your blessing. Once you've done that, contact me again."

Dejected, I hung up the phone, wondering what to do next.

Since I was still recovering and confined to my small apartment, I devoured books by Indigenous authors, learning about a broad spectrum of Indigenous cultures. I didn't understand why I felt so compelled to pursue them, but I went with it. Something was guiding me.

Once I returned to riding the summer following my crash, I returned to travel writing. One of my Ontario-based tourism clients accepted my proposal to write articles with Indigenous themes. That gave me opportunities to meet in person with an Anishinaabe scholar and a Chief and brought life to traditions I'd only read about. It also validated my course of action.

When I heard the Ontario MCC—the Mennonite Central Committee, the charity organization founded in the 1920s to feed starving Russian Mennonites—was hosting an Anishinaabe speaker, I was elated. This collaboration, I thought, must reflect a spiritual reconciliation. The MCC representatives would understand my perspective. The teachings I'd grown up with viewed humans as separate, even superior, to all other life. Perhaps this move by a Mennonite organization signaled a wider acceptance of humans as an integral part of nature, conscious of our role and effect on our environment, and ready to embody a way of life congruent with the sacredness of our Earth.

The event was an outcome of Canada's Truth and Reconciliation Commission (TRC) mandated "to educate people about the history and legacy of the Indian Residential Schools system, and share and honour the experiences of former students and their families." The official report concluded the school system amounted to "cultural genocide." Mennonites had operated three residential schools in northern Ontario.

The Anishinaabe speaker, a Professor Emerita and Instructor in Indigenous Studies, told stories from her culture, educating the handful of listeners. After, I tried to engage with the MCC representatives but was met with indifference, a sharp contrast with the national MCC's official response to the TRC. It felt like the Ontario MCC viewed collaboration as a Missions project. They were going through the motions but appeared uninterested in understanding another culture. Disappointed to the core, I'd run into another dead end.

I knew I carried the experiences of my ancestors in my energetic DNA. However, since the earth is a living being, I also must carry the experiences of the lands my ancestors and I walked. Those experiences helped shape me. And the Wisdomkeepers of those lands were the Indigenous Peoples, which explained my drive to understand them. I didn't feel compelled to go to what is now Ukraine, but local Indigenous people could tell me about the area around my parents' farm where I grew up. The Niitsitapi (Blackfoot) People, indigenous to the area in Alberta where Dad and Mom had lived as children, could shed light on the energy of this land my parents had lived on and how it may have influenced them, and me.

Since it had been a year, I followed up with the local Elder I'd spoken with, thinking she'd appreciate my new insights. I tried to explain that, as much as I respected her culture, I didn't want to adopt it. Rather, I wanted to understand our personal relationship with nature. I was again disappointed. She was respectful, and not the least bit interested in what I said.

I emailed Quinton, recounting my frustration and inability to connect with an Elder who could advise me.

"Tell you what," he said. "There's a Blackfoot Fair at Siksika in August. Go there, offer tobacco, ask to speak with an Elder, and explain your situation."

Up to that point in time, I wasn't sure how my quest would continue. Now, the desire to attend the Siksika Pow-wow put the wheels in motion for the Ancestor Trail trip, and became the reason why the dates for the Fair were central to my plans.

8

In the first week of August 2016, after 3,000 miles of travel, I'd reached Dalmeny, north of Saskatoon, Saskatchewan. Campland RV Park, my home for the night, sat on the outskirts of town, right off the Yellowhead Highway. Although Gerhard and Susa had been destined for Langham, two rail stops west, they talked about their two years in Dalmeny the most. As anxious as I was to find the farm they'd lived on, my first order of business was to set up camp and off-load my luggage. The clothing, utensils, and provisions I carried on my bike were not much less than what was in the two trunks that held all Gerhard and Susa's possessions. Although a tent was my home on the road, at least I had a furnished haven to return to.

Now a fifth-generation family farm, the Schultz's was the first stop on the Ancestor Trail. I'd visited there in 2003 when I was traveling around the country after leaving my marriage and career. At that time, I'd contacted eighty-eight-year-old Rudy Schultz and his wife Martha, son and daughter-in-law of the people who'd taken in Gerhard and Susa. Rudy, an adolescent when they were there, remembered them. Rudy and Martha had driven into nearby Saskatoon to pick me up for the drive to the farm. After that we'd gone back to their place for a dinner of boiled potatoes and local Mennonite sausage.

Since then, I'd lost touch with the Schultzes and had no idea how to find the farm, but Dalmeny was a small town and someone would know. As I cruised the streets weighing my options, I scanned for buildings that might have been here in the late 1920s. Gerhard and Susa may not have gotten into town often, but it was neat to envision them walking these streets as young adults.

I started at the post office. They referred me to the pharmacy and when I struck out there, I went to the Town office, located along the railway tracks, once the lifeline of these small prairie locales. The clerks told me to call Peter Schultz and handed me a phone book. If anyone would know, it would be Peter, they said. I'd struck gold. He was a cousin to the family I was looking for and he'd be delighted to show me around. In less than fifteen minutes, he was at the Town office. After brief introductions, he hopped in his pickup and instructed me to follow him.

My anxiety level spiked. Heading deep into farm country, we'd likely encounter treacherous gravel roads. There was no sense worrying until I needed to, and I talked my anxiety down. But only a few miles later, we were into the same kind of deep loose stuff I'd crashed in.

I tried to find traction on the more packed, narrow shoulder but my anxiety skyrocketed as my confidence plummeted. Though the dusty gap between Peter and me widened, I wasn't going to force myself to continue until I crashed. Jaguar, who'd already seen me crash once, agreed. This wasn't the time or place to push my limits.

I had to get out to that farm, but it wasn't going to be on two wheels. I stopped and sat there defeated, gasping for air while I waited for Peter to return. I explained my post-crash fear of gravel and knew he'd have a solution. Dalmeny is a Mennonite enclave and everyone knows everyone else. He knew people nearby who had a barn where I might be able to park my bike while Peter toured me in his truck. Swallowing my pride, I agreed.

I followed Peter into the driveway and waited while he knocked on the door of the bungalow and spoke with the young woman who opened it. A few minutes later, Harry, her husband, appeared in the back yard near the barn. "Park it right over there beside mine," he said, pointing to a dusty motorcycle, idle during harvest season.

In another pickup and another dusty ride across prairie grain country, reminiscent of my post-crash ride to the hospital two years earlier, Peter chatted freely about his family history, unaware I'd brought four passengers with me. I listened with one ear, but my thoughts were with Gerhard and Susa. Ninety years ago, in their mid-20s, they'd been driven out to this farm, their new home, miles from the nearest town.

As we pulled into the driveway, I tried to imagine what they would have been thinking. I knew through Susa's letters they were glad to be together again. They'd been living in Langham, with Gerhard's brother Abram and his wife Liese. Susa was so lonely there because Gerhard could only get home from work on the weekends.

"There used to be a white two-story house, right over there," I said, pointing toward a tangle of greenery. "It was standing when I was here in 2003 with Rudy and Martha. It's where Mom was born."

"They took it down two years ago, and built that bungalow," Peter said.

"But those trees would have been here," I said, surveying the tall trees that had shaded my grandparents.

Peter nodded in agreement. "All this land," he said, sweeping his arm over fields of crops surrounding the house, "was pastureland for beef cattle."

Walt Schultz, the current steward of the land, was on his way to a combine crisis on a remote field. The machine had broken down while harvesting and he didn't have much time to chat. He was too young to have known my grandparents, but he'd heard stories telling how his grandparents had taken people in.

"Gerhard told us he picked stones out of the fields," I said.

"We don't have any stones," Walt said.

"That's because Gerhard got them all," I said, smiling.

At Gerhard's urging, I told Walt that Gerhard had always spoken highly of his grandparents, with much gratitude for taking him and Susa under their wing and giving them a start.

It was energetically powerful to have been with the Schultzes at their farm. I didn't learn any new facts about Gerhard and Susa's life here by visiting the space they'd lived in, but I felt a deeper heart connection with them.

Afterward, Peter took a circuitous cross-country route back to my bike. He was eager to show me the Schultz farms in the area, established as the family had prospered and grown. We even stopped at the Mennonite cemetery where the family, including Rudy and Martha, was buried. When we arrived back at Harry's place, and I guided my motorcycle out of the barn, the gravel wasn't the greatest hazard. That honor went to the litters of black barn kittens that darted from everywhere.

Evening was falling as I returned to Campland RV Park. The site was as flat as the prairie it lay on. With nothing to interrupt the view, my illuminated tent was silhouetted against a fiery orange sunset. The evening was magical and calming. As stars emerged, slowly at first, then by the thousands, I gazed upward.

Gerhard and Susa had been as comfortable as they could be with the Schultzes, who were also MBs and part of a community and church. Although they treated them very well, the Schultzes were *Kanadiers* (Mennonites who had immigrated from Russia to North America in the 1870s), not *Russlanders* (the name given to the later wave of immigrants my grandparents belonged to), and they weren't blood. During the fifty years since the *Kanadiers* had come to America and Canada, the *Russlanders* had had very different life experiences. Although they were all Mennonites, their religious and cultural practices had evolved differently.

Susa's father Heinrich and his wife Helena, along with five of her sisters and two brothers had settled in nearby Waldheim but found it hard to be accepted amongst the *Kanadiers*. After only a few months, Heinrich moved his family to Dominion City, in southern Manitoba, where more *Russlanders* lived, while Gerhard and Susa stayed in Dalmeny with the Schultzes. Even though he missed Susa, Heinrich valued his family dearly and wanted to keep them together in a place that welcomed them. He wanted to farm, and his sons to farm, too.

Even though life situations may be a fit at one time, circumstances change, and our souls may yearn to leave the nest and take flight, even when that nest looks like home. My restlessness was no different than that of my ancestors. Only the circumstances were different.

I slept comforted by the same stars they'd slept under. Something in the air had told them, and now me, that all was well, even if we couldn't appreciate it at the time, or it took a while to arrive.

The next day, I left Dalmeny and began a two-day ride west and north to Beaverlodge in the Peace River District of northern Alberta. Gerhard and Susa's month-long travel from Russia had ended in Langham, Saskatchewan, right on the way, one block off the Yellowhead Highway. A few buildings from their time must still exist. I had to stop.

Look for the grain elevators in prairie towns and you'll find the train tracks. Most elevators are defunct, but Langham's still houses an operation that mixes, packages, and sells birdseed. Other than being moved away from the south side of the tracks, the Langham Station, built in 1905 and now a museum, stood as it had in 1924 when Gerhard and Susa arrived, spruced up with a coat of grey paint and white trim. The wooden Arrivals and Departures board hung empty, the last train having left the station decades ago. Abram would have forgone the benches, pacing the platform, glancing down the track, listening for the train whistle, and waiting to throw his arms around his brother and sister-in-law. Huge planters overflowed with petunias, Gerhard's favorite garden flower.

Sixteen months separated Gerhard from his younger brother and the two were always close. Here in Langham, Abram and his wife Liese had taken Gerhard and Susa in until they could get themselves established. What a joyous reunion that was!

A six-sided Peace Pole stood sentry, strong and proud, a testament to the townspeople and those they'd welcomed, including me. The prayer on its faces—*May Peace Prevail on Earth*—beamed the languages, including *Plautdietsch*, and dialects of the cultures that had settled here: Cree, English, Norwegian, Doukhobors, Hutterites, and Mennonites. This was the first one I'd seen, but there are tens of thousands in 180 countries, dedicated as monuments of peace. Bowing my head, I joined my four companions in voicing a prayer of gratitude for this land.

It's rare to see strange women riding through town on a motorcycle. Noticing that my wanderings had caught the attention of one of the few other people on the broad street, I rode over to where he and a couple of others were unloading a trailer. They might be able to answer questions about the town's history.

Robert Anderson greeted me warmly. A retired university professor, he operates a thriving bee operation across the tracks from the grain elevator. Our brief meeting conveyed his extensive knowledge of the area's history, which predated the arrival of Europeans. As I said good-bye, he ran over to his truck and returned carrying a couple of jars of local honey. I hope Gerhard and Susa received the same hospitality from the locals as Robert showed me.

On my way back to the highway, I stopped at Zoar Mennonite Church, a large, simple white clapboard structure constructed in 1911, where Gerhard and Susa likely would have worshipped. The gratitude, grief, and hope poured out to God in German hymns and prayers from its wooden pews still resonated through its walls.

A curious woman from a small bungalow across the street approached me, the floral ribbon from her straw hat tied loosely under her chin. She wondered why I was there. Having lived in Langham for more than fifty years, she could easily sense a stranger. She couldn't reconcile me with her stereotype of a woman who's been raised Mennonite, or rides a motorcycle, let alone both. As we chatted amicably, and I told her of my grandparents' time here, her incredulity turned to fascination, acceptance, and respect. Gerhard and Susa nodded and smiled, bowled over to hear their few months in Langham touched strangers ninety-two years later. The woman would have kept me there all morning, but my passengers were antsy to get going. Beaverlodge, Alberta, where Johann and Liese landed, was still two days away and I wanted to leave enough time to explore the area. We *had* to be back in southern Alberta for the Blackfoot Pow-wow, which started in five days.

Most of the day I enjoyed riding across the open prairie. You could see forever, through time. Broad river valleys had carved wide contours through the otherwise flat landscape. The Yellowhead is the only highway through the area, and with little danger of getting lost, I didn't have to pay attention to road signs, other than the speed limit. When we weren't chatting, we quietly enjoyed the ride, and each other's company.

I should have paid more attention. I got wrapped up and turned around in a massive Edmonton road construction project, and then caught in afternoon city traffic. It cost me an hour when all I wanted was to get out of town and find a place to camp. Once back on track, I found several RV parks, but they were either private or wouldn't allow tents. I'd be riding through sparsely populated, remote country the rest of the way. Without knowing if or where I'd find a suitable campsite, I grudgingly found a motel. It exceeded my budget and I loathe the impersonality and isolation of motel rooms. Campsites, where I can pitch my tent, breathe fresh air, and meet interesting people, are much more to my liking.

It was a clean, warm, and safe place to stay, though, but I was glad to be on the road again the next morning. Especially because we'd soon be in Beaverlodge, Johann and Liese's first home in Canada. They, too, must have felt anxious to arrive at the end of their arduous trip.

Johann's parents stayed in Russia and he never saw them again. Three Klassen first cousins did make the move and homesteaded near them in northern Alberta. Liese's brother Jacob, and sister Helena and their families came to Canada, but she said good-bye forever to her father and four sisters. The best news was that Liese carried another child, my father, who would be born here. Dad liked to say he snuck through the border.

Their arrival in Canada had been three months later than planned because Johann was detained in Southampton to treat his trachoma, an eye infection, while Liese waited, her anxiety and their baby growing inside her. Others in their group had gone before and were waiting to take them in. Heading into a remote wilderness in the middle of winter, not sure what awaited them or where they'd live, was not the right situation for

Liese to give birth. Instead, they waited in Swalwell, Alberta, until Bernhard John, affectionately called Benny, was born two months later, before completing their journey.

WILDERNESS PARTED as I rode north to Peace River Country, 300 miles north of Edmonton. It was the furthest north I'd ever been by motorcycle. Wild country. Beautiful. Unpredictable. The highway followed a broad valley and the river that had courageously carved its way through the boreal forest eons ago. Between the road and the river ran the train track, a steel ribbon, defying the elements. River, rail, and now road. Fingers that reached out, transporting explorers, families, and prospectors to their dreams.

Beaverlodge was named Redlow during their time, but my family always called it Peace River, no doubt in unconscious deference to finally finding a land of peace. When they arrived, barely a year after the railroad extension was completed, fewer than 200 people lived here, clustered around a post office, school, and a few stores. In 1929, it received its current name, after the lodges built along the river by the Beaver Indians (now known as the Dane zaa).

I couldn't imagine what it would have been like to arrive here in 1926. The wilderness was beautiful and the remoteness calming, but I was on a motorcycle, not arriving as a refugee trying to make a home for my family.

Johann must have wondered where God was leading them. All he'd be able to see from the train window were forests, sometimes a lake or marsh. How could he farm here? Swalwell, where Benny was born, was surrounded by fertile farmland like they'd had in Russia. Most of the way up to Edmonton was like that too, before they entered this wilderness.

He and Liese must have questioned if they'd made the right

decision for their family. In Russia, they'd lived in a big brick farmhouse in a small village but the communities were as one. Family was always near. Now they'd be with fewer than twenty families, spread out across the countryside. Still, with a name like Peace River District, it had to be a good sign.

It wasn't much further along that the land began to transition. Johann must have been so relieved to see it change from forest to field. Then he could picture their farm and home here. It would be hard at first, but nothing compared to what they'd already been through. It would be a good life for their family. They'd stay with Johann's cousin until he could get their own place built.

Beaverlodge's population has grown to 2,465, but it retains that pioneer edge. As I rode along the railway tracks on the main route through town, massive, mud-covered four-wheel-drive pickup trucks dwarfed me. Even the pavement had a film of slick mud on this sunny August day, vestiges of forays into surrounding fields.

A more convivial aspect of frontier towns is the welcome they extend to strangers, especially women on motorcycles traveling alone. Like most northern municipalities, the town maintains a spartan campground. The Beaverlodge Pioneer Campground sat beside the IGA grocery store, tucked behind a former one-room log schoolhouse. This would be my home for the next three days.

Travelers have stopped by Beaverlodge for more than a hundred years, although their faces have changed. At one time, prospectors seeking their fortune passed through on their way to gold fields. In the late 1920s, newcomers poured out of rail cars to homestead land of the Treaty 8 region, traditional territories of the Cree, Beaver, and Chipewyan, that had become more "accessible." Now the campsite sees pick-ups hauling fifth wheels and vacationing retirees, as well as families. Three young men from New Brunswick who'd come to work in the oil fields occupied a corner site. And one motorcyclist in a tent found a quiet, shaded, grassy spot along the back corridor. With a solid picnic table, clean showers, electricity, and free Wi-Fi from the secondary school behind me, it was perfect.

It's easy to understand why this land appealed to farmers. Prairie grasslands rolled up from the south in gentle undulations, creating a sense of openness. Foothills of the Rockies flanked the western exposure and abundant forests protected the northern and eastern edges. A small stream squiggled its way through as if trying to have as much fun as possible before joining the modest Beaverlodge River. The land would have been rife with deer, elk, moose, black bear, small mammals, waterfowl, and songbirds; the rivers teeming with fish. Even in August, the area felt lush, and dense crops covered fields maturing for harvest.

Soil was fertile and supportive of growing grain, but it had to be cleared. Johann and Liese would repay their credit for their farm loan and the *Reiseschuld*, their transportation debt, from the proceeds of their crops. Johann's first priority, though, was to build a shelter for his family and animals.

I'd ridden to the south end of town and the statue of the larger-than-life beaver sitting on the giant felled tree he'd chewed. It made a good photo op. The town sign offered hope with its slogan: *A Place to Build Dreams*.

My campsite vantage point looked southeast from the town to the golden fields where Johann and Liese had farmed. I sat on the picnic table gazing at their fields of dreams. They must have been so grateful to be here. Perfect climate and soil conditions produced a high yield that first summer. They'd survived extreme hardship, but they'd persevered and now their family could live in freedom. Everything looked so promising.

Then Johann's cough and night sweats started. Stoic as he

was, he probably tried to ignore them for as long as he could. He was young and healthy and could beat this. But in those days, tuberculosis was incurable. As a last resort, he was moved twenty-five miles to the hospital in Grande Prairie, away from Liese and Benny.

Johann had survived many challenges, but he didn't have the physical strength to overcome this one. Years of malnutrition, overwork, and stress made him vulnerable to illness. He died on February 7th, 1928, less than two years after arriving in this land of peace.

I had vague instructions to help me find the exact homestead location. The woman at the Visitor's Center told me to turn south at Foster's Feed and Seed, continue over the bridge, and look for a grove of trees with a sign marking the Mennonite cemetery. My grandparents had lived near there.

I cruised south slowly, crossing the concrete bridge, taking in the surroundings and not wanting to miss an overgrown plot. My passengers kept an eye out, too. I needn't have worried. The sign on the east side of the road was much larger than I expected, worn and tired, but standing proud against a backdrop of tall poplars, eclipsed by one towering pine. The gravel shoulder was too narrow and sloped to park on, so in the absence of other vehicles, I crowded the edge of the pavement, kicked out the side stand, and activated Trudy's four-way flashers. Dismounting, I removed my helmet as one would doff a hat out of respect. I pocketed the pouch of tobacco I'd carried from Manitoulin Island, then walked across the road, reading the sign across the deep ditch, a chasm of time.

Beaverlodge River Mennonite Cemetery

The Mennonite families purchased land in this area in the late 1920s, establishing their cemetery on this site, and further north, their church. It served them until roads and transportation improved, and they centralized near La Glace. This graveyard, not being registered, was partially destroyed with the building of the present bridge and road.

Rest in Peace.

County of Grande Prairie, 1977

Johann had been laid to rest here. I knew that at least some of the eight unmarked graves, now indistinguishable in the trees and undergrowth, had inadvertently been disturbed and his remains had likely been moved during road renovations, but to stand there taking it in overwhelmed me. Johann, the grandfather I never met, lay here. It had been such a short period of Dad's life and one he rarely spoke of. What few stories he'd heard opened painful wounds. If not for Johann's endurance in getting his family here, my story would be completely different. With utmost reverence, I laid down a gift of tobacco, grateful to Spirit for delivering my ancestors to this land and grateful for their sacrifices and courage. Lastly, I asked for blessings in exploring my family history in this area.

I carry Johann's blood, and his experiences and strengths live in me. In 1926 he walked land near here. But where?

A small frame house on this side of the bridge caught my attention so I made a U-turn, stopping at the mailbox. A large mongrel loped up the muddy, rutted driveway, barking and seemingly friendly. I wasn't willing to test his demeanor by pulling into a situation I couldn't easily get out of, though. As I stopped to consider my next move, a middle-aged woman approached, wind-blown, frayed blonde hair curling at her shoulders and rubber boots poking out from under baggy pants. She listened intently as I described my mission, then invited me to join the family gathered in the side yard.

Her grandfather and his brother had purchased large tracts

of land in the area around 1914, homesteading and eventually making homesteading arrangements with other newcomers. She knew vaguely of the Mennonite families who had landed here, had seen pictures of their log homes and gatherings, but couldn't be more specific with how I might find out exactly where my grandparents and infant father had called home.

Land records are archived at the county seat in Grande Prairie, twenty-five miles east. The ride there took me back through the bucolic route I'd come. Mary, the archivist, who knew every dusty document in the library, pulled out huge ledger books filled with meticulous entries penned by some clerk wielding a fountain pen dispensing fine black ink. I pored through them, deciphering the elaborate cursive, but no title bore my grandfather's name. Ironically, the only record of him being in the area was an official entry for what was purported to be an unregistered cemetery; he was the second of eight people interred there, including one other man and six infants. In a bizarre twist, Mary, the archivist who found the records, began coughing uncontrollably when I told her he died of a respiratory disease. She'd been fine immediately before that.

Disappointed but not defeated, I returned to Beaverlodge. Knowing they'd lived close to the cemetery, I'd use my intuition to guide me. I traced the grid of Township roads up, down, and across, pausing at regular intervals to get off Trudy, walk around, and take in the view. As much as my passengers loved to chat while we rolled down the road, uncharacteristic quiet prevailed. Maybe it wasn't for me to know now, but I sensed I walked the same land they'd walked.

MY HEART NEEDED time to absorb what I'd learned and felt. A good long motorcycle ride through this area would help. We were still many miles from the mighty Peace River, the district's namesake. Tomorrow I'd ride further north than I'd ever been, to lay eyes on this iconic waterway.

Heavy fog had blanketed the town while I slept. A check of the weather station showed it would clear fifteen miles north, so I waited for it to dissipate, then set out. The wind that eventually cleared it stayed with me the entire day, threatening and teasing, with roiling clouds adding to the primordial ambiance.

Mother Earth has been particularly prolific and generous in sustaining life in Peace River country. Prime farmland produces high yields from her surface. Beneath that, a network of pipes draws oil from her depths. Tanker trucks trundle down gravel roads and traverse farm fields to sidle up to pumping stations. After gorging on liquid gold, they deliver it to larger pumping stations or refineries. Further north, the harvest turns to lumber, and tankers are replaced with logging trucks, their racks bulging with freshly felled trees.

Then the land drops away and the road sweeps right as it descends into a dramatic valley, where the majestic Peace River flows through its heart as it has for eons. Mighty. Broad. Languid. Powerful.

There's no designated place to stop, but I had to. With little traffic and good visibility, I hit Trudy's kill switch and balanced on the side of the road to take in the view, the air, and the energy.

There's a benefit to flat terrain—you can see clear across the country. Most of the day I'd miraculously avoided the rain. I'd ride on wet roads minutes after a cloudburst had passed, or skirt ahead, narrowly missing another one. On the way home, the sky to the south was again dark and angry. With such acute visibility, I could watch the clouds and track the weather, strategizing which roads to take to avoid the worst of it.

Johann and Liese had survived turbulent times in their homeland by watching the storm clouds and adapting to the best of their ability. The river evoked the power of peace, the peace my ancestors had stood for even during times of turmoil, and the freedom they had found, without conflict.

Content and grounded once again, I continued on, returning to my Beaverlodge campsite late in the evening. It had been a powerful day. Just as the energy of place had filled me with gratitude under the prairie sky in Saskatchewan where Gerhard and Susa had started their new life, so too had the power of the place where Johann and Liese had found a home.

A peaceful sleep under another northern sky quickly overcame me, preparing me for my final day in Beaverlodge.

WITH ONE DAY LEFT, I wanted to savor the area and make one more visit. The woman in the tourist office had put me in touch with eighty-three-year-old Lydia Wiens, who lived in Grande Prairie but had grown up in Beaverlodge. It had taken a couple of days, but we'd connected at the eleventh hour. Lydia, spry and with short white hair combed back from her face, welcomed me like long-lost family. She'd even invited her sister Agatha over to meet me. A three-foot-wide rectangular plaque above the kitchen cupboards, visible from anywhere in the living-dining area, affirmed *FAMILIES ARE FOREVER*. Her parents had been part of the original group of Mennonite refugees that included Johann and Liese. Lydia's father had planted the pine tree that now towered over the poplars in the Mennonite cemetery when her parents buried their five-month-old daughter, the first person to be laid to rest there. Johann was the next.

I thought she might be able to tell me where Johann and Liese had homesteaded, but she didn't have anything to offer. After a wonderful visit with Lydia and Agatha, during which Lydia shared photos of her family's early days in Beaverlodge, I left to pay final respects to my ancestors. Riding out to the cemetery, on the same side of the road, I noted a culvert for farm access nearby. It gave me a safer parking spot and access to the site without having to climb through the ditch.

This time, I walked to the back of the cemetery copse along rutted farm equipment tracks. The mowed corridor between tree line and fence line, used to access the adjacent wheat field, gave me privacy for my thoughts. The drone from beehives stacked beside the trees provided background music as I regarded the scene. Other than the sign at the road, occluded by trees from where I stood, nothing indicated that anyone had ever been interred there. I wondered about the experiences of the people who had tried to tame this land. The people whose dreams had set the stage for future generations.

But only one person interested me. After everything Johann had been through, getting to this land, getting his family here, and then leaving them to fend for themselves, what had he thought as he prepared to leave this world? Did he have a calm or troubled passing?

Softly, I called to him. "Opa, are you here?"

And from nowhere, a bird appeared high above my head, soaring toward the trees in front of me, then swooping away, back to where it came from. A messenger.

"No, little one, not in the trees, but I'm here with you and in the wind. I'm at peace."

Johann had found the serenity he'd sought for himself and his family.

"Thank you, Opa. We are well. Rest in Peace."

Slowly, I made my way back to Trudy. I'd connected with a grandfather I'd never known, in a way I couldn't have imagined.

9

At age eight, I had three brothers and a sister. Out of necessity, I'd begun pitching in with household chores and looking after the little ones. Dad needed Mom to help run the farm.

Fruits and vegetables were picked fresh and canned or frozen for the winter. Our large vegetable garden grew tomatoes and rows of corn higher than my head. I spent many hot steamy summer evenings husking corn, dropping naked cobs in boiling water, cutting the kernels off, filling plastic bags, sealing them with a twist tie, and stacking them in the deep freezer in the basement. I marveled when I'd be at my friends' houses for dinner and their food wasn't home-grown or baked.

My parents mustered resources to feed us healthy food on a tight budget. As crops ripened, Mom canned the fruit of the week and all winter we'd have our own tomatoes, peaches, and cherries. And jam! Lots of yummy jam, which we had every morning on our toast. They discovered that the National Bakery in St. Catharines sold leftovers at the end of each day for fifty percent off. They put their name on the store's list and when it came up, someone from the bakery would call, tell us what was in the order and Mom would decide if we'd take it. She'd pass on fancy pastries and wait for an order of mostly bread and meat pies. They started buying beef by the half from Good's Butcher Shop in Vineland, another order that helped fill the freezer, and our stomachs, over the winter. Needless to say, they soon invested in a second chest freezer.

Dinners always included dessert—something Mom had canned or baked. Many of my friends' mothers bought canned or frozen fruit at the store that was never as good, nor were their mothers as good as mine. Our diet was wholesome out of financial necessity, even before we knew the ill effects of highly processed foods. We still had our share of sugar, but wore it off with work and play.

At age eight, my cousin Jude and I started summer camp, hosted by Eden Christian College, a church-run secondary school in Niagara-on-the-Lake, about twelve miles from our home. The gymnasium floor became the sleeping area for everyone, with rows of sleeping bags arranged by campers' ages. As a public relations gesture, the Niagara Falls Cyanamid Plant, producers of pesticides and fertilizers, converted their water storage facility into a swimming pool and opened it free of charge to the public. The pool actually had a current, generated as two million liters of water an hour were diverted from the nearby hydro canal, fed by the mighty Niagara River. Cyanamid even supplied an on-duty nurse and two lifeguards. The minimal registration fee for a week at camp was still a financial stretch for my parents, but because it was for my spiritual edification, it was a sacrifice they were happy to make.

After that, I went to Camp Cherith, a Christian non-denominational girl's camp in southern Ontario. Mom's youngest brother, my favorite uncle, Uncle Peewee (Walt), and his wife drove me up in his new burgundy Corvair. I didn't know a soul or what to expect, but managed to find my way to my austere cabin and throw my things on a stark wooden lower bunk. I dreaded swimming in the pond with the gooey, mucky bottom. Archery lessons helped pass the time, but lots of enforced Bible reading put a damper on the fun. Every day started with personal devotions. We'd hunt for a solitary location, spread out a plastic ground sheet to separate us from the dew, read our Bible, and pray—heady stuff for a week that should have been playful. I was a lonely little girl, away from home for the first time by myself, and didn't know what to do. The chapel service later in the day irked me too, but scanning the woods surrounding the outdoor sanctuary kept my fertile imagination occupied. I wondered how deep the forest went, what birds and animals lurked in the shadows, where the paths led, and where the streams flowed.

Other friends went too, but on a different week, and after two years, my parents stopped sending me. I'd started to realize that I wasn't like everyone else, even within Mennonite circles. I was curious, loved to explore the outdoors, especially in the woods, and questioned what we were taught. That gave me a wider perspective, something that has served me well in later life.

In spite of a tight budget, Mom and Dad managed to fit in family holidays, working around the farm and harvest schedule. For several years, they and a group of friends rented cottages on a northern lake. The rudimentary structures had indoor plumbing, an exposed interior framework, and eight-foot walls exposed to the rafters, voiding any secrets. Someone always had a boat and towed us around the lake on a board or water skis. Dad could come up only on weekends because we went during cherry season, but he'd take us there on Saturday, leave Sunday afternoon, and come back the following Saturday to get us.

In early October 1967, after the harvest and during the long Canadian Thanksgiving weekend, my parents rented a fourteen-foot house trailer, hitched it to their dark turquoise Ford Galaxy 500 and took us to Expo 67 in Montreal. Mary was only two, so she stayed with Gerhard and Susa, and the remaining seven of us—my parents and five children ages five to thirteen—packed into the car and trailer like sardines. Architecturally striking pavilions depicting cultures from countries all around the world, staffed by people of all colors and sizes dressed in traditional regalia, captivated my imagination. There was no way we could get to them all, but we saw enough to open our eyes to the fact that not everyone lived, or thought, like we did. I didn't grasp the importance of these excursions, or how lucky we were. Hardly anyone I knew went away on family holidays.

The next year, eight of us piled into the Galaxy, five in the back seat, three in the front, and drove 1,400 miles to Fort Lauderdale, Florida, for Christmas vacation. My parents hadn't thought to make overnight room reservations for a hotel or motel somewhere along the way. Storms, compounded by lines of traffic from road construction, made for a harrowing drive and a wicked migraine for my mother. As Mom and Dad tried repeatedly to find a place to stop for night, we referenced the Christmas story and joked that there was no room at the inn. I doubt my parents laughed. Our family ended up sleeping on cots, divided between the second and third floor hallways of a rickety hotel in the Appalachian Mountains.

Florida was as new to us as staying in a motel. The small family-run place had a pool, and we only had to cross the road to access the beach. It was the first time I saw an automatic dishwasher and a garbage disposal built into the kitchen sink. It was also my first experience getting stung by a Portuguese Man-of-War.

If family and church were central values, the threads of hard work, achievement, and earning my way held everything together. During school season, homework and piano lessons, including daily practice, took up much of my time. Being the oldest and a girl followed by three brothers, I learned early to cook, clean, and do dishes. The boys were exempt from household chores. During my adolescence, Mom returned to nursing part time, working on the farm in the mornings, then going in for a shift at the hospital. I picked up cooking and caring for the family. I know she loved the work, but we also needed her pay to make ends meet. I always felt like I'd raised a family and as a result, never wanted children of my own.

We were expected to behave and do above average, but not stellar, work in school. At times I focused on output at the expense of details. My second grade report card noted: *Elizabeth is doing very well, however sometimes accuracy suffers at the expense of speed.* By seventh grade, I'd caught on: *Elizabeth is a good, hardworking pupil.*

As much as I'd vowed in second grade to never become a writer, I won my first writing award at age ten. Five schools in the township held a contest to write an essay about Sir John A. MacDonald, Canada's first Prime Minister. I spent much time putting something together and then the day before the deadline, I lost it. Digital copies were unheard of, leaving me one option. I scrambled to recreate my work from memory. Thankfully, the content was still fresh in my mind, and I managed to pull off a win at the fifth-grade level.

Other than piano lessons, which most Mennonite girls took, artistic pursuits were not valued or encouraged. My parents and grandparents had to prioritize how to allocate limited funds. Always they gave to the church and charity, but beyond that, there had to be a practical reason to part with scarce funds. Art was a luxury, not a necessity.

When it came time for secondary school, I had choices: the public Beamsville District High School sixteen miles west, or the church-run, privately funded Eden Christian College, sixteen miles east. It's unnerving enough to cross the threshold into ninth grade without having to make a decision of that magnitude. I was scared of going to a public school. If I went, I'd go into the five-year Arts and Science stream because I was smart. But "secular" people went there, and I didn't know how to act around them. I already knew I didn't fit into my culture, but I didn't know where I *did* fit, and for a thirteen-year-old, that's unsettling.

Eden, with its familiar setting and rules of engagement, made a secure safety net. I'd know others there from the church. I didn't want to go, but it was the lesser of two discomforts. Once there, though, I faltered. The bare bones academic curriculum lacked the course selection available in larger public schools. We learned German rather than French, and Bible was a required course. Every day of the six-day schedule had a different mix of classes, except for morning chapel. That was carved into the first period in stone, one day out of six in German. I had an okay alto voice and chose to sing in the optional choir, but I really wanted to accompany the choir on the piano. Unfortunately, someone more senior always got it and I was much too timid to ask for a turn. We wore uniforms—navy jumpers over the blouse of our choice, and knee socks. The bottom hem had to fall a certain distance above your knee, but a few girls always managed to get it hiked up higher. I followed the rules.

My two years at Eden cemented the stifling sensation evoked by the religion of my culture. I grew to despise going, although my marks didn't suffer. When a new high school, West Park Secondary School, opened in St. Catharines and I learned I was in the catchment area, I refused to return to Eden. West Park started with ninth to eleventh grades, adding a grade every year. That meant for three years, I'd be in the senior class.

Because West Park was new, it drew students from four

diverse schools, so the culture hadn't been established yet—good news for a girl looking for a place to fit in. Ellen, my best friend from elementary school, was there. She was non-Mennonite but had been raised in an even more conservative, fundamentalist religion. We didn't have classes together because we were in different academic streams, but we took the same bus and shared lunches and breaks as often as we could. She already had a boyfriend who took up most of her social time.

Gone were the uniforms and liturgical classes, replaced by homemade miniskirts and dances. A sprawling, brightly-lit two-story building with modern lab equipment and a cafeteria replaced a few cramped classrooms and dark hallways with squeaky hardwood floors and lockers in a cement basement. By now, the other kids had experienced the fun of school dances. That was way beyond my comfort zone, not just because I'd never been, but because the belief that dancing was a sin was embedded in my psyche.

Ellen liked to go out a lot more than I did. Occasionally, she'd convince me to join her in the party atmosphere and dancing she loved. At seventeen and sixteen, we hadn't reached the legal drinking age of twenty-one, but that didn't stop us. Her phony ID cards got us past the bouncers. This wasn't my world, either, and it made me uncomfortable. Not because I'd sinned and disobeyed my parents. I simply didn't enjoy it. No matter where I went, I was the odd one out.

Having a boyfriend didn't interest me, mostly because I thought no one would find me appealing. Besides, I didn't know what to do with a boy. I'd never get married. No one would want me. It never occurred to me that those I dated weren't worthy of me. It pleased my parents if the boy had a Mennonite name, but even then, I rarely dated.

I made other good friends at West Park, some of whom are with me to this day. I also have friends from elementary school, but none that I stay in contact with from Eden, save my cousin Jude, who has always been like my sister.

As soon as school recessed for summer, full-time farm work began. There's something profoundly fulfilling when you get paid for work. The harder you work, the more you get paid. I admired that I could work and earn money while most other kids played all summer. Strawberries ripened first and if Dad didn't have any, I'd ride my bicycle to the farm of another Mennonite a few miles away.

Sweet cherries came next and Dad always had those. We'd plant cash crops, like squash and rhubarb, and as soon as they sprouted, we'd dig weeds. I prided myself as an exceptional worker. I'd hoe the soil and aerate it for the tender young squash plants without damaging them and get every weed out. I also learned to drive the blue Ford tractor, so I could help with more advanced chores. Dad appreciated our hard work, long hours, and doing what it took to get the job done. It's how he grew up to be a successful farmer.

Nothing stopped me from doing one of the "boy's" jobs—like driving a tractor or the forklift. In the house, though, traditional gender roles ruled. It was rare to see a male in the kitchen, other than during mealtimes. And they didn't do any cleaning, laundry, or childcare.

As a small-scale farmer, Dad found markets that took all his peaches. Selling to the co-op was always a last resort because they paid him less. Cudmore's in Burlington and Hollydean in Bronte, both thirty miles away, were his staples. Hollydean, a professional grocer, looked pristine and organized but sold less. Cudmore's, where rows of fruit baskets sat haphazardly on the ground or makeshift stands, and a thick wad of cash weighed down the owner's saggy front pocket, sold way more. We loved getting a turn to go along because Dad would stop at Tastee-Freez for ice cream. Cudmore's was a good gig for many years, until a few farmers tried to get in on the action and undercut his prices. One of them, another Mennonite, even called Dad to ask if they could collaborate, but Dad would have nothing to do with it. He found another market and taught us about resourcefulness and persistence.

For a while he took peaches to a canning factory that produced the Del Monte brand. Curious, I asked Dad what Del Monte meant. "Kill the farmer," he said. To this day, that's what I think of when I see the label.

THE SAME THINGS that held the *Russlanders* together during times of extreme hardship—conformity, prioritizing the group—drove me away from the religion. My grandparents lived with imminent threats to their physical survival during their final seven years in the Molochna. The early years in Canada, when their community had been dispersed across a strange land, were also arduous. Mennonites in North America had come to their rescue to help them immigrate and get started. But as much as people tried to help, the cohesiveness didn't come close to the homogenous communities the *Russlanders* had enjoyed in the Molochna.

When the group's priority is survival, there's no room for individual expression. The rules of conduct have to be followed by everyone. Otherwise, individuals put their lives and the life of the group at even greater risk. Their strong faith bound them together and they clung to that through their prayers, songs, and German language. Precise rules delineated right from wrong, based on their literal interpretation of the Bible. Those Anabaptist roots, planted 400 years earlier and nurtured ever since, went deep. Having survived dire times, the Mennonite culture grew even stronger.

Even though I was born thirty years after my grandparents

arrived here, the culture, inured by decades of adversity, still operated under the same rules. Other than falling off my bicycle or into the creek behind the farm, my physical survival was never in jeopardy. Yet my parents and the church passed on those same teachings and the spiritual consequences of going against the grain. It's what they knew and it had kept them and their parents alive. The community, bonded by the common religion, served to help each other through tough times. As each generation passed down their beliefs and practices to their children, they did the best they could with what had worked for them. And it came from a place of deep love.

It didn't work for me. I grew up fearful, in spite of having nothing to fear from events in my lifetime. But before my world could open up, my cast had been set. My deep-seated fear lived in the energetic DNA I'd inherited from my ancestors. It shaped my perspective and choices and took decades for me to come out from under it.

WHILE WE EARNED money at home, we earned salvation at church. Family and church inextricably fused into a single unit. To question religious teachings shook the foundations of my family structure. As much as I enjoyed a happy childhood, I soon learned that I was powerless. God had all the power. It kind of defeats the purpose of working hard to achieve something when it could be taken away in an instant. These are contradictory, entrenched concepts. No wonder I was confused.

I'd found the fundamentalist MB religion constrictive and exclusionary. While I embraced the strong underlying values like kindness, compassion, integrity, community, living peacefully, and respect for others, it didn't make sense that MBs had it right and everyone else was wrong, even other Mennonites. As much as they purported a God of love and kindness, incurring the wrath of God for sinning, even inadvertently, predominated their message. If something unpleasant or even tragic happened, someone's sin was to blame. The experience served to punish, teach a lesson, or both.

Following God's teachings in the Christian Bible, as the church interpreted them, happened from a rote sense of duty and forced compliance. Those practices may have helped others develop a close relationship with God, but they didn't work for me. I didn't feel the deep sacredness or connection with Spirit until much later in life, and not through church. Followers of the MB doctrine failed to see the dichotomy between the original teachings of Christ and how organized religion had mutated them for the purposes of control. I didn't understand until decades later that accepting Christ into my heart really meant accepting myself.

MY PARENTS FELT SO much love for us, their children, even though fear undermined their beliefs. Although they were both born in Canada, they were closer to the terror of my grandparents than I. No one talked about it. Mom and Dad wanted only the best, which included eternal salvation, for their children. But as a child, I saw only fear and anger if we didn't obey the Lord, and them. Now I see the deep love. To them, not believing had dire consequences, and they'd do whatever it took to make sure their children got to heaven.

Long before I consciously realized it, I began to question church teachings. Dread gnawed beneath the playful facade of a freckled red-headed little girl. The specter of the imminent Second Coming reminded us to follow the rules. You'd be judged when you got to heaven's gate and, if found wanting, could be sentenced to an eternity in hell. If you were alive when the rapture happened and not ready, you'd get left behind for

1,000 years of suffering, no questions asked. No second chances. The righteous would vanish. Books like *Left Behind*, which had nothing to do with the message of Christ or Christianity, sensationalized the Apocalypse and fed the fear. I'd heard stories of what my grandparents had been through and in no way did I want to be caught up in something like that! On the other hand, I feared getting tortured for being Mennonite when the end times came, as had happened to my grandparents and their families.

When Dad would pray during our daily family devotions, he'd always include, "And we know Your coming is very near." And then I'd be scared. What was going to happen to us? Was I going to be tortured and starved? Was I going to go to hell forever? Would I be left behind?

The prohibition on questioning the Church's teachings compounded the effects of the rhetoric. Questioning not only showed weakness, it was a sin. Blind faith and acceptance were expected, unequivocally. I hated being terrified all the time so I kept those thoughts and fears to myself. It's no wonder I had migraines. I feared getting ridiculed for speaking my truth. Although I had lots of friends in school, I felt uneasy if they didn't come from a Christian family and portray themselves as believers. When push came to shove in the end times and things got tough, they could turn me in to the authorities in a heartbeat and I could be tortured. Or worse.

It didn't help that my parents would take us to evangelical crusades featuring Billy Graham clones. We'd go down to the St. Catharines Arena, which would be jammed to the rafters. On stage, a preacher would whip the crowd into an emotional frenzy, then end with a call to come forward and accept Jesus, while the choir sang *Just as I am, Without One Plea*. If you weren't a born-again Christian, unrelenting pressure almost dragged you out of your seat to walk to the altar, where someone waited to counsel and convert you. Radical acceptance went to those who stepped forward, into the fold.

Calls to the altar occurred on a smaller scale in individual churches. There'd be singing and an evangelical sermon, followed by a call to action—coming forward. I think I went up once or twice, just to vent the pressure. It brought relief, never joy. Even thinking of the lyrics makes me cringe now.

The implicit pressure to conform—first by becoming a Christian, and then a church member—was potent. With membership came status; you'd now joined the ranks of the righteous and left the others behind. Dad served as a church Elder; Mom led girls' clubs. They did so much for me. How could I embarrass them in front of their Mennonite peers by going my own way?

Adult baptism at the so-called age of reason, usually one's early teens, was a foundation of the Mennonite faith—a differentiator of the Anabaptist religions. Once baptized, you became a church member. How could anyone who had known only one religious path, and been discouraged from asking questions or exploring anything different, make an objective decision?

I took the plunge around age thirteen out of a sense of expectation, not because I'd felt a calling. I thought there must be something wrong with me that I didn't embrace it like my friends and relatives did. I didn't feel it. Reluctance made me one of the last holdouts amongst my peers, but I didn't have the courage or will to divulge that I didn't feel what others expected me to feel. That would mean I'd lost contact with God or had darkness in my heart. It would inflict a deep wound on my parents.

The Church didn't make getting baptized easy. First, I had to tell my parents I'd made the decision, then I had to pass muster at the church, become a baptismal candidate, and, finally, get baptized. The process started with an appearance before the

Church Council—elected Elders—all men, all stern, including my father. I had to tell them of my decision, give my testimony, and then defend why I was ready to become a member. Like most of my peers, I passed the nerve-racking scrutiny the first time. Next came an appearance in front of the church members, which could be several hundred, to repeat my testimony and answer their questions. It terrified me. I'd leave the sanctuary and they'd vote on my candidacy. Acceptance cleared the way for baptism. Everyone would congratulate me on my decision to come to the right side and my parents would be joyous.

I dreaded testimony time, a regular part of the Sunday evening service. People would stand up and recount a special spiritual experience, demonstrating how they'd shared Christ with someone, usually in a vulnerable position—someone seriously ill or going through a rough spot. It embarrassed me that they'd have gone to someone in need with the primary intent of saving their soul, not to relieve their hunger, or illness, or poverty. Their intervention assuaged them but did little to relieve the other person's suffering.

Sometimes someone would get up and spill their guts with a juicy experience God had helped them through, or forgiven them for, and I'd squirm in my seat, wishing the service over. Why were there conditions attached to helping someone labeled a non-believer? Why couldn't you extend kindness because it was the right thing to do?

My parents didn't see my discomfort because I wasn't upfront about my misgivings. They'd grown up believing their way was the only way, so it was needless to explore alternatives. The best talks I had with Mom happened when we did dishes, alone in the kitchen. She washed, and I dried. That was the closest we got to heart-to-heart, but it never went too deep. The walls went up when I ventured into spiritual territory, so I learned not to ask personal questions about God and Jesus, or what made Mennonites right and everyone else wrong. I'd already been told it was because the Mennonite interpretation of the Bible was right. End of discussion.

Another unspoken reason for accepting the church's teachings stemmed from my feelings for my beloved grandparents. I understood they'd been persecuted because they had been open about their faith and refused to deny their Christianity. If they were willing to die for it, their belief system must have been extremely powerful. How could I question that? I wanted to be loyal to their sacrifices and beliefs. It was too soon to understand that their beliefs were only part of the story, or that tangible fears drove their fervent prayers. Death stared them in the face every day. The Second Coming and the Apocalypse were the least of their concerns.

Gerhard, Susa, and Liese spoke almost nothing about what had happened in Russia, only enough to acknowledge difficult times intensified by bandits, the Reds, and the Whites. All were evil incarnate, dressed in different colors. They were so grateful to be away from there, nothing could be worse. We believed this phenomenon affected only Mennonites. Later, I learned how other Russians had suffered through those times, too.

Still, my grandparents didn't live as if a fear of God ruled them, or they were victims. They projected a trust that in spite of a litany of bad experiences, God looked out for them. Every day, they gave thanks for living in a country of freedom. Only in Gerhard's final years, when mild cognitive impairment took him back to his last years in Russia, did memories and fears torment him.

The chronic fear was worse for my parents because their enemy was unseen and undefined. They grew up in a land of freedom and opportunity, albeit in poverty. They didn't suffer their parents' pain, but they carried their fear. Mennonites had known peaceful times for more than 100 years before the man-made apocalypse caught them by surprise. The Russian Revolution, Civil War, famine, and the Bolshevik regime broke new ground, and the Mennonite people, including my grandparents, handled it the best way they could—through their faith in God.

It showed up differently in me. Turmoil churned my insides, belied by the calm, joyful demeanor I showed to the world. Ironically, expressing my individuality and unique gifts was exactly what Spirit wanted. Following my heart was how I would leave my mark, thrive, and find peace.

I learned that if you ignore Christ's invitations, after a while He stops calling, which means you're lost forever. Your heart gets hardened like a rock. In fact, it was my soul that cried for attention but was continuously being thwarted and suppressed. It took decades before I had the courage to do anything about it and step into my power. I never wanted to hurt anyone's feelings, and I didn't want to get hurt myself, so the easiest thing was to acquiesce. And so, my spirit went to sleep for thirty years.

10

I dismantled my Beaverlodge campsite with deliberation. I was unlikely to return and wanted to absorb as much energy as possible from this place that held profound personal history. Had I stuck to my original plans to go directly to southern Alberta after Dalmeny without visiting Beaverlodge, I would have missed strengthening this soul connection to my lineage and getting to know a big part of the heritage I wore.

My trip timelines revolved around the Blackfoot Siksika Fair, which began on August 11th, one day away. For years, I'd studied Indigenous wisdom from books, trying to understand how the interconnectedness between all life defines us. After futile attempts to get the answers I was looking for from a First Nations' Elder near my home, Quinton Crow Shoe had suggested I seek counsel at the annual Siksika Fair and Pow-wow. The Siksika people had lived on the land where my grand-parents had farmed and my parents spent formative childhood years. No one was in a better position to explain the relationship with the land than someone from their community. No other dates on the Ancestor Trail were carved in stone but I *had* to be at that Fair.

After adjusting for the 850 miles added by traveling to Beaverlodge, I still hadn't pushed myself too hard—and that was an accomplishment. Now, though, I'd used up the buffer days built into my schedule and the Fair started the next day. I almost couldn't believe how close I was to finding answers I'd waited years for. I could ride the 550 miles to Siksika in a day, but it would be much more enjoyable and less taxing to do it in two. The Fair ran for four days, so arriving a day later than planned still left plenty of time to meet with an Elder. Beyond Quinton's suggestion, I hadn't made any arrangements. I was confident that Spirit was leading me and the meeting would happen by following divine guidance.

Rather than go back to southern Alberta the way I'd come, I stayed further west on Highway 40. It added sixty miles but skirted the spectacular Rocky Mountains, a minor tradeoff. Not only was the route new to me, but none of my passengers had been there either. Midway between Beaverlodge and Siksika, a large KOA campground west of the town of Hinton would make a good place to overnight.

A final sweep of my campsite assured me I hadn't forgotten anything. Before turning in the night before, I'd checked the tire pressure, tire tread, and given Trudy the once over, scanning for irregularities, as I did before every departure. Everyone was on board and ready to roll. I climbed onto Trudy, sent up my prayers, and pulled away, my heart imbued with Beaverlodge forever.

As I settled into the saddle, ready for a day of riding through wilderness, I imagined Liese leaving here eighty-eight years earlier. My time in Beaverlodge suffused me with overwhelming peace. In contrast, Liese was besieged by profound grief, despair, and loneliness, such that she'd never known.

Liese had journaled that *having God take away our two daughters was too hard to take and I strove against God.* What she'd described as *hard and difficult times for my husband* in Beaver-lodge must have been excruciating for her. But Liese's departure from Beaverlodge marked the most dire time in her life. She'd admired Johann's words of comfort when their daughters had just died and they were preparing to leave for Canada. She'd written that she was so angry, but Johann was strong and said, *The Lord Gives and He also takes away. We want to praise the Lord.* Now, though, even Johann had been taken away.

Johann had not left a will, which meant the estate had to go through probate. For Liese, who for good reason mistrusted and feared authority, who knew nothing of the ways of this country, and who spoke little English, the process was arduous and terri-fying. But this paled compared to the threat that she and Benny could be deported to Russia because Johann had died from a communicable disease. Dad's only memory from Beaverlodge is Liese cradling him in bed, crying herself to sleep. She couldn't escape the darkness, even with her faith and strong constitution.

Again, the community looked after its own and a Mennonite neighbor took Liese under his wing to help her with legal proceedings. Johann and Liese had shared an interest in six quarter-sections with three other families. But no one had money and the partners couldn't compensate her for Johann's part of the land. The proceedings were complicated, drawn out over seven months, and she walked away empty-handed. Again.

On top of that, Mennonites were allowed to immigrate under the condition they not be a drain on the public purse for five years. That meant no government help of any kind, including health care. She was in debt for Johann's treatment and hospital-ization, although it was likely forgiven, a common practice. Physicians and others were compassionate, especially in such desperate situations. Mostly, the Mennonites looked after each other.

Out of necessity, Liese's hardiness and resilience supplanted the numbness of grief. She had to figure out a way to keep herself and Benny clothed and fed. With this foremost in her mind, she'd done laundry for the railway workers hired to install tracks in the area. She'd haul water from a well and heat it over a wood fire, scrub the filthy clothes by hand, rinse them, and hang them to dry on a clothes line, before exchanging the load for another.

This period of her life would have been even worse than when she and Johann left Russia. She was leaving the love of her life behind in wild, northern Alberta, all their hopes for a new life buried with him. Her brother Jake had moved to Peace River District and helped as he could, but he had his own young family to care for and land to clear. Her sister Helen was in British Columbia with her family. All she had was Benny, her faith, and an empathetic community that offered what support they could. She had no choice but to keep going.

The same Mennonite safety net had comforted Gerhard and Susa six years earlier when their little Ellie died days before they left Russia. Others had experienced tragedy, too, and were leaving at the same time. Many had gathered from the surrounding villages to say good-bye and wish them safe travels in the new country. On Sunday, the day after Ellie's funeral, the congregation assembled for the last time many of them would see each other. Surviving seven years of terror and devastation had fused their community into a tight group. At Gerhard's request they sang a song of hope, *Wenn der Herr die Gefangenen Zion* (When the Lord Releases the Prisoners of Zion). They took comfort in the lyrics, "Those who sow with tears will reap with joy." Then they got on the train.

Gerhard, Susa, and Liese had surmounted those times and I imagined what their life had been like as Trudy carried me through the land that had inured Liese to struggle. Pristine forests, fed by crystal clear streams and rivers set against a cloudless sky evoked a spontaneous shout of "Thank you!" to Spirit, through my closed helmet. I loved being open to the elements, but I didn't have to worry about finding food, fuel, or shelter. This smooth, paved highway wouldn't have been here in Liese's time. She arrived soon after the rail bed was laid and her only means of local transportation would have been a cart to take her along the rutted roads.

My Hummingbird guide, who helps me see the wisdom and learn the lessons in ancestral stories, encouraged me to consider what my grandparents had to teach me from how they handled profound loss. The faith, courage, and gratitude worn during these hard times were the hallmarks by which I framed them. Could I have shown such forbearance in their circumstances? Have I honored the teachings they lived?

Their stoicism would have been of little comfort to me. They couldn't afford to let grief, regret, or self-pity bog them down. They'd had to move forward so they and their families would survive in the new land. They clung to their faith for survival. I'd inherited their quiet fortitude in my energetic DNA, but I had no basis to embody it as they had. Survival needs had never crossed my mind, yet I still knew to suppress my feelings. I'd known that self-pity wouldn't help me when I'd broken my ankle, and that I should concentrate, instead, on healing.

Liese had to be closer to civilization so she could earn better money and care for their son. She'd bundled up their paltry belongings in the small wooden valise Johann had made long ago to hold their dreams, the inside of the lid inscribed with his signature. For years, it sat in the living room of our farmhouse. That and another larger wooden suitcase—five cubic feet—that he'd built, his initials riveted into the top, were the only material possessions Dad had from his father.

With gratitude, Liese took up a position as a housekeeper with the Bauers in Beiseker, not far from Swalwell where Benny had been born. I'd visit their descendants after the Pow-wow. She and Benny lived in a room in the family's home in exchange for her housekeeping services. Many Mennonites had set up farms in the area and even an MB church in Linden, twenty miles north. While Liese was getting back on her feet again following Johann's death, Peter Jansen, a bachelor three years her senior, was establishing a farm forty-two miles further south. Two years later they married, and Liese and Benny moved away to start again.

LIKE RIDING ACROSS THE PRAIRIES, it was easy to stay on course on the road from Beaverlodge to Hinton, even while daydreaming. We traveled the only main road for hundreds of miles. The greatest hazards were from oncoming oil tankers, lumber trucks, and errant elk or moose, so I did have to be wary, but it wasn't like driving in Toronto traffic. As if to remind me to keep my attention on the road, a stone flew up from a big rig ahead of me, taking a chip out of the surface of my helmet.

Settlements are rare along that stretch of highway, so when I arrived at the Grande Cache Tourism and Interpretive Center, I pulled over and refueled at the adjacent gas station. Gazebos with picnic tables dotted a wide apron of grass, the perfect spot to eat my lunch and nap. Wandering through the displays inside offered a glimpse into the area's natural history and culture, rife with stories of Aboriginal peoples, hunting, and the fur trade. Beyond the grandeur, the environment can be harsh and unforgiving, yet people have lived here for thousands of years.

Hinton lay another 100 miles down the road, so I didn't dawdle. I'd rather arrive, get my tent set up, and relax for the evening. I refilled my water reservoir, repacked my lunch cooler, checked to make sure my load was secure, and got back on the road.

Until lunch we'd been in the foothills. Now we climbed to higher elevations, curvaceous roads, and breathtaking mountainscapes. Gerhard, Susa, Johann, and Liese gawked at the Rockies and speculated about the Pow-wow. They'd never been to one. Strength, peace, joy, gratitude, and exhilaration melded into one in me. I was miniscule yet powerful, unmistakably one with Spirit. My Eagle guide lofted high above me, soaring the thermals, emulating the expansiveness I felt. Serpent did her part by keeping me grounded and focused on the road.

My religious upbringing was devoid of this relationship to nature. The holiness of the mountains, earth, sky, and rivers nourished my soul later, as I studied Shamanic Energy Medicine. Seeking to understand this relationship with nature and the land led me to explore Indigenous wisdom. While ancient stories from Indigenous Peoples around the world differ, common themes at their heart held the key to the connection my soul yearned for. For the Siksika people, it is a way of life rather than a belief system.

I felt immediately at home in circles that honored the cycles of nature and revered all life. As a child, I'd learned fundamentalist Christianity held the only path to God and salvation. In nature, there was no path. We were already there. One. Different names for one's Higher Power, rituals, and ceremonies were only in the details. Individual spiritual journeys were like different roads with unique scenery leading to the same destination.

ARRIVING AT THE HINTON KOA, I was on the eve of finding the guidance and answers I'd pursued for so long. The next day, Thursday, I'd reach southern Alberta, camp near the Siksika reserve, and make my way to the grounds on Friday.

After setting up my campsite, I rode into town for gas, along with groceries for dinner and the next day's breakfast and lunch.

I wanted to be ready to go in the morning. Trudy takes premium high octane gasoline, and whenever possible I fill up at a Shell station because, in Canada, their premium blend is free of ethanol, which can damage your engine over time. I pulled up to the old-style pump dispensing V-Power, Shell's premium blend, double-checking the signage to make sure I had the right nozzle. Trudy's tank was still one-third full, but I topped it up, went inside to pay, and then headed off to the grocery store.

Trudy hesitated a bit before purring to life. Since that had happened once or twice, I thought nothing of it. Once back at my campsite, I checked her over and locked her for the night. My site faced west toward the mountains, an outstanding backdrop for my outdoor dinner. Other campers, out for their evening stroll and curious about a woman traveling alone by motorcycle, stopped to chat. Soon after, those ancient landforms cradled me to sleep and sent me to dreamtime.

Morning came early. Today's travels would take me to southern Alberta and to Siksika. Condensation had collected on the inside of the rain fly as cool night air met the warm air generated by my body heat. Unless you're in the desert, it's a regular occurrence. My tent dries fast, so I packed up the contents, spread the tent on a picnic table, and enjoyed breakfast while it dried. In silence, I sipped my tea, made from mountain water boiled on my little cook stove, drinking in the majesty of the Rockies. More sunshine, blue skies, and cool temperatures heralded another picture-perfect day.

Breakfast over, I secured my load onto Trudy and gave my passengers the five-minute warning. It took that long for me to don riding pants, boots, heated jacket liner, riding jacket, ear plugs, helmet, and gloves. Gear is designed for riding, not standing around, so once it's on, I want to get going.

After a final circle check of Trudy and her load, I hopped on and sent up my prayers as I did every morning. Except this time, she wouldn't start. She'd try, but the engine wouldn't catch. A few times she'd sputter, then cough and die.

She'd been so reliable and there'd been no sign of trouble. Puzzled, I removed my helmet and jacket and sat down to figure out the next steps. If I waited a few minutes, and tried again, the problem might clear.

No such luck.

In every area, there's always someone else around with motorcycle experience. I had to find that person. My inquiry at the KOA office for a local mechanic led me to Mike, a long-time rider who worked at the campground. All he got from pressing the start switch was thick black stinky exhaust before the engine died again. Another camper came over and tried, also to no avail. Nobody could diagnose the problem. I questioned if I'd filled the tank with diesel fuel, but I'd been so careful, so I brushed it off. The two guys even smelled the fuel but couldn't detect the distinct diesel odor.

I was six miles outside of a small town in northern Alberta with a motorcycle that wouldn't run. The town's one motorcycle mechanic had gone to the annual rally in Sturgis, South Dakota. The nearest Triumph dealer was in Edmonton, 200 miles east.

Blackfoot Motorsports, who'd buried my Ténéré after its crash, was 400 miles south in Calgary. But because I knew them, and already had an appointment for routine servicing next week, I tried them first. The service person walked me through a couple of scenarios, but it was impossible to diagnose over the phone. I called Echo Cycle in Edmonton and explained my situation. They'd assess my bike, but it would be tomorrow. If they had to order parts, those would take another day or two to arrive.

I could not believe this was happening. I *had* to be at the Pow-wow tomorrow. For months I'd planned around it and now everything was falling apart!

Taking a deep breath, I coached myself not to catastrophize. Take one step at a time, get accurate information, and use it to take the next step. My Jaguar guide, an expert in tracking, helped me troubleshoot without wasting time. I had to get Trudy to a shop with expertise and diagnostic equipment. The closest was Edmonton. Towing was expensive, over $1,000, according to two separate quotes. The roadside assistance that came with my AMA (American Motorcyclist Association) membership would cover thirty-five miles, a fraction of the distance.

Mike had another idea. Griffiths Ford, a local dealer, rented vehicles. They might have a solution. And they did. Renée, the rental manager, asked me Trudy's measurements and calculated the smallest vehicle I needed. I'd have to pay a drop fee, but the rental cost for a Ford Transit van would be $375 plus fuel. Renée and Joe, a coworker, drove the van out to the campsite. We removed Trudy's mirrors, loosened and lowered her windscreen, and Joe and Mike shoe-horned her in. Luggage and gear crammed whatever space remained. Thankfully, Gerhard, Susa, Johann, and Liese, and my animal guides didn't take up any physical space. Besides, Eagle wanted to soar, not be cramped up inside.

It didn't surprise me that everyone who helped was a rider—Mike, Renée, and Joe, and fellow campers who'd pitched in. My community had come together again to help a fellow traveler in need. By mid-morning, my precious cargo and I were underway. With any luck, I'd reach Echo Cycle in time for them to at least assess her before closing.

Trudy's headlight stared at me through the rear-view mirror as if gazing into my perplexed mind. Once again, I'd been stopped while on the cusp of experiencing a culture other than my own. The first time I'd crashed. When Barbara and I had stopped at Blackfoot Crossing after the crash, on my way back to

Ontario, the person I'd wanted to see hadn't been there. Now this. What was I missing? Maybe I wasn't supposed to go, yet I felt so guided to do so.

I still met monthly with Oriah and didn't typically call her between our monthly appointments, but extraordinary times call for extraordinary measures.

I phoned her from the van.

"You're not going to believe this!"

She's not one to ascribe meaning to every event, but she, too, couldn't mistake symbolic neon lights. "Be alert to who crosses your path now," she said. "Watch for the people and experiences you otherwise would not have had were it not for this detour."

Already, I'd been reminded of the power of community in Hinton. I was suspicious that I'd given Trudy the wrong fuel. Was I also giving myself the wrong type of spiritual fuel?

As much as I liked to be in control of a situation, people and events could come along that influenced my world and changed my trajectory. The reliable motorcycle I'd chosen and scrupulously maintained was jammed in behind me, refusing to run.

My grandparents had learned about control. They'd lived a simple life out of the limelight, minded their own business, and espoused high moral values, kindness, and compassion. The upheaval that consumed them was completely outside of their control and changed their lives forever.

In reality, there's little we control. Thoughts and beliefs passed down through generations influence our choices, even if we're not aware of them. We make careful plans, which get disrupted when the unexpected creates chaos. The trick is to create a center of calm in the midst of that chaos, the kind of energy my Serpent guide excels in. That's what I decided to do as I tracked east toward Edmonton. My passengers nodded their heads and smiled. The sun shone beyond blue skies and the traffic was sparse. In spite of the upset, the moment was serene. Answers would come when I was ready.

Nearing Edmonton, almost at my destination, the traffic slowed and crawled to a stop. As I inched forward, I could see there'd been a horrendous crash and traffic was being diverted onto a service road. I reminded myself to stay focused on the road, although I couldn't help but ponder the delay in getting Trudy assessed.

I pulled into Echo Cycle's parking lot thirty minutes before closing. They were expecting me but didn't think they could fit me in until first thing the next morning. Even if they could fix it right away, I wasn't traveling any further today. I resigned myself to another hotel room.

I'd explained my suspicions on the phone. While I was getting Trudy admitted to the shop, they'd wheeled her into the back, drained the gas tank, and refilled it with gasoline. She started right up. I'd filled it with diesel, after all. And not even regular diesel. Premium diesel. I didn't even know diesel came in premium, but in this part of the country where diesel-fueled engines are the norm, it was common.

I had to laugh in spite of the situation. A motorcycle, my spiritual guide since age sixteen, had led me to a new insight. I knew further clarity would be forthcoming, but for the time being, I got the message: Make sure I was feeding my body and spirit the fuel that was right for me as I explored another culture.

My van rental ran for twenty-four hours. Rather than navigate through a strange city on my motorcycle and leave it sitting out in a hotel parking lot overnight, I was grateful when Echo agreed to let me pick it up in the morning. I found a place to stay, not too far away, and at a reasonable rate. I'd lost another day of the Pow-wow, but two days remained. It still gave me plenty of time.

11

That night I tossed and turned in the Edmonton hotel room, excited, curious, and still uncertain about the significance of the delay in getting to Siksika. In the morning, I'd drop off the van and pick up a refueled Trudy, ride 200 miles to southern Alberta, and find a campsite near the Siksika Nation Fair. That would put me in a good position to get to the celebrations Saturday morning, its second-to-last day.

Then further delays cropped up. No trollies were available to move my bags from my fourth-floor room to the lobby. I waited in line at the checkout for almost twenty minutes to ask where to find one. Spotting another guest ferrying his luggage to the car, I followed him and retrieved his as soon as he'd unloaded it.

Renée, Mike, and Joe had been angels of mercy and I wanted to leave them a token of appreciation. Tim Horton's coffee shops are de rigueur in Canada. Even Hinton had one. I hoped they'd appreciate the gift cards I'd leave in the van. But I missed the Tim Horton's driveway on my first approach and had to go back around the block and try again, only to discover it was closed for renovations. At least the drive-through was open and could sell me gift cards.

Finally, I had the van back at Echo Cycle. They'd agreed to keep it in their secure parking lot over the weekend until someone from Griffiths could pick it up on Monday. Ironically, I'd forgotten to fill the gas tank. Out I went again to find a gas station. Coming back, I missed my street turn. By this time, the delays were completely laughable, and I wondered what was next. I recognized them as messages to slow down and be more mindful, especially with where my journey was taking me next. All I wanted to do was get back on the road. With Trudy.

At long last, packed and ready to go, the only thing left to do was turn the van keys over to Echo's service manager. Somehow, I'd misplaced them. When I finally found them, they were on my motorcycle seat, under three bags of luggage. Replacing the bags and securing them once again, I did a final check of the bike.

Then I did another check in with my animal guides. They'd been with me the whole time, but I'd been more preoccupied with my grandparents. All were in place and ready to go— Serpent on the engine pan, Jaguar on top of the bags where he could sleep in the sun, Hummingbird tucked in the dash, guiding me, and Eagle on my helmet to help me keep perspective—and a perfect launch pad for the soaring he loved.

Slight trepidation lingered, though. Was something else going to stop me? Offering up a prayer to Spirit in gratitude, and requesting continued protection and guidance, I pulled out of the parking lot.

I KNEW my personal fuel didn't come from the Mennonite religious teachings. Over time, my spirit had gone to sleep, reflected in my life choices of education, marriage partner, and career. Without knowing or intending it, I'd built my life on a facade. Rather than shed my skin and grow, like Serpent, I'd confined myself in skin that no longer fit. Then I projected that persona to the world, attracted people based on that persona, and made decisions without knowing who I was.

As much as my parents had nurtured and supported my independence, that independence had always been within the confines of the religion. They trusted me, within the context that God was in control. I prided myself on my self-sufficiency, ability to achieve what I set out to do, and willingness to explore new places, but always set the bar way too low, inside that religious box. My goal was to move through life without causing any waves or hurting or offending my parents, specifically Dad. His God-given duty was to make sure his children were safe for eternity and he took his job seriously, with the highest of intentions.

In his deep desire to save me, starting in my teens and adulthood, he'd ask me about my spiritual life. I dreaded being alone with him because the answers to the questions he sought weren't what lived in my heart. He believed he was right and any other perspective was wrong, so that made trying to explain or reason difficult—and emotional. He wouldn't understand my perspective, and I didn't have the courage to speak my mind. My responses were evasive and defensive because I didn't want to disappoint him, yet I felt guilty because I wasn't open. I hated those feelings. He didn't realize you couldn't reach someone's heart through fear or guilt. My heart ached for him because he was as tortured as I, in a different, even more stifling way. Mom always supported him, but she never questioned me the way he did.

They didn't realize that every time they brought up salvation, it widened the gap between us and pushed me further away from the church. If only they would love me for who I was and what I stood for. But the acid test to accepting me was whether I was a Believer. I didn't understand why they couldn't see what I saw in the fear-based ideology. It's ironic that in a culture that purports non-resistance, they were always on the offensive, trying to make converts.

As soon as I turned sixteen, I took driving lessons and got my license. I could shuttle my brothers around to school and sporting events, freeing up my parents' time for other things. So my parents didn't blink an eye when I met my first motorcycle at age sixteen. John and Robert bought a little Honda 50 from my classmate, another Mennonite, for ninety dollars, for fun and to get around on the farm. Somehow, they let me ride it. I never thought about it. It was merely something I did, and Mom and Dad didn't raise an eyebrow. I don't remember my first ride or having any fear. At sixteen, you're invincible.

A motorcycle became my companion through life's ups and downs, always there, ready to teach me what I needed to learn about myself. Or to take me away.

Without knowing it, I'd entered a time of mediocrity. I could work hard and get good marks in school, but I underutilized my gifts. I feared and averted risk. In the end, God controlled everything, so why bother trying something different? And why risk a new venture when Christ's Second Coming was imminent? Stay with what's safe, predictable, and pleasing. That fear of persecution and loss, which had been so acute earlier in life, had subsided to a dull ache.

At age seventeen, I met Daniel, my future husband. He'd switched to West Park and we were in some of the same classes. Daniel was a non-Mennonite, a must for any romance. He aspired to attend university, rode a motorcycle, too, and was intelligent, fun, outspoken, a hard worker, resourceful, and as socially inept as I. He could make things and figure out machinery. He'd worked as a farm laborer for many years to buy his car, an Austin Mini, and his Bridgestone motorcycle.

It amazed me that someone had an interest in me, especially someone from outside my cultural circle. Somehow that seemed like a success. My best friend Ellen worked and had a steady boyfriend, so Daniel and I spent quite a bit of time together, often with his guy friends. We both graduated from secondary school and went away to the same city for our post-secondary education.

Dread of university matched my earlier fear of attending a secular secondary school. I didn't know how to act in a world where everyone would be worldly, dating, and partying. Besides, I didn't value myself enough to have high expectations for an education or career. My comfort zone had a small radius and I wasn't confident enough to push through it. I didn't belong in the Mennonite world, but I still didn't know where I did fit.

Even if I could get a student loan and grant, I didn't know how I'd pay for university. Now I see that rather than looking at what I wanted and finding a way to make it happen, which is how Gerhard and Susa got Mom through nursing school and university, or how Dad and Mom started farming, I looked at the obstacles and ruled it out before I tried.

My parents offered to help but only if I went to a Bible School like their friends' children. But I couldn't wait to get out of Eden. No way was I going to back into that morass. Instead, I played it safe again, and enrolled in nurse's training thirty miles away. I had some interest in it, though not the same passion as my mother, saw it as a respectable profession, and knew it would provide a good living.

Schools of Nursing were affiliated with teaching hospitals. Rarely did anyone go to university to become a nurse unless they wanted to work in management or administration. I moved to study at the Hamilton General Hospital, rather than stay in my hometown. It's where Mom had graduated and it had an esteemed reputation. It was also in the city where Daniel planned to attend university to study Engineering.

Mom was thrilled, proud, and eager to move me into residence, but I wasn't having any part of it. I was a big girl and had a boyfriend with a car. He'd help me move in. Her feelings were hurt, but I'd been independent for so long that her sudden mothering surprised me.

I loved my newfound freedom. After a year of Engineering, Daniel switched to a Commerce program and another university in St. Catharines, our hometown, while I completed my Nursing program. Another student and I rented a derelict apartment on Hamilton's main street in a seedy area of town. The building was a firetrap, and something I could afford. I'm not sure how my parents allowed me to live there, but after all, I was paying my own way. Besides, they still had five other kids who needed their attention. Being away for extended periods gave me a face-saving excuse for skipping church. I attended once in a while, but those intervals got further apart.

Nursing jobs were plentiful when I graduated, yet again I knowingly sold myself short and moved back to St. Catharines, where Daniel had another two years to complete his undergrad. I could have worked in a large university hospital, but chose a small hospital, once a tuberculosis (TB) sanatorium, where Gerhard had recovered from glandular TB the year I was born. Most patients were there long term, some with active TB, but the majority suffered from chronic chest conditions. Many were refugees from Eastern Europe who had worked in poorly venti-lated mines in northern Ontario. Years of inhaling toxic dust had left them with little lung capacity and they gasped and wheezed, even when speaking. At least my grandparents had been out in the fresh farm air and not underground.

After graduation, I moved back into my parents' home and bought my first car with a loan Dad co-signed, a brand-new brown 1974 Toyota Corolla. Two years earlier, my parents had extended the house with a basement bedroom shared by Robert and Mark, a main floor bathroom with our first shower, and a family room with large sliding doors. Eight people crowded it, but I had my own room back.

By the following spring, I felt the need to be back out on my own and found an apartment in a quaint four-plex in an older part of town. Soon after, I bought the first motorcycle I could call my own: a 175cc Honda XL, which I rode around the countryside and, in nice weather, for the ten-minute commute to work.

Even though I made good money, working in a small-town chronic care hospital with no future was a poor fit for a young woman whose heart wanted something different. I had no idea what that was, only that it wasn't what I was doing. I was always good in math and had a good sense of logic. Maybe I would become an accountant. So I enrolled in university and began taking business courses part time, the same program Daniel had switched to, although he had a different major. I was already feeling disappointed for selling myself short by not going to university, instead defaulting into a nursing career. I enjoyed parts of it and it's a noble calling, but it wasn't mine. After a year and a half at the TB hospital, I moved to a larger active hospital an hour's commute away, which would allow me to continue my business courses.

At the same time, I grew ashamed of the religious practices of my parents and grandparents, although never the family and friends in it. Guilt tormented me because I knew how much the religion meant to them, but I didn't want anyone at work, school, or social circles to know of my Mennonite background. I didn't want anyone to label me with the stereotype. Now that I worked and rarely attended church anymore, it felt like a fresh start. Daniel disdained organized religion and couldn't possibly understand how it was so intricately woven into the Mennonite culture, even though he attended family functions and got to know my extended family. With only my dissident view and his family rift—caused when his Catholic mother and Anglican father married—for perspective, he endorsed the reasons for the widening schism separating me from my culture.

My marriage in 1977 came about as a matter of pragmatism more than passion. Daniel had graduated from university and accepted a job in Oshawa, a few hours away from our hometown. I wasn't comfortable cohabiting and knew my parents would have a fit, so I put my part-time business studies on hold and we decided to get married. Adopting a non-Mennonite surname added relief and disguised me from others and myself.

Planning the wedding was a nightmare. My family would not allow liquor or dancing, which Daniel's family expected. Most Mennonites held weddings in the church, with spartan receptions served in the adjoining gymnasium. We settled on a morning church wedding with lunch at a restaurant overlooking Lake Ontario. The whole thing felt like a pressure cooker. Daniel called it the worst day of his life.

On the night before the ceremony, my intuition tried to get my attention at the rehearsal. As the wedding party assembled at the front of the church, Daniel's brother stepped outside to pass gas and the door locked behind him. Amidst great laughter I joked, "I can't go through with this!" I don't know where it came from, but it caught everyone, including the minister, off guard. The silence was deafening. All eyes turned to me.

"Just kidding!"

Unconsciously, a part of me knew it to be the truth, even though I didn't understand or accept it at the time. The person I showed to the world, including my partner, was based on the roles I'd adopted to protect my spirit. I went through with the wedding, but how could a relationship built on a facade last, let alone thrive? It would be twenty-five years before I'd have the courage to say, "Enough."

The first year taxed my physical, emotional, and mental energy. We rented a small apartment and Daniel started his entry-level career job as a supervisor at a large General Motors assembly plant. The unionized workers initiated the green, idealistic university grad with a difficult start. Meanwhile, I started nursing full time at the local hospital. Within months, I started having panic attacks and contracted mononucleosis. The virus kept me off work for three months, until two days before Christmas.

On Christmas, I worked the day shift and came home fatigued. Daniel sat in the dark, blinds pulled, still in his pajamas. Depressed. We'd been invited to the home of friends for dinner and managed to get there, but the times in Oshawa didn't get much better. After a year at GM he resigned, and we moved back to St. Catharines. He got another job, and I got a part-time job working full-time hours in the hospital.

Permanent nursing jobs had become scarce, so a year later when I received an offer to work as an occupational health nurse in a nearby steel plant with 2,000 employees, I took it. I already knew I didn't want to do shiftwork in a hospital for the rest of my life, so it seemed like a good opportunity to take a Monday to Friday job, with two shifts, days and afternoons. I was so under-utilized, but I stuck it out until I got downsized during the 1981 recession. Eventually, the owners closed and razed the plant, but it got my foot in the corporate door and would lead to other things.

When we'd moved back to St. Catharines, I resumed my business studies at university. Since I worked in occupational health, it made sense to switch to an Occupational Health program. Through the course transfer I lost credits, so I settled for completing my Occupational Health certificate and a general Bachelor of Arts, the minimum degree I could have and still say I had a university degree.

I could have done anything with my life, but already felt trapped, restless, and dissatisfied with my career and relationship. Four years into our marriage, we started counseling. Daniel never seemed concerned, but our relationship lacked the closeness I expected. Nothing came of our appointments and we soldiered on. The thought of separating never crossed my mind.

Still, our marriage had its satisfactions. We both enjoyed motorcycle travel and attending motorcycle events, we earned good incomes, and purchased our first house. Somehow, I believed, things would get better.

For our wedding gift to each other, we'd bought a new 650cc Yamaha motorcycle. After sharing it for four years, I'd long been ready for my own again. So, one August weekend when Daniel went away with friends, I bought a used 750 BMW for him and from then on, we each had our own bike. I didn't realize my spirit guide had answered the call of my restless spirit by getting me a ride of my own.

During the early years, we travelled by motorcycle to the East Coast, around Ontario, Quebec, and New England. We both worked full time and didn't have a lot of vacation time, especially since we were either starting our careers or in a new job with only two weeks' vacation per year, which limited our range, but we did what we could.

To his credit, Daniel supported anything I wanted to try, so after the steel plant downsized me, I bought a franchise for a home health care business, which I ran out of our house for three years. I enjoyed the patient and family contact, but it required me to be on call 24/7 and rely on employees who were either between jobs or didn't aspire to do much. It reminded me of Dad's woes getting good help on the farm.

Daniel had been looking for a change and found a job in Toronto. With relief, I turned the franchise back to the owners. We moved to Newmarket, an hour north of Toronto, and I got a job as an occupational health nurse with a sporting goods manufacturer. The factory of 1,000 people introduced me to a diverse immigrant workforce, with foreign cultures and beliefs. It wasn't long before I moved into the Human Resources Department, managing the Health and Safety program. I drifted through the day, the week, the month. I worked steady days and earned a good salary, but the work didn't engage my soul. Looking back, I don't even recognize that person. I felt drab, hollow, frustrated that these peak years, which should have been full of vitality, were passing me by, but not knowing what to do about it.

That job also evaporated in a restructuring, but I had another, again as an occupational health nurse, without missing a paycheck. Warning signs plastered that decision, too. I'd walked into a large, archaic, patriarchal organization with a friendly but controlling and patronizing site General Manager. Still, I was floating aimlessly through life and the job suited my needs at the time.

Except for a few ill-advised investments, Daniel and I made wise financial decisions, which gave us a good foundation during our marriage, and after. Never was there any friction about money. We both earned good salaries, his always much more than mine; we never had a budget, and never overspent our means. Everything went into the same pot and came out without question. Yet even though we had so much financially, I feared having it wiped out. After our marriage ended, he said I should be thankful we'd made wise financial choices because it gave me a good cushion. I thought, but didn't say, "Imagine what I could have done had I listened to my heart in the first place."

Daniel was keen at thinking things through and had an eye for quality construction and materials, and I have learned from him in this respect. It's helped me develop a strong sense of a product's environmental impact from cradle to grave, something I factor into my purchasing decisions. He could look at a piece of furniture and discern the craftsmanship and potential longevity by the wood, joints, and finish. My own sense of discernment had begun when Mom taught me how to sew and how important it was for a seamstress to match up the stripes when joining two pieces of fabric; it still jars my eye to see clothes with mismatched patterns. Daniel and I both preferred quality over quantity and would wait and pay more for something well-made that would last. Consequently, we kept vehicles, appliances, furniture, and clothing for a long time.

I enjoyed working around the house—painting, wallpapering, and building things. Helping with house renovations, plumbing and electrical work, and carpentry taught me how things functioned, how to troubleshoot, and what to look for. When Daniel and I did the work, I always knew it had been done right. That interest carried over to our motorcycles. Daniel did most of the routine maintenance, although I'd often watch to understand the process. Once I was single again, I worked on my own bikes, albeit under his tutelage. As much as he would have done it for me, I wanted to learn how to do it myself. The interest and intuition that were urging me to learn were also preparing me for things to come. That knowledge would help me when I was on my own, and I would use it to teach others to gain confidence in trying something new. Oil and filter changes and brake pad or air filter replacements were a cinch. Replacing sprockets and chains or a clutch cable got more complicated. Even after our divorce, we worked together to adjust the valve clearances on my FZ1, Super Ténéré, and Triumph (Trudy). Excluding computerized electronics, mechanical work is logical. As long as you're methodical and organized in taking stuff apart, it goes together in the reverse order, with no leftover parts. I knew what to do in an emergency and that boosted my confidence.

Daniel was reliable, honest to a tee, trustworthy, and giving, but our partnership lacked the heart connection necessary for an intimate, soul relationship. You can have everything else, but if that connection isn't solid, it doesn't work. My spirit cried for attention.

For the time being, I focused on gratitude for what I had, something I learned from Gerhard. I had my freedom, lived in a country of peace, enjoyed a pleasant lifestyle, and had a kind and caring husband. Daniel would tell friends about our wonderful relationship, citing our lack of arguments as proof. It was true that we never argued, and I never got angry on the outside, except for the time I was so angry with him I threw a soft-boiled egg against the kitchen wall during our first Christmas. When he boasted about our lack of conflict in private, I'd counter that never arguing was not a good thing. It meant that things were going unspoken and getting bottled up. On that point, we disagreed. Many times, my insides were tied up in knots. Years of coping with my family's belief systems made me excellent at suppressing my feelings, and I'd ask myself what I could possibly be dissatisfied about. Many people would give anything to have my life, I reasoned. Look at how my grandparents had lived.

Daniel always wanted children. I never did, even though for a while we tried. I felt I'd already raised a family—my siblings— and didn't want to do it again. Besides, for an unknown reason, I feared I'd die if I became pregnant. Even deeper in the dark recesses of my mind lurked another horror: What if the end times came during my pregnancy or when I had a small child, and we couldn't get food, or lived in danger of being killed for our beliefs? I didn't understand how people, Christians, could have children, bringing them into a world where such terror could break out at any time. I might get away as an adult, but how would I manage with small children, and why would I risk that when the end times were near? None of it made sense, but those thoughts would come out of hiding to haunt me.

Those fears have long since vaporized and have no more hold on me. It took many years, but I realized that the imminent Second Coming message had been around since the days of the early Christians, 2,000 years ago. I learned, instead, to embody what my grandparents practiced—to live each day for all it is worth. The afterlife will take care of itself.

Daniel and I had always dreamt of owning a home in the country. After twelve years of marriage, we bought a treed lot on a gravel road an hour northwest of Toronto and built a custom post-and-beam house with stone walkways and lovely gardens. Although we hired a general contractor, we did a lot of finishing work ourselves. Building it with the best materials and to the highest standards was a priority for both of us. We stained each piece of wooden clapboard and each wooden window before it went up and each floorboard before it went down. Pine planks fashioned the main floor's ceiling as well as the second-storey flooring and cathedral ceiling. My favorite feature, a large ground to roof fiddlehead window, graced the southern wall. During many sleepless nights, I would gaze out at the moon and stars.

We moved into a shell, with unfinished drywall and plywood floors on the main level, and no kitchen cabinets. French doors opened west from the eating area onto a large deck that faced the trees. On the south side, the living room ran the width of the house and benefited from floor to ceiling windows. One end became the sitting area and I envisioned a beautiful grand piano at the other. In the late nineties, a beautiful ornate, antique rose-wood grand filled that spot. I resumed piano lessons and joined a social group for get-togethers of music nights and fun.

Other than my religious-based terrors, I had two big fears: flying and cats. I couldn't be in the same room with a cat, likely because of the way I'd seen barn cats and kittens treated and maimed through the tough life on the farm. But Daniel loved them and he talked me into getting two adorable kittens, Mickey and Maurice, born in a woodpile a few miles away. They were so tiny, yet they frightened me so. When they were ready to leave their mom, we brought them home in a cardboard box. Daniel held the box on his lap while I drove, watching their every move. Of course, they tried to climb out of the box, driving me to the brink of hysteria. I soon adored them, though, along with Abigail and Oliver who came later.

At the same time, I had to deal with my fear of flying. I'd been at my new job for two months and had to go on a business trip with my boss and his boss to the company's head office in Connecticut. When Daniel and I had traveled to the Caribbean, I'd taken 20 milligrams of Valium before the flight. That kept the anxiety at a manageable level, but I couldn't do that with my new bosses. I had to go stone-cold sober. Even worse, we sat stuffed across the back row of a Dash 8, a turboprop with a capacity for less than fifty passengers. The two-hour flight felt like two days. Focusing on how safe airplanes were, especially compared to motorcycles, I managed, at least, the nearly over-whelming, immediate panic.

Over the years, the stark house grew into its beauty. But I was restless. If this was the way life was going to be, I concluded, then we should travel and get to know other cultures and parts of the world. We'd traveled the country a lot by motorcycle, but it was time to move beyond that. We'd already taken trips to resorts on five Caribbean islands and Mexico, but those didn't count. They were touristy and not an accurate reflection of the country, even if we did venture out on excursions.

Overseas travel started in the '90s with a trip to Ireland. It was the shortest distance I could fly while still crossing the Atlantic and I had to test my phobia. I never got comfortable, but it became tolerable without drugs or alcohol. The Ireland trip gave me the courage to travel further abroad, and every year after that we traveled to countries in South and Central America, Asia, and Europe.

We enjoyed camping, too, and bought a lightweight sixteen-foot fiberglass canoe to paddle into the backcountry. I'd never wilderness camped or been in a canoe so I had some learning to do. I loved being out in the woods, along with being out on my motorcycle in nature. We equipped ourselves with a lightweight tent, sleeping bags, sleeping pads, pots and pans, dishes, and dry bags. Those four- to seven-day trips were soul-nourishing quiet time, bobbing in the canoe, poking into small lakes and streams, and getting away from everything.

During that time, we fit in two white water canoe trips in the pristine Yukon wilderness, with six other adventurers and two guides. On our inaugural trip, an outfitter dropped us off near the put-in point. After a short but onerous portage, we reached the South MacMillan River to start a twelve-day paddle, and learned vigilance in reading the river. A few years later, my heart in my mouth, we flew in on a 1951 Beaver (single propeller) airplane, our canoes lashed to the pontoons. Wild Ernie, the bush pilot, flew low beneath the cloud cover to maintain visibility as he navigated between the mountains. We landed on the Snake River, our lifeline for the next ten days.

The wilderness exhilarated me and quenched my soul. We never capsized, but whitewater canoeing was one of two things Daniel and I couldn't coordinate. The other was ballroom dancing. We tried lessons but couldn't get the hang of it. Both activities require you to be in synch and move together, something we were never good at.

To the observer, we had an ideal life. We had rewarding careers, good health, four cats, a car, pickup and two motorcycles, and we traveled around the world. He claimed he was happy; I was not. I could not understand how he could be. He'd suggest moving, but never with a concrete plan or for a logical reason. That beautiful home in the country grounded me, yet I was uncomfortably anchored to it. For years, I'd had a recurring dream in which I moved to a different place. Always, it was unsuitable and usually dark, dilapidated, and a dump, and I'd kick myself for moving. Always, I'd wake up troubled.

IT TOOK twenty-five years of gradual decline, until only a shell remained, to summon the courage and start peeling back the layers to find the joyous redheaded, freckle-faced little girl. Life felt meaningless, unfulfilled, and colorless. I'd gained fifty pounds and lived in a rut, going through the motions, but not living, feeling, or experiencing. I wasn't going to live the rest of my life like this. I had no concept yet of ancestral energy or energetic imprints, but that would come.

I'd even lost my interest in motorcycling and sold my bike. Between work and our travels, Daniel didn't ride his, either, so he sold it. But bikelessness was fleeting. Three years later, I still had no interest, but he wanted to get back into it. It didn't make sense to buy two bikes, so we decided he'd get one large enough for me to ride comfortably as a pillion.

Not long after, we took a five-day ride through Eastern Ontario. When we got back, we stopped in a parking lot and he encouraged me to try it. One lap around the parking lot and I knew I had to have my own motorcycle again. Without knowing what I wanted, I purchased a Honda Spirit. I completely missed the symbolism that it had arrived to help my spirit wake up.

On a lazy Sunday afternoon in 1998, I lay on the sofa looking up at the massive beams and the house I'd waited so long for and worked so hard to finish. Did I really think this house on this particular plot of land was the only place on God's earth where I could be happy? Of course not! I suspected I'd have to leave our relationship to reclaim myself and find happiness, but even after twenty-eight years of being together, I wasn't ready to give up without one last try.

I shocked myself by even considering that my marriage was ending. This wasn't supposed to happen to me. We began counseling, but after a few sessions, I continued alone. Daniel didn't see any problems, but I needed to resolve whatever was eating at me. I felt trapped, alone, and so lonely.

AT WORK, I'd assumed increasing responsibility for Human Resources, Health and Safety, and Training and Development. The organization hadn't changed with the times, making them ripe for a buyout. My ancestors had been oblivious to the social changes around them and got caught up in a civil war. On a different scale, our senior managers were over-compensated, complacent, and archaic, unaware of their peril. A far more progressive company with a youthful culture scooped it up and began making changes.

I welcomed the news. This could be the break I'd sought, where I could finally tap into my potential. I was in my mid-forties and past the pinnacle of a traditional career. I'd earned a degree and professional certifications, but I hadn't pushed myself or stretched my comfort zone. Nearing the low point of my self-worth, esteem, and confidence, I jumped at an offer to move to a different location in a Human Resources role, with lots of potential for meaningful work. I loved the new company, an international consumer packaged goods corporation, and its values. My immediate boss, who portrayed himself as a collaborative coach, was another issue. I didn't trust him. We clashed on ethics, but if it came down to it, he'd be believed before me. Determined to succeed, I poured my best into my work and the culture transition. But a year into the new regime, we sat at the table in my office for my performance review. I listened as he told me I was failing. It was the shot of energy I needed. No one calls me a failure! Especially someone whose opinion I didn't value.

I'd known for some time that the Human Resources path was a poor fit, in spite of my proficiency. I'd begun to feel stifled, and like the serpent that sheds its skin when it grows, it was time for me to start thinking about another career.

Trent, the site manager, and I had a cordial, professional relationship based on shared values. We also shared a love of reading and would exchange books. In 1992, Mom had gifted Daniel with a book titled *My Harp is Turned to Mourning*, a novel based on the experiences of the Russian Mennonites in the years leading up to their emigration. Nine years later, I'd picked it up and read it, and thought it might be one Trent would be interested in.

The book hand-off marked a turning point in my life. For twenty-five years, my non-Mennonite surname had helped me conceal the past. Now I was ready to expose my secrets to someone from outside the religion, someone in a position of authority over me. The image of our hands on the book, mine offering and his accepting, cracked the wall around my spirit and let in a sliver of light.

My soul yearned to sing. It had been so long since young Elizabeth had begun to close down and build that wall around her. Even before I knew about Serpent, my skin was beginning to feel tight.

Other things began to happen. Although our marriage was on tenuous ground, that year Daniel and I travelled to China and stopped in Xi'an at the site of the Terracotta Army. Thousands of life-sized clay soldiers, with individual facial expressions, horses and chariots positioned by rank in battle array, waited in marching columns. They're part of an elaborate mausoleum created 2,200 years earlier to accompany, safeguard, and serve First Emperor Qin into the afterlife. We'd seen cultural protectorates of the afterlife in the Mayan tombs in Mexico and Guatemala, and the pyramids of Giza in Egypt, built well before Christ walked the earth. But the visual effect of these life-size beings struck me like a bolt of lightning. Here was a culture polar opposite to the one I came from. These guys were afraid of dying. The Christian story was no different, just more modern. It was ludicrous to think that clay figures could protect the emperor in the afterlife, but no more so than some of the stories I'd heard. Didn't it make a lot more sense to focus on making the most of this life, rather than using it up by preparing for an unknown afterlife? It didn't seem right that we were sent here solely to prepare for another life.

This epiphany awakened me to the cross-cultural fear of the afterlife. The Christian story, dispersed by the Mennonites, had no exclusivity over frightening people into following their teachings, no matter how altruistic they were. Carrying that fear another moment meant carrying an unnecessary weight.

Close to the same time, a glimpse into a Mennonite history book whose title I can't remember offered another key to help me loosen fear's grip. Somehow, I stumbled across a passage describing a fire and brimstone sermon from the late 1800s. It could have been a page from my childhood. I recognized the rhetoric from the pulpit that scared me so much, and realized that the threat of imminent apocalypse had been going on for at least 100 years, yet the earth and her inhabitants were still intact.

Both of those events dislodged an irrational and pervasive fear of imminent doom. I felt liberated, and the first stirrings of awakening to the real me, and where my power lay.

MY HONDA SPIRIT accompanied me for two years, until it could hand me off to a sportier, more powerful motorcycle that would match the power that awakened in me. My new Yamaha FZ1, outfitted with hard side-bags and a trunk, was an all-purpose bike, well-suited for travel. Daniel said it had too much power for me and that I'd be popping wheelies. He was right in that it did have a lot of power, but not as much as I did. I never popped a wheelie or crashed during my 130,000 miles with that bike.

In spite of ongoing counseling and trying to work things out with Daniel, the reparation wasn't happening. We'd been together for more than thirty years, but prolonging something that no longer worked was pointless. In my heart, I knew I'd exhausted my options and would have to leave my marriage to find the relationship my soul craved, beginning with the relationship to myself.

In my late forties, I'd evolved into roles in both my marriage and career that weren't me, molded by the thoughts and expectations of other people. It was the same pattern I'd followed as a young girl when I'd adopted roles for others that didn't suit me. There had to be more than this emotional flatness. A lot of living awaited!

Drifting through life, I'd adapted to uncomfortable situations by glossing them over or trying to replace them with something else, as well as sticking with them too long. Avoidance allowed events to accumulate to the point where I felt pushed to the wall. I could no longer take the emptiness in my marriage or career. Handing off *My Harp is Turned to Mourning* to Trent initiated the slow process of exploring the heritage I'd been ashamed of and tried to bury for so long. My Honda Spirit had come to rescue me, but changes had to start within me, for the survival of my soul.

Telling Daniel I was leaving was the hardest and most painful conversation I've had in my life, but I had no other choice. It was like when I used to protect my parents' feelings at the expense of my own, and I couldn't let that happen any longer. I knew he wouldn't understand, and he'd be so hurt. As I expected, he was shocked. We'd booked a trip to Cambodia, Laos, and Thailand and decided to go anyway. He didn't want to come home. I did.

On December 11th, 2002, I moved into a country home apartment that led out into a garden surrounded by wildflowers and trees. Set back from the road, with a garage to store my motorcycle, it was the haven I needed. I lay on the sofa in front of the gas fireplace, warm and cozy, watching the gentle snowfall, at peace. I still had the job to tend to, but that could wait.

GERHARD SHOWED ME THE WAY, with a far more intense spiritual struggle from his youth. Mennonites had held on to their tenet of non-resistance for hundreds of years, through horrendous times when many died. Even in the Russian Civil War, most didn't want to fight back. Their non-violent stance tormented some of them more as reports of escalating brutality spread throughout their colonies. They prayed and asked God for guidance, then a small group decided to take action. They could no longer stand by while innocent unarmed civilians were tortured, slaughtered, and buried in mass graves, while villages were plundered and women raped.

In a highly contentious move, the *Selbstschutz,* an armed unit, was formed for defensive purposes only, out of necessity, as an ideal. A verse from Scripture supported Gerhard's decision to join: *But understand this: If the owner of the house had known at what time of night the thief was coming, he would have kept watch and would not have let his house be broken into.*

Growing up, I'd taken issue with this literal interpretation of Scripture. I couldn't argue against it here. Would I have found such courage in that circumstance? Could I have stood against centuries of spiritual beliefs? Could I have killed terrorists? I was in no position to offer a moral judgment from my safe perch in a land of peace and plenty.

When the battle signal sounded for the gathering of the *Selbstschutz* in the street of his village of Lichtfelde, he answered the call. He was only seventeen and trained as a teacher, not a soldier. His trembling, yet supportive, family awaited his return. It was only a matter of time until the *Selbstschutz* got drawn into conflict, siding with the Whites (anti-Communist). When the Reds (Bolsheviks) drove them out, opportunistic Makhno, the terrorist leader, sided with the Reds. At that point, both armies turned against the *Selbstschutz*, swarming the country like locusts. Ultimately, the *Selbstschutz* fought the Makhnovtsy and the Reds who would one day rule them. That didn't bode well for their future.

Things that happened in Russia didn't disappear from your memory banks when you left. Even here in Canada, people remembered who participated and who didn't. That point of friction lingered for decades.

LEAVING A JOB WAS A BIG DECISION, but certainly not on the scale of the decision my ancestors made to leave their homeland. By the summer of 1919, the Bolsheviks had gained the upper hand and some semblance of calm had returned to the colonies. People began to hope that things would improve. But economically, religiously, administratively, and nationally, the Mennonite way of life clashed with Bolshevism. Many could see more erosion of their lifestyle coming. Others thought things would get better, or felt God wanted them to stay in Russia. Had the government guaranteed their religious freedom, they might have adapted to the dramatic changes and given up their traditional land holdings. But in their hearts, they remained concerned for their physical survival. More importantly, they knew their souls would starve in the New Russia where they'd lost their religious freedom.

TAKING the step of leaving my marriage had made leaving my job easier. Early in 2003, my supervisor increasingly expected me to support decisions I viewed as unethical; for me, this was the final straw. I wrestled with my options, questioning the right action, until I was clear. I *had* to leave. My soul would starve if I stayed.

Three months after that realization, I gave my notice, a move that liberated and empowered me, although it astounded family, friends, and co-workers. They called me brave, courageous, and asked if I was scared. It's one thing to leave a long-term marriage, but to give up an established career when I now had to support myself added a new dimension to people's perception of risk. Many colleagues had decades of seniority and planned to stay until retirement. They couldn't understand why I'd walk away from what they called a good thing, or how remaining in the wrong roles drained my life energy. At age forty-eight, I had a blank slate on which to write whatever I wanted. When a serpent sheds its skin, the whole thing comes off in one piece. My tender new skin was ready for new growth.

August 1st, 2003, my last day on the job, was a Friday leading into the busiest summer holiday weekend of the year. Most of the salaried employees, including everyone in my department, had taken the day off. It's unconventional to leave someone alone on her last day of work, especially with access to personnel files and confidential records. It's extremely poor practice from a security perspective, but they counted on my strong work ethic, knowing I'd work to the end of the day and fulfill my obligation. When it came time to leave, I closed down my laptop, shut my office door behind me, and turned in my laptop, keys, and security passes as instructed. Then I closed the door and walked forward, filled with gratitude. I'd completed hard lessons and no longer had to drag them through the rest of my life.

My soul was as famished as my ancestors' physical bodies had been after their years of upheaval in Russia. Their souls were intact, nourished by their culture and religious beliefs. It was time for me to find the right fuel that would nourish me.

12

O nce Trudy had been refilled with the right fuel, she didn't cough or sputter once. The ride from Edmonton to Strathmore, the closest town to Siksika, went quickly. It's amazing how exquisitely we run when we nourish our souls with the right ingredients, and how quickly things can sour when we force something that isn't a good fit.

I had a general idea where I wanted to camp but hadn't made a reservation. The sun was still high in the afternoon sky and by mid-Friday afternoon, I'd reached Strathmore, near Siksika where tomorrow I'd finally get to the Fair I'd planned this whole trip around. There, I was confident I'd speak with an Elder who would offer guidance and insights in response to my questions. I pondered how best to find this Elder. I'd been to pow-wows before but didn't know what to anticipate here. I knew I couldn't walk in cold, clasping my gift of tobacco, and expect an open-armed welcome. My best approach was to assess the lay of the land once I got there. I'd been guided this far. I trusted I'd be guided once I arrived.

I pulled out the tattered Alberta Accommodation Guide I'd picked up when I entered the province. I'd gotten into the routine of using it to narrow down choices, then gathering more information from the respective websites. I also had a campground app, or I'd Google nearby campsites. The area around Strathmore held three campgrounds and I chose Eagle Lake RV Resort. The pictures looked lovely, although online pictures can be misleading. It was four miles south of the Trans-Canada Highway, so traffic noise would be minimal. It was the nearest I could get to Siksika, had a five-star rating, and was on a paved road. Mostly paved.

The only warning sign I had that the tarmac was about to change was the sudden dust kicked up from a car I was following at a distance. Not sure what to expect, I slowed down from fifty-five miles per hour and stopped when I saw what lay in front of me. Unmarked. One hundred feet of road had been dug up and replaced by deep, loose, gravel, exactly like the stuff I'd crashed in two years ago only forty miles from where I sat. Adrenaline coursed through me, leaving a taste in my mouth like an old penny. I had two options. Go through slowly, or retrace my steps back to the highway, head west and circumnavigate the concession on paved roads, approaching the resort from the south. Here was another reminder to proceed slowly and mindfully on my journey.

I closed my eyes, took a few deep breaths, and got my fear under control. It seemed silly to go all the way around. I could walk my bike through the gravel if I had to, even with the load I carried. I sent a quick request to my Jaguar animal guide to help me track the best course through the gravel, took another deep breath, and headed for the most packed surface. Though my entire body was tense with anxiety, I forced myself to keep a loose grip on the handlebars, look ahead, and keep going. As soon as I was back on pavement, I let out a huge sigh of relief, expelling the momentary tension and exhaustion that had overcome me. With a firm footing under me, I was back in my groove.

Eagle Lake Resort was as pretty as the pictures portrayed. Half the campers were seasonal, creating a temporary community on nicely tended plots of home. It was tranquil, yet vibrant, with friendly staff. Mature trees shaded the flat sites, each within a minute's walk to the lake. While checking in, I learned that a motorcycle had wiped out on that gravel section a few days ago and the rider and passenger were still in hospital. I'd already sent up a prayer of gratitude for getting me through and for the car ahead that had alerted me, but this news merited another.

As soon as my tent was set up and my "home" the way I liked it, I headed back into Strathmore for groceries. With my bags off, it was easier to maneuver and carry extra supplies. I'd be staying here two nights so could stock up a bit. This time, I took the longer way around, avoiding the gravel trap. I'd understood the message and didn't need it repeated.

Once back, I kicked off my boots, removed my gear, and relaxed. I longed to chat with Mom, but dementia had eroded her ability to carry on a meaningful conversation. Dad was hale and hearty, though, and following my travels. I called to check in and let him know where I was. I knew it was close to Namaka and the farm he and Liese had moved to when she remarried, but I didn't realize how close. He told me that in the 1930s, the Mennonite kids in the area used to gather and go skating on Eagle Lake, right where I was. His family was too poor to afford skates so he couldn't join in, but he'd be there with his friends, watching. It made me sad to think the Jansens were the poorest of the poor.

After the Fair, I'd spend a few days exploring the area and

this part of his and Liese's history. For now, I walked down to the lake where the surface reflected the setting sun. Except for the season and the absence of the campground, it wouldn't have looked much different eighty years ago when a lonely figure sat on the sidelines watching his friends play hockey. Turning in for the night, the feeling was much the same as I'd felt camping in Dalmeny, Saskatchewan, near where Gerhard and Susa lived, or near Johann and Liese's land in Beaverlodge in northern Alberta. It felt familiar, even though I'd never been here. The excitement was building even with my grandparents. They'd never been to a pow-wow and were eager for the next day to arrive.

THE FAIRGROUNDS WEREN'T hard to find. All I had to do was ask the first person I came to on Siksika Nation land. "Turn right at the next intersection. Go down a ways and you'll see it on the left. Can't miss it!"

He was right. Dozens of tipis set up on the grass flanked the round arena's western and southern exposures. White, yellow, and red backgrounds, painted with beautiful designs to honor animal spirits and spirits of nature, stood out against a brilliant blue sky. RV camping was relegated to behind the tipis. Access to the parking area in the field on the east side was via a gravel path, this one easy for Trudy and me to navigate. Admission was free. Everyone was welcome, although I didn't see any other sixty-two-year-old white women or motorcycles.

The grounds buzzed with celebratory energy. Not knowing which way to go, and obviously a visitor, I joined a line of others heading into the dancing arbor, pulled by crescendoing energy. The dancing hadn't started but the wooden bleachers surrounding the arbor were packed with observers. I climbed two thirds of the way up and made myself comfortable. Families were settled in for the day with coolers, blankets, and toys to keep their children occupied. My grandparents were agog at the euphony of sound, color, and participants of all ages. It looked nothing like a Mennonite celebration!

A few minutes after I got seated, the parade began, signaling the beginning of the day's proceedings. Tribal Elders, men all wearing similar elaborate, eagle-feathered headdresses led the way into the arena, accompanied by drum beats and traditional singing. Dancers wearing regalia followed, their outfits resplendent with an array of intricate beadwork, porcupine quills, tin jingles, and other meaningful objects. Women carried eagle feather fans as they danced around the circle. The men's dancing incorporated leaping, twirling, crouching, and rising. As the floor filled with dancers, the energy became frenetic, as if I could feel the heartbeat of Mother Earth herself. Even the children were parading in their little regalia. My ancestral spirits were fascinated and delighted, and with so much going on, didn't know where to look next. They felt the energy, too, but stopped short of joining the dancers.

Watching the dances for a few hours, I was mesmerized, but my mission stayed foremost in my mind. The Elders were involved in the festivities, so approaching one would be inappropriate. People were gathered around the announcer's stage, but that didn't seem like the right place to go to ask for an Elder. My best option looked like the security office.

I started at midafternoon. Walking over, I explained my reason for being there, that I had a gift of tobacco, and asked to speak with an Elder. The security person told me to come back at 4 p.m. when an Elder who lived near the land Dad had lived on would be there. When I returned at 4 p.m., she said he was needed to help with parking and to come back at 4:30. When he still wasn't back, another person advised me to check the Elders' tent, as she pointed to the south side of the arena. When I got there, the tent was empty.

It may take me a while to get a message, but it was becoming impossible to ignore that this was trending in an unfavorable direction.

"They're busy with the celebrations," I was told. "Come back at the end of the day when things wind down." That was 10 p.m.!

"Please," I implored. "I've waited a long time and come a long way. I'd like to speak with someone."

I had full confidence that things would work out as they were meant to, but I was beginning to question whether that might look completely different than what I'd expected. I sent up a silent prayer, asking Spirit to facilitate this meeting.

Finally, the security supervisor took me under her wing. "Wait here. I'll be right back."

She returned with the best news of the day.

"My grandmother will speak with you."

She led me through the crowd clustered around the dancing circle to the spot where her grandmother sat in a collapsible chair at the edge. "She's hard of hearing, so speak loudly." Thanking her profusely, I took the empty seat Grandmother offered beside her.

Offering her the tobacco, I began, trying to make myself heard and understood over the din. Again, I asked Spirit for help, this time to articulate my message so I'd be understood, in as few words as possible.

"My father grew up in this area," I said. "His stepfather's farm bordered the reserve, but they had to walk away from it in 1937. I'm trying to understand how the spirit of this land lives in me."

"Go and talk to the people who live there now," she stated, clasping the tobacco.

I wasn't sure she understood my line of thought. She thought I was trying to get the land back. I recognized that the land the Jansens, and many of the Mennonites, had lived on had once been Blackfoot land, taken away by the government for colonists while the Blackfoot people were herded onto a reserve. To no avail, I tried to rephrase my wording to be clearer. "I'm trying to understand how the energy of my ancestors lives in me," I said, almost pleading.

"Check the archives in Strathmore to find land ownership," she replied. "Or speak to Mr. and Mrs. Watson who lived in that area for a long time. They're white. English."

Seriously? I'd waited so long for this day and held out such high hope. I'd been counseled to come here by a Blackfoot man whose grandfather was an Elder. He himself was not an Elder but he'd offered me advice from a place of cultural wisdom.

While we sat there and I wracked my brain for a more productive approach, another woman came around brandishing a stack of five-dollar bills, handing them out randomly. I wasn't sure what to do when she offered me one, but Grandmother advised, "Take it. She's a white woman married to a Blackfoot man and she does this all the time." You don't question gifts, so I did as I was told, accepting the message of abundance with gratitude.

Grandmother then called over her friend, another grandmother and asked me to explain why I was there. I got an identical response. I resigned myself to the fact I was not going to get the answer I sought.

I thanked them both and walked away, back to Trudy, deeply disappointed.

The security guard who'd led me to her grandmother saw me leaving. "Did you find out what you wanted?" she asked, her voice compassionate.

"It wasn't what I wanted to hear, but it was evidently what I needed to hear," I answered, smiling sadly, and thanking her.

Once I got back to the campground, I phoned Oriah to seek her counsel. Her advice was sagacious and insightful, as always. She pointed out that it's hard to surrender what doesn't line up with other expectations and feelings, partly because we don't understand what the feelings are telling us or where they're directing us. It's our attachment to those expectations that closes us to any message not consistent with where our minds have decided we're going. She acknowledged that holding expectations lightly is exceedingly difficult.

The Indigenous people I'd consulted since the crash had told me the answers were within my culture. The earth-based spirituality I sought wasn't addressed in my culture, but I couldn't make them understand that. I'd also been told by non-Indigenous spiritual teachers my journey would unfold in ways that weren't logical.

I'd had such high hopes for what I expected to hear at the Pow-wow, not even considering the answers lay elsewhere. For now, I'd had enough of doors closing in front of me. It was so disappointing, but in a way, it simplified things. I could concentrate on my family. I still didn't think that's where the answers lay, but it was the only thing to do. I reasoned with myself, knowing the answer hadn't dawned on me yet, and it would arrive in a way I hadn't anticipated. I needed to let it go and trust I'd gain understanding when the time was right. "Thank you, Great Spirit," I breathed.

I didn't realize how much emotional capital I'd invested in the day. The Pow-wow had been spectacular, with a more authentic, homogenous, and less touristy feel than another I'd attended in Ontario before I left. The ride back to Eagle Lake Resort revived me somewhat, but I arrived exhausted. That night I slept through a terrific windstorm that blew someone's boat off his truck. Trudy was untouched, and my tent held fast. I was protected.

THE HAMLET OF NAMAKA, Alberta, once a thriving rail-siding, still comes up on Google maps, but other than a small directional sign on the TCH, you wouldn't know it was there. An old schoolhouse and a handful of modern houses were only a few miles from my campsite at Eagle Lake. Dad spent his formative years, from age four to eleven, on this farmland south of the hamlet. Walking this land was a must, guided by the rudimentary map he had sketched for me, complete with landmarks.

A preliminary scouting of the area revealed many gravel roads of the same treacherous nature as the one I'd crashed on. My grandparents had not given up in the face of adversity, and I may have been able to navigate those roads, but I wasn't willing to risk my safety when it wasn't necessary and chose to find another way. Instead, I'd go to nearby Strathmore and rent a car for the next day, Monday.

Tonight, friends from the motorcycle community, Karen and Richard Reynolds, would host me. Although we'd never met in person, Karen and I had followed each other on Twitter for years. I'd known she lived somewhere near Calgary, but until a year ago, I hadn't known she'd lived near where I crashed. Even more serendipitously, Bill Cormier, the Good Samaritan who rescued me from the ditch and drove me to the hospital, had attended elementary school with Richard. Bill and his wife Laura had invited us all over for dinner on Monday evening.

Karen ran her own consulting practice and Richard farmed, the fifth generation of stewards of their land. Pulling into the driveway, an intriguing array of sensations met me, making it feel like home. The farmhouse and barn were like the ones on Dad and Mom's farm. This land produced grains, which Dad had grown up with and always wanted to go back to.

The evening was lovely as Karen, Richard, and I sat around

sharing stories of motorcycling and diverse family histories. Karen offered to drive me around the next day, which was fine with me. I was happy to share my exploration with her. Besides, I had come to find out that Strathmore had no car rental agencies.

IN LATE 1926, Russian Mennonite refugees were offered farms on a large ranch, known as the Namaka Farm, on traditional territories of the Niitsitapi (Blackfoot) of the Treaty 7 region in southern Alberta, after the owner went bankrupt. The hamlet of Namaka to the north, the Bow River to the south, and the Blackfoot reserve (now Siksika Nation) to the east bounded the 13,000-acre farm on an eight-mile tract of land. Anxious to have what was considered mostly virgin land under cultivation, the Alberta Government partitioned it into cookie-cutter quarter-section (160-acre) farms and negotiated mutually attractive deals with the Mennonites. Thirty-six immigrant families settled here, making it almost twice the community Liese had been part of in Beaverlodge. These immigrants had no money, but they had hope, opportunity, and a reputation for a strong work ethic. Generally, they had to agree to farm it for three years and pay for it by turning over one third of the proceeds of the crops.

My father's stepfather, Peter Jansen, grew up in a Russian Mennonite colony near the Sea of Azov, in what is now Ukraine. He was estranged from his family, ran away from home, and at age seventeen served a very short stint with the Cossacks, fighting with the Whites against the Reds. After spending three years in a Bulgarian prisoner of war camp, he made his way to Germany. There, Hitler was beginning to send ominous signals, and Peter foresaw trouble. Not wanting to bring attention to the fact he was of German ethnicity, the ticket that probably got him into Germany in the first place, he changed the spelling of his surname from Jantzen to Jansen.

Peter arrived in Saskatoon in 1926 and hung around for at least a year, harvesting and threshing grain, earning enough to buy a new car—a Model T Ford. It didn't take him long to upset and demolish it. In 1928, he appeared on horseback in Namaka where he stayed with an aunt and uncle until he could get his hands on a quarter-section that had become available. Located right near the Bow River Valley, the farm bordered the Blackfoot reserve. That first year, the wheat yield was so high the sheaves clogged the binders. It's not known how he and Liese, who lived forty-two miles away, met. It's safe to assume the Mennonite network went into high gear to connect a young widowed mother with a small son and a bachelor with a farm.

Benny was four years old when Peter and Liese married and not pleased to be uprooted for the third time in his short life. He'd have to start all over with a new father.

KAREN HAD a few emails to answer and people to follow up with on Monday morning, so I used the time to catch up on messages and journaling. By noon we were on the road.

From Dad's map, I knew within a quarter-section where the farm had been, even though no evidence of the houses, farm buildings, or fence lines remained. As soon as we crossed the railway tracks heading south on Range Road 250, the farm had been on the left. An invisible line at the back of the farm marked the border with the Siksika reserve. Where in the 1930s a family farm, with house, barns, and granaries had existed on each quarter-section, now the land was one big grain field.

Dad's map showed us where to stop. Karen and I walked across a culvert onto the land, our unseen passengers just as inquisitive. Karen hung back while I walked further into the field along a small turn-around for farm equipment. Afternoon breezes rippled the waist-high grain that surrounded me.

The barn and granaries had probably stood near the property line, near where the poplars now grew. The house would have sat closer to the road. The kitchen was the largest room. Benny slept in the living room, Peter and Liese in the bedroom. As the others arrived, they put them wherever they fit. They even took in boarders, including the schoolteacher, Miss Hinz. Peter was hardworking and honest, but not a natural father. He loved to play with his children, though. Albert was born nine months after their wedding, followed over the next five years by Hilda and Irma.

They always had food to eat, even during the drought when this land was parched. Although grasshoppers and Russian thistles proliferated, wiping out any hope of a crop, they were resourceful. Since there was no grain, they cut green thistles into silage, salted it, and fed it to the farm animals. They slaughtered two 300-pound pigs a year, had their own chickens, and ate pigeon breasts from the birds Peter shot off the roof of the barn with his .22. When they had company, they'd send Benny out to guillotine a chicken with a special wire gizmo designed specifically for that purpose. Guests would have to wait until dinner was cleaned and cooked.

They did what they had to do. Everyone was in the same boat. They thought being poor was normal, and besides, they had no other choice. I'd heard that before. When adversity strikes, you keep going as best you can. You don't let it overwhelm you or define you. During my post-crash months, I didn't have a lot of choice. I wasn't going to let myself languish and had to manage as best I could, focusing on healing so I could get mobile again.

During those Dirty Thirty years, Peter, like the other Mennonite farmers, couldn't make a go of it. They worked the land as they had in Russia, creating the biggest dust storm in their history. They didn't realize this was different soil and a different climate, both of which required farming techniques better suited for this terrain. In any case, a quarter-section wasn't enough to feed a family and the farm animals, as well as pay back the *Reiseschuld,* (transportation debt), and turn a profit to pay off the farm debt.

Dad had told me that one Christmas Liese had the house spick and span, until a storm came up and covered the inside with dust. It settled right on the sills and in the cracks of the windows. She cried and cried because everything was so filthy.

Things on the farm were going from bad to worse. Peter had relatives in the Niagara area of Ontario and they'd sent word that the fruit farms there were flourishing. In 1937, he became the first Mennonite to walk away from the Namaka farm, turning it back over to the bank.

The Jansens got on the train and headed east, but eleven-year-old Benny's heart stayed behind. He'd enjoyed the endless wheat fields and open sky of the prairies, and the small horse called Pony that he rode bareback. As an adult, he'd long to return, but life took him in other directions.

What strength and resilience my ancestors had to survive, year after year, each one bleaker than the one before. In gratitude for their protection and the example they'd held out for me, I laid down a gift of tobacco to Spirit.

We returned to the car and continued our tour of the area. Further north on Range Road 250, south from their church, now a dwelling, sat the Mennonite cemetery. Meticulously manicured, it's maintained by descendants of Namaka Farm Mennonites.

The bonds of community and friendship between the Namaka families lasted a lifetime. Like the Jansens, many of them moved to the Niagara area of Ontario. Once, I asked Dad why those relationships were so special. "Simple," he said. "We needed each other to survive."

Karen and I returned home with barely enough time to relax for a few minutes before heading out for dinner. With anticipation tempered by apprehension, I wondered if I'd even recognize Bill, my Good Samaritan. We'd spent ninety minutes together in his pickup, and he'd waited for Paul, my moto friend from Calgary, to arrive at the hospital before handing me off. Most of that time I was in shock.

Shock is a survival mechanism, designed to redirect blood supply to vital organs under times of extreme duress. Survival instincts had kicked in to direct me to turn my motorcycle off, climb up to the road, and flag down a stranger for help. I'd been able to give him directions to remove my helmet and gather my belongings strewn around the crash site, then make a few important phone calls, before my body cried, "No more!"

My survival instincts were rooted, in part, in this area. Liese, who'd struggled to survive her whole life, found brief solace in Beaverlodge before her dreams—and life—were dashed. Here in southern Alberta, life had been one challenge after another, most of it out of her control. Yet none of this defeated her. Her faith, community, and tenacity kept her going. The physical lands she'd left behind had recovered and, with the right care, thrived, but for her to survive physically and spiritually, she'd had to move on, something I'd also learned through my divorce and career changes.

As it turned out, I would have recognized Bill anywhere. He and Laura welcomed me warmly into their rural home. Karen must have told them of my dietary preferences. They'd gone to a lot of work to meet them—vegetarian chili, gluten-free biscuits, and a fresh beet salad. Bill and Richard, Karen's husband, live only a few miles apart but hadn't seen each other in years and enjoyed reconnecting.

Seventy years earlier, my family was learning how to survive by being part of a community of others who shared their cultural heritage and spiritual beliefs. Here I was, surrounded by a different kind of community, but, nonetheless, one that had come to aid me. Again, the kindness of strangers overwhelmed me, our interconnectedness unmistakable.

T wo days later, after having Trudy serviced in Calgary, we were heading east towards Drumheller, basking in the expansiveness of the prairie landscape. Like a bolt out of the blue, my soul understood why I was so drawn to Indigenous spirituality. The message the grandmother at the Pow-wow and the other teachers over the years had delivered sank in as I rode east between Calgary and Drumheller across the plains. They'd conveyed the words, and now those words had found meaning.

And it was so simple!

To understand how I'm shaped by my culture, why I've made the choices I have, and the history behind my beliefs, I need look only at my ancestors. In my case, my Mennonite background. Up until my late forties, I had distanced myself from it, never wanting anyone to know that's how I was raised. But that was my physical and energetic DNA. It was time to embrace it.

The Indigenous Peoples' experiences were a mirror to show me what happens when one becomes disconnected from one's culture. When Indigenous Peoples were systematically and forcibly removed from their cultures, not only did it decimate their way of life, it destroyed individuals for generations. I'd left my culture voluntarily, and did not endure the trauma over generations, but it was still a disconnection from my roots. Roots nourish us and help us thrive.

Whether I agreed or disagreed with their religious beliefs, the blood of Gerhard, Susa, Johann and Liese, and our ancestors before them, ran through me. Their experiences lived in me energetically. To understand who I've become, that's where I need to go. That was the lesson Hummingbird was here to show me.

I'd also learned much about how to live in balance with nature, including my own nature, and what happens when I don't. I can let go and move on, open to Divine guidance in a new way. It seems for life's major lessons, I have to be shown them repeatedly. When I'm unable to read them, the lessons become more explicit, dramatic, and direct. Spirit was trying for so long to guide me to the answer, but I hadn't been ready to hear it.

Eagle, my guide to seeing both the big picture and the details, had done his job and helped me realign my spirit, while soaring high above me. He rarely touched down except to rest.

Like Quinton had advised, "Ask for a blessing and the way will become clear." It took two years, but now I knew.

As I did my routine scan and checked my rear-view mirrors, four sets of eyes looked back at me, smiling. They knew too.

DRUMHELLER LIES in the Red Deer River valley, central to Michichi, where Gerhard and Susa had farmed after they left Dalmeny, Swalwell, where Dad was born, and Beiseker, where Liese and Benny lived for two years after moving south following Johann's death. The surrounding area is reminiscent of the Russian steppes that housed Mennonite colonies for generations. Many Mennonite immigrants settled in southern Alberta, Saskatchewan, and Manitoba because that's where they were sent, but it also felt like home.

Trudy was rejuvenated after being serviced. Gerhard, Susa, Johann, and Liese were ready for more riding, and Serpent, Jaguar, Hummingbird, and Eagle were in position, ready to guide me on the next phase of my journey.

The whole trip seemed unreal. It was as if the lives of my ancestors had reignited as I'd followed their migrations and walked the land they'd walked. The four of them continued to chat as I rode along, reminiscing, swapping tall tales, and laughing. It was good to see them like this.

We were almost at the turnoff for Beiseker, where I hoped to find the place Liese and Benny had lived. She'd worked here as a housekeeper for a family called Bauer who were Seventh Day Adventists. Other than that, I had little to go on. Although 819 people called the village home, its broad streets were empty, and it looked one breath away from extinction. Against the railway tracks, the Town Hall and Museum sat in what was once the train station, defying the town's sleepy first impression. With a profusion of planters and baskets bursting with bloom, it exuded the small-town welcome I'd come to know. It was a good place to start my search.

Although Sandra, the petite, vivacious, and youthful town clerk, had no knowledge of the Bauer family, she tried hard to dig up clues. Local history books in the museum offered some information about the family, but it was from the same era Liese and Benny were here, eighty-eight years ago. I was looking for something more current. Dad told me descendants still lived in the area, so I was persistent.

So was Sandra. She contacted Betty, an elderly woman who'd lived there her entire life, and came up with an answer—Kurt and Erika Meyer.

"Erika is the granddaughter of Hans and Frieda Bauer and lives out there," Sandra said.

"Out there?" I'd always thought the home was in town. Any farmers I knew didn't have housekeepers.

"They farmed twelve miles east and four miles south of here," she said. "A lot of Seventh Day Adventists live in that area."

Not only had Liese moved away from anything that was familiar, she'd moved into the middle of nowhere with strangers whose community had customs and beliefs different than her own. At least they spoke German. How lonely she must have been—twenty-seven-years old and widowed, impoverished, and on her own. There must have been some kind of Mennonite connection somewhere. I'd try and find it.

I placed a call to Erika Meyer but got her voice mail. Briefly, I described my interest and left my call-back number.

Sandra suggested I call Lina Hoffman to see if she had more to offer. Lina was younger than Betty but was on the Museum Board and knew each resident and their history. Unfortunately, she had no more to offer about the Bauers, but became excited when she learned I was on a motorcycle.

"My daughter Marianne and her live-in, Jessie, ride, and they live in Drumheller. Give them a call when you get there."

I loved it! Such a welcome to a stranger, as if I was family or had lived there forever. This had been my experience throughout my trip, but it always warmed my heart when it happened. People were so interested in my quest. They wanted to help—and share their stories and often their homes.

Out of ideas, I retraced my steps to the main highway. As I headed east out of town toward Drumheller, we got a kick out of a statue of Squirt the Skunk, the Village mascot standing sentry in the campground on the eastern outskirts. Each prairie community seemed to hold its own quirky charm.

With approximate coordinates of the Bauer farmhouse deduced from historical records, I'd try to find it. It was right off the main road, but I stopped as soon as I turned. As with most of the rural side roads, it was deep, heavy gravel, more than I was willing to risk. I'd have to find another way.

I continued to the nearby hamlet of Swalwell, home to ninety-five people. With any luck, I'd see some old buildings, maybe one reminiscent of what Liese called a nursing home where she and Johann had waited out her pregnancy, and where she'd given birth to Dad. Unfortunately, I came up empty. Amongst the smattering of modernish houses, some evolved from mobile homes, others more permanent, nothing looked old. Other than the nearby dam and fishing hole, I couldn't see a reason that people would live here, although Swalwell may have been larger when it served as a nursery for immigrants. I had to be satisfied with a photo of Trudy parked against the Swalwell sign, next to the railway tracks, once the lifeline of these prairies. Then I continued east to Drumheller.

The campground was south of town, with leafy, manicured lots. The only downside was that most of the lot, including the elevated tent site, was graveled for easy maintenance. It didn't make for a comfortable carpet, but it would do as my home for the next six nights. And it was quiet. After setting up, I called Marianne and we had a delightful chat. She and Jessie had an RV parked in the nearby hamlet of Wayne and invited me to join them at their campfire on the weekend. In 1912, Wayne became a boomtown when coal mining was taking off. The population swelled to 2,500 and the Rosedeer Hotel and its Last Chance Saloon opened. Now, officially, twenty-seven people lived there, not counting the apparitions who stayed behind. The Wild West history and charm draws visitors from around the world, though, and it's a popular biker destination.

Later that evening Erika Meyer returned my call. We chatted

briefly and amicably, like old friends. Thursday and Friday she was busy helping on the farm, and Saturday was her holy day, so she offered to show me the Bauer farmhouse on Sunday. That was four days away, but I was elated! I sat in my camp chair with my feet up on the picnic table. It had been another awesome day.

THE AWESOMENESS CONTINUED into the next day. I'd had picture-perfect weather for most of my trip—sunshine, blue skies, and warm, but not hot, temperatures. Staying in one place for more than a night meant I didn't have to pack everything up and load Trudy every morning, and the lightened load made traveling easier. Today promised more of the same, ideal for hunting down the land Gerhard and Susa had farmed. In my dream, they were around the breakfast picnic table with me.

Both Dad and Uncle Peewee, Gerhard's youngest son, had told me Gerhard was an okay farmer, but he wasn't impassioned by it. He would have loved to be a teacher as he'd been trained to be in Russia, but that wasn't likely to happen. They needed to make a living and a place for family. Farming was their only choice, and if they were going to do that, they wanted their own land.

I never had to make a choice like that. I could have done whatever I wanted but was afraid of doing anything perceived as risky when I was starting out. Their only option was to take a chance. A gust of wind blew my map off the table and I ran to retrieve it. I put it back and weighed it down with my water bottle.

They longed for the tight communities of family and friends they'd enjoyed in Russia. The Schultzes in Dalmeny had been very good to them, but Susa missed her family desperately. Gerhard's father Heinrich, brother Abram, sister Sara, and their families had lived close to them, but that was not her *Freund-schaft*. Gerhard worked long hours outside and Susa was alone with a baby. It was hard for everyone. In 1927, they left the Schultzes and moved 600 miles southeast to join Susa's family, the Koops, on their farm in Manitoba. It was wonderful for them to be reunited, and comforting to be in a familiar church community. Yet, while spiritually their life was rich, physically, they were still struggling to survive.

That season it rained so much that standing water separated the house and barn. On top of that, the implements were of poor quality and kept breaking down. They needed to be replaced, but there had been no profits for two years. The future was bleak. In 1928, Susa's father packed up the farm and most of the family and moved east to Ontario. Gerhard and Susa went west.

Gerhard had gotten word that crops in southern Alberta were good, with a high yield and decent prices. Land similar to where they'd come from in the Molochna was available. Gerhard's brother Abram, who'd stayed near Dalmeny, Saskatchewan, also wanted to farm, so the two of them purchased a place in Michichi, Alberta, near Drumheller, both families sharing one ramshackle house.

These weren't short moves. They'd zigzagged across a huge area—first to Dalmeny in central Saskatchewan, then back to southern Manitoba, and then another 800 miles west here to Alberta, doing what they had to do.

MICHICHI WAS nothing more than a main street and two cross streets in Starland County, also part of the extensive traditional territories of the Blackfoot people of the Treaty 7 region in southern Alberta. Land archives would be somewhere central, here, but finding them was my first challenge. They turned out to be in Morrin, a hamlet north of Drumheller. Dorothy, the archivist, tried to help with my unusual request. She hauled out old area maps showing land titles, but there wasn't one for the years Gerhard and Susa were there. To find the exact location, I needed to know the lot and concession number. Of course, if I knew that, I wouldn't be there. With little hope of success, she offered to continue searching and call me if she turned up anything.

In the meantime, I'd ride out to Michichi and satisfy my curiosity about its character. Some of the rural roads started out paved; however, once the population they serviced grew too sparse for the township to justify maintaining a road surface that farm implements and heavy trucks would chew up, they became varying textures of gravel, from hard-packed to wash-board, loose, and deep. I'd gained confidence on gravel after my crash, to a point. These roads extended beyond that point, and I faced a ride of ten miles inland to where I needed to go. It didn't make sense to push myself so far past my comfort level and risk a wipeout on a road where no one might find me. I had nothing to prove. My Jaguar intuition held me back. It wasn't worth the risk. Landing in a remote Alberta ditch once was more than enough for me. Unfortunately, two approaches from different directions yielded the same results.

Finally, I stopped on the most packed part of the road and got off Trudy, leaving her near the middle of the road. There were no vehicles in either direction, and you could see for miles, so I had lots of time to move her if I saw someone approaching. I knew I was looking in the general direction of the farm, even if I didn't have the specifics. Out of gratitude to Spirit and the Indigenous Peoples of the land, I laid down tobacco at the road-side, the wind picking it up and carrying it across the ditch and over the field.

Every time they watched this tradition, my grandparents were delighted with this tactile expression of reverence and gratitude. The concept of tobacco as a sacred medicine was new to them. They'd shown gratitude and reverence in different ways, but they'd learned that what counted was in one's heart, not the particular tradition.

If things had gone differently, their farm would have looked like the fields of gold that surrounded us.

They started from nothing. *Nuscht!* as Gerhard would say. No equity. Only a transportation debt to his brother Peter, who'd borrowed the money from International Harvester, his employer. As with many of the Mennonite farmers, Abram and Gerhard bought three quarter-sections for one dollar down on a $23,655 mortgage at five percent interest, which they agreed to repay out of the proceeds of the crops. They were hopeful and thought this was the start they'd waited and worked so hard for.

That first August, the yield and the prices were both high, but an early, heavy frost iced the windows of their home and froze the seeds for the following year's crops. The 1929 crop was smaller, and wheat that had sold for $2.17 a bushel in 1925 fell to $0.58 cents a bushel. Half of that had to go toward their land purchase. In 1930, the price for a bushel of wheat was between seven and eight cents, but on the positive side, they could keep it all for themselves.

Gerhard began working at an open-pit coal mine east of here, riding his horse seventeen miles each way through the bitter cold. As the snow whipped around him in the harsh wind and frigid temperatures, I'm sure he asked God daily, "What could you possibly have in store for me in this desolate land?" just as he had when crossing the Atlantic. They took one day at a time and no matter how hard it got, thanked God for their freedom and trusted Him to take care of them.

While they may not have realized it, my grandparents already knew what has emerged from eastern religions and earth-based spirituality: They'd embodied living in the present moment. While they always had hope, they appreciated everything they had in the moment, most of it not material. They knew if they could look after the present, the future would look after itself.

In spring, the rains and cold temperatures prevented them from getting on the land. Finally, by 1931, when they again had no money coming in, Gerhard and Abram had to forfeit the farm. As hard as it was for the brothers to separate, they decided the best thing for their families was to follow their wives' people. This meant that Abram and his wife, also named Liese, would move west to British Columbia with her family. Susa and Gerhard would move east to Kingsville, Ontario, where most of the Koops lived. Gerhard had to swallow his pride and ask Susa's father for a loan to cover their moving expenses. They couldn't get much poorer.

And I worried about gravel roads. And money. I wasn't wealthy, but I always had more than enough for what I needed.

They'd been in Canada for seven years and still weren't on their fiscal feet. Except they'd survived, and always had hope. It was infinitely better than what they'd left behind. Every day they gave thanks for living in a country of peace and freedom. Any hardships were tolerable when measured against that bar.

14

My Drumheller campsite had been home for four nights, longer than any spot I stayed at during this trip. Today, Sunday, I'd meet Erika Meyer, granddaughter of the people who had taken in Liese as domestic help when she'd moved from Beaverlodge after Johann's death. Of course, they took in Benny with her.

Harvesting had started the day before and Erika's husband Kurt, his brother Joe and crew were combining. She could meet me once she'd helped shuttle heavy equipment between farms. After I'd explained my reluctance to ride gravel roads, she arranged for me to park Trudy at Joe's farm. His driveway was right off the main paved road and she'd pick me up there.

I headed west across the flat grasslands turned farms, the morning sun on my back.

Liese had landed in a wonderful place. The Bauers spoke German and were very kind to her. Mr. Bauer took two-year-old Benny under his wing, especially when Benny got under the skin of their teenage sons. The Bauers were Seventh-Day Adventists and when Liese found out their holy day was Saturday, she explained she didn't want to celebrate her Sabbath then; she wanted to honor it on Sunday. Mrs. Bauer said it was no problem. She could have both days off.

I sent up a silent prayer of gratitude for these strangers who had taken her and Dad in.

Meeting Erika was like meeting a sister. We'd both grown up on farms, understood the urgency of a crop ready for harvest, and knew how to work. Our fathers had lived and probably played together. She was a few years older and a few inches shorter, but we agreed it felt like we'd known each other forever. I climbed into her metallic grey Ford four-by-four pickup and she deftly navigated the roads across the flat land, sliding around on the gravel like a pro. I was glad I hadn't tried it with Trudy.

We went directly to the Bauer homestead. The farm had been passed down to Erika's parents and now she and Kurt managed it. The white farmhouse with a south-facing porch stood tall and proud, a watchtower over the surrounding fields. Purchased through Eaton's catalog (a popular mail order catalog published by a Canadian retailer between 1884 and 1976), the house looked much as it had when Liese was here. The interior had undergone renovations but would still have been recognizable to her.

In sharp contrast to the times throughout its 100-year life when it had been filled beyond capacity, it stood vacant. Most recently, Erika and Kurt had loaned it out to a family who'd been displaced following a major forest fire that had enveloped their hometown of Fort McMurray in northern Alberta. The family had been there two months and just left. The generous spirit of Erika's grandparents in helping others in need lived in their descendants.

In the 1920s, Erika's grandfather had remarried after the death of his first wife. The new wife came with a family and at one point, twenty-two children lived here. Most of them were gone by the time Liese and Benny arrived, but it wasn't hard to see why the Bauers needed extra help. The kitchen and parlor were of modest size. Five bedrooms on the second floor, each with a metal room number tacked to them, lined up around the wooden-banistered stairwell. The house must have been crammed to the rafters.

The big red barn across a large yard sat in stark contrast to the blue sky. Little Benny would have had a heyday running and playing out there. The house, barn, and a few small outbuildings added contour to the otherwise flat landscape. Nothing else was visible for miles.

I didn't hesitate when Erika asked if I'd like a tour of the area. She showed me her and Kurt's farm, their church, the cemetery where her grandparents were buried and the local school. Our family stories had come full circle—granddaughters of disparate families who lived here eighty-six years ago, separated by 2,000 miles, had connected as friends. I'd gained a new appreciation for Liese's isolation and resilience. Erika, who'd not known of the Bauer's role with my ancestors until my phone call, learned something new about her grandparents' compassion.

Neither of us could explain how the two families came together, but there had to be a link somewhere. Liese didn't have relatives in this area, but I wondered if Johann had.

This was Seventh Day Adventists' country, but many Mennonites had settled north of here. Both the women I spoke with in Beiseker earlier that week had told me to go to Linden, thirty minutes north. "There are lots of Klassens up there," they said, speaking of Johann's family name. "One family owns a big feedlot. There's also a popular family restaurant, Country Cousins, where someone may be able to help you."

Erika finished our sightseeing excursion by early afternoon. That left plenty of time to see what I could find in Linden. With a current population of 828, everyone had to know everyone else and their families.

I shouldn't have been surprised to find everything closed up on Sunday, including Country Cousins. Traditional values, with Sunday as a day of worship and rest, prevailed. Except for me, nothing in the village moved. I'd have to return during the week. Since it was such a beautiful summer day, I decided to let Trudy go where she wanted as I explored the area.

My quest for ancestral history had taken me back hundreds of years before bringing me here to the area around Drumheller, Alberta, where the history goes back to antiquity. Dramatic landforms, scoured and eroded over millennia in what is called Canada's Badlands, have exposed rich deposits of fossils, including bones from the dinosaurs that roamed here seventy million years ago. The roads cut through valleys, their sides striated with millions of years of wisdom. As I rode, I imagined the life that once thrived here, the knowledge in those fossils, and the energy of the place. Mother Earth had supported life for millions of years. Dinosaurs had come and gone. My ancestors had come and gone, and one day I'd be gone, too. What a reminder to make every moment count and leave a positive legacy for those who have yet to come.

Overnight, the temperature dropped from 80°F to 60°F, accompanied by threatening clouds, strong winds, and occasional showers. The winds buffeted me all over the road, slightly less when I traveled west heading into them, significantly more when I turned north and they became forceful crosswinds with unpredictable gusts. I was glad I didn't have further than forty miles to my destination. I stayed warm and dry but pictured a bowl of *Borscht* waiting for me when I got there. Was there any chance Country Cousins served it?

Borscht owes its origins to Ukraine. That's where the Mennonites would have adopted it before bringing it to North

America. A cabbage, potato, onion, and tomato soup, it's flavored with fresh dill and pepper. Generally, the Mennonite version differs from the Ukrainian in that Mennonites don't add beets. They also use a soup bone to make the base, and you can usually track down remnants of beef intermixed with the shredded cabbage. *Borscht*, with a dollop of sour cream, and *Zwieback* with lots of butter, made a hearty—and delicious—meal. I'd never made either.

Pickup trucks lined the street in front of Country Cousins, their drivers inside for lunch. Trudy doesn't need much room, and I found a spot right up front. Other than the wait staff, I was the only woman there.

Luck smiled on me. Fresh *Borscht* is served every day. I squealed with delight before ordering a large bowl. While I waited, I asked my server if she knew any Klassens whose roots in the area might go back to the late 1920s. She didn't, but she connected me with Brian Enns, sitting two tables away. His wife was a Klassen and her parents lived a block up the street. Brian came over and after we chatted, he made a phone call, setting me up with a visit to his in-laws, both ninety years old.

In the meantime, my bowl of *Borscht* arrived. With the first spoonful, memories of my childhood, of meals prepared by Susa, Liese, and Mom, flooded over me. The *Borscht* went directly to my soul. Hymn singing is the strongest tie to my culture, but traditional food is a close second. It took me back to being a little girl, when all was right with my world, before I began to question the religious teachings of my parents and realize they weren't a fit for me, before I lost touch with my self.

The Elder and grandmother's advice of going back to my roots to discover who I was took on an even deeper understanding. Like I recognized the "me" riding a motorcycle, so, too, I innately knew the woman who ate *Borscht*.

I took my time, savoring the memories before walking up the

street to the Klassens. They were expecting me and eager to share stories. They reminded me of my parents—Henry was a retired farmer and Tina had mild dementia. We had a delightful visit, but unfortunately, the mystery of how Liese got to Beiseker remained intact. These Klassens were no relation to Johann, nor were any other Klassens in Linden. Ironically, Tina and her family had lived in Beaverlodge and two nephews still farmed there.

Undoubtedly, the Mennonite community had done for Liese what it did so instinctively: extended compassion to one of its own and arranged to have her needs met.

MY TIME in Drumheller was a turning point. No longer did I feel compelled to search. I knew who I was. Although I still had much to learn about myself, now I could focus on deepening and strengthening that relationship. Confidence replaced uncertainty and became a new normal through which I saw myself and the world—a perspective that had always been there, buried for safekeeping under layers of outdated stories and myths. Johann, Liese, Gerhard, and Susa remained with me, but their roles changed. They were companions along for the ride, still there if I needed them, but more subdued.

By late August, I'd visited the lands my ancestors had lived on in Western Canada before moving to Ontario, except for Gerhard and Susa's brief stay in Manitoba. I'd had the "aha" moment when the words of the Elder and Siksika grandmother sunk in.

Before I returned to Ontario, it was time for the Ancestor Trail to swing further west and for me to visit relatives and reunite with my other community—the adventure motorcyclists. Gerhard and Susa loved to go on road trips, locally or across the country to visit *Freundschaft* in Alberta and British

Columbia. They'd cobble together a route by figuring out how to visit the most family along the way. Liese and Johann would have done the same had they the opportunity, or the relatives.

Horizons Unlimited's four-day travelers' meeting was being held at the end of August in the mountain town of Nakusp, British Columbia, in the Kootenays, not too far over the border from Alberta. I'd been there two years ago, days before crashing. Besides meeting up with friends from far and near and making a couple of presentations, returning there on my motorcycle felt like the completion of a cycle. A triumph. Staying overnight in Calgary with Charlotte Williams on the way there was another. When I'd been there after my crash, I was recuperating from surgery and my motorcycle had been written off. It felt good to pull into her driveway on my new motorcycle, under my own steam. After leaving a joyful reunion with Charlotte, I then had a monumental part of the trip ahead of me.

Rugged, majestic, spectacular, and mind-blowing are just a few ways to describe the Rocky Mountains. To get to Nakusp, I needed to cross them, something I've done numerous times, so the feeling of being hemmed in by walls on both sides of me caught me off guard. I'd just spent four weeks on the prairies where you can see for miles. The mountains hadn't lost any of their magnificence, I just couldn't see as far. My ancestors had not lived in the mountains. Perhaps my comfort with the plains made the mountains seem like a foreign country.

Ever gregarious Gerhard loved this side trip. He and Susa had driven to the west coast to visit his brother Abram and his family, and other nieces and nephews. But riding through the mountains on a motorcycle was new to my grandparents and they were excited. A few times I heard whoops of glee, or intakes of breath as we rounded a corner and entered a spectacular vista. Again, they chattered away in *Plautdietsch* but I let them go. I had to focus on the road.

The gathering of more than 350 adventure motorcycle enthusiasts felt like home. People who have ridden all over the world, are dreaming of it, or are looking to connect with others of like mind, converge to learn the intricacies of traveling overland by motorcycle and other means.

The event fascinated my grandparents. Any get-togethers in their lifetime would have been only Mennonites and centered on the church. Here the surnames were foreign to them, as were the activities, but they couldn't escape the vitality and energy. They loved it and understood why I felt at home here.

Visiting inner and outer ancestral worlds is a rich, powerful experience. The side trip with my motorcycle community refreshed me but felt oddly like an interruption. I'd been in such a different place and time; shifting into the present in a different community was disorientating. Even during the trip, my priorities and perspective had changed. By following the Ancestor Trail, walking the land that had welcomed my young grandparents, I'd reconnected with my roots in a way I hadn't thought possible. The Horizons Unlimited event was fantastic, but my heart kept pulling me back to my ancestors.

On the way home, I planned to loop further south in Alberta so I could visit Gerhard's niece, Elvira Dueck in Coaldale. Her mother, Sara, had been his older sister. Another niece, Hedy Reimer, daughter of his younger brother Abram, lived in Abbotsford, British Columbia, almost at the Pacific coast. Hedy had led an exciting life and had invited me to stay with her, but the extra 600 miles seemed too much to add to an already jam-packed trip.

Then Elvira emailed and asked me if I could wait an extra day or two because she was having minor surgery. That gave me time to visit Hedy. Both women were ninety, mentally sharp, driving their cars, and active in their communities. I knew I'd enjoy their company and they might be able to add new stories.

Gerhard, Abram and families had lived together for much of their time in Alberta; Sara and her husband had lived nearby for a while. This might be my only chance to hear Hedy and Elvira's family stories.

Only three months separated the births of cousins Hedy, Elvira, and Mom. They'd grown up together, much like Jude and me, and remained close friends over the miles and years. Hedy spent much of her career as a Public Health Nurse in Central and South America, working with CUSO (Canadian University Services Overseas), often flying in puddle jumpers to remote jungle villages. When she could, she'd traveled by motorcycle, long before it was in vogue. Only recently has she stopped tutoring people in Spanish, but she still enjoys international travels.

When I contacted her to let her know I'd be coming, she cautioned me that her fourth bout of cancer made her tired. She didn't have her usual energy and I'd have to make my own bed. I laughed. I'd never expect her to do that, but it was kind of her to consider it. It reminded me of another Reimer trait I loved—direct communication. No sense sugarcoating the message.

Low energy for Hedy at ninety is still above anyone else's average. Touring me around in her car, the first stop was a visit with *Freundschaft*—her sister, brother-in-law, and another cousin. I was *Onkel* Gerhard and *Tante* Susa's granddaughter, and even though I'd never met some of them, we knew each other. Gerhard and Susa gazed lovingly at the scene. The family laughter and conviviality were exactly what they treasured.

We returned to Hedy's for lunch and a *Mittagsschlaf,* a traditional afternoon nap, before heading out again, to land where Hedy's parents, Abram and Liese, had farmed berries. Later, we made a stop at the Mennonite Heritage Museum, where the Mennonite story—from Anabaptist origins in 16th-century

Europe, to personal stories of refugees who settled in British Columbia's Fraser Valley—comes to life.

When it was time to leave the next morning, Hedy escorted me from her third-floor condo. She had to get a photo of me and Trudy, loaded for the road. I was so glad I'd made the trip. She'd lived her life to the fullest and according to her own compass, unconcerned with what others thought of her. Throughout her long life, she'd touched the lives of so many others, including mine. She'd mothered me as if I was her own and it felt wonderful. As great as self-sufficiency and independence feel, it sure feels nice to be looked after sometimes.

Even the mountains cradled me on the two-day trip east to Coaldale, Alberta, and Elvira. Hedy and Elvira were still spry, alert, and vivacious, even driving their own cars! Though nearly the same age, Mom had had to move into long-term care earlier in the year because of dementia. Why? How was she different? What switch had been flipped in her that the others had averted?

Tears coursed down my cheeks inside my helmet as grief poured out. She'd worked hard her whole life and been very charitable with her time and skills. Now, she couldn't function in the life her cousins enjoyed. She and Dad had been separated at the time they needed each other most. She, who'd been so smart, couldn't figure out where she was or why she couldn't go home. I wanted to share my quest with her and let her see how happy I was. I grieved for the loss of the mother I wanted, and for what she had lost.

Mountains and my motorcycle came together to nurture and heal. I camped in Grand Forks in the West Kootenay Mountains, in a municipal campground with other riders. All night, the mountains held me, and I slept like a child.

September dawned late the next morning. Tonight, I'd stay with Mom's cousin Elvira in Coaldale, Alberta, another MB stronghold. At its height in 1939, the church there seated 1,000 worshippers.

Elvira lives in a fourth-floor condo and usually walks the stairs rather than take the elevator. That day she'd been featured on local TV for more than fifty years of volunteering at the thrift store. And that's only one example of her generosity.

A few days before, when she'd asked what I'd like to eat, I'd hoped for *Borscht.* I'd loved the way it had made my heart feel when I had it in Linden, and to have it prepared by Gerhard's niece would be extra special. Sure enough, when I arrived for lunch, Elvira had *Borscht* and *Zwieback* with butter. Then *Stollen,* a sweet yeast bread coated in sugar for dessert. All baked fresh.

Elvira and her husband John had once farmed and produced nine children. I gladly agreed to her invitation for a guided tour of the area, including her farmstead. Two of her seven sons now operate the farm, and it was a pleasure to meet these men descended from the same ancestors—Gerhard's parents. It was harvest time and the combine needed maintenance, so time for social banter was at a premium. I did get to climb up into the combine's cab, though. I loved watching this family in action, the sons living the legacy left by their parents and, in turn, preparing to pass it on to the next generation.

Elvira used to play with Hedy and Mom when her parents drove the family to visit *Onkel* Gerhard and *Onkel* Abram's farm in Michichi, north of Drumheller. No matter how hard times got, she remembered laughter and good-natured teasing between Gerhard and his siblings.

Always, they sang in German, the language of the heart and the medicine that brought healing to these *Russlanders. Heimatlieder* were songs of home, usually referring to heaven, but could also mean folk songs from the Golden Age they'd enjoyed for a century in Russia before the Revolution. All the Mennonites knew these songs and they'd sing together on the spur of the moment, longing for "home." You couldn't find a dry eye when these songs were sung. Everyone had been touched by loss in Russia, either by death or leaving loved ones behind, knowing the next time they'd meet would be in heaven.

Elvira had invited her brother Arnold and his wife, Hannah, for dinner. Were it not for Hannah's celiac disease, we would have had another home-cooked Mennonite specialty: *Wernicke*, a dumpling much like a perogi. Still, we enjoyed Mennonite sausage from the local butcher. I hadn't told Elvira that I avoided cow dairy, sugar, gluten and any processed food. Nor did I feel it necessary to tell her the only meat I ate came from a source where I could verify it was organic and had been humanely raised and butchered. That day, it didn't matter. Nothing could detract from the goodness of that soul food, prepared and served in the traditional way, with love.

When I left in the morning, it was with a *Wernicke* doggy-bag for lunch.

Two days of travel across the flat prairies with their big open sky awaited. My next visit with Mennonite *Freundschaft* was in Winnipeg, Manitoba, with a cousin, Karl Koop, and dinner with my sister Susan. I'd be staying with non-Mennonite motorcycling friends in a town thirty minutes outside the city. The city stop represented a hybrid of my communities.

Karl's father, Jake, was Susa's youngest brother, sixteen years her junior. Only ten years old when their father Heinrich Koop brought his family to Canada, Jake had followed the migration from Saskatchewan to Manitoba and Ontario before settling in Jordan, Ontario.

There, Heinrich started what is now a sixth-generation large-egg farm operation. Heinrich passed away in 1949 and the farm passed to Karl's father, Jake, and his wife, Hilda. As children, Jude and I would visit, playing in the yard with Karl, who was younger than us, and two sisters who were older.

In 1931, eighty-five years before Karl and I met for coffee in Winnipeg, my grandparents—his *Tante* Susa and *Onkel* Gerhard—had stopped not far from where we sat, on their way east to another start. Other than their three children, what they carried with them didn't amount to much more than what they'd arrived with in Canada. Like me, they'd stopped to visit *Freundschaft*—Susa's older sisters and Karl's *Tanten,* Sara and Tina.

The sisters lived and worked together their entire lives. Tina was a housekeeper; Sara, a nurse. Sara had been trained as a deaconess (a nurse who ministered to physical and spiritual needs) in Russia and held senior management hospital positions. Here in Winnipeg, she'd gone back to high school to be able to requalify for nurse's training, work she was already so proficient in. In her journal, she'd articulated the difficulties experienced by immigrants establishing a life in a new setting. In spite of her advanced education, it had been hard to get accepted into nurse's training. She was too Russian, too Mennonite, and was told she was too old to keep up with the theory.

But Heinrich had raised strong women. Sara was persistent, finally gaining acceptance into St. Boniface Hospital, across the Red River from where Karl and I sat. Upon graduation in 1934, at age thirty-eight, she was awarded a Gold Medal for highest standing in theory.

The same blood that ran in her ran through me.

To be sitting with adult Karl at Starbucks in downtown Winnipeg's Osborne Village required a paradigm shift. As with other relatives I'd visited on this trip, that undeniable heart connection and an unspoken awareness of our blood connection felt like home.

Beyond that, Karl had researched and authored *Experiences of My Grandfather Heinrich Koop (1869-1949) and Family* in 1977.

He'd been crucial in bringing the Koop history to life and helping me understand the Mennonite culture.

Karl has his PhD in Theology, with a special interest in Anabaptist history. He's a Director of the Graduate School of Theology and Ministry, and a Professor of History and Theology at Canadian Mennonite University in Winnipeg. He had a wealth of information, both personal and broader, and an in-depth understanding of the times that had formed us both. Descended from the same culture, our paths were widely divergent.

Even though they were with me now in spirit, Gerhard and Susa were as thrilled to see the adult Karl as they would have been had the meeting taken place when they walked the earth in human form. Eager to learn about his life and work, they knew he could teach them much about Mennonite history.

A story of Karl's epitomized one of Gerhard and Susa's greatest gifts to me—their ability to see the big picture. The history went way back to 1860 in Russia, when the Mennonite church split over what some of the members viewed as inconsistent and unspiritual conduct by others. They insisted on church discipline. The original Mennonite Church in Russia was known as the *Kirchliche Gemeinde* (KG). In 1860, a breakaway, more fundamentalist group became the Mennonite Brethren (MB) Church, the tradition I was born into.

The acrimony that fell from the separation lasted for decades. A major sticking point was the method of baptism—MBs insisted on full immersion while KGs were satisfied with the symbolism of pouring water over the candidate's head.

The Koops were KGs; Reimers were MBs. When Gerhard and Susa married, she was required to join the MB Church and the only way to do that was through rebaptism by immersion. Because she'd been raised as a KG, and had been baptized, albeit by pouring, she felt it unnecessary and refused to cede. In the end, she won. That was a huge statement, especially for a woman. Her twin, Anna, did the same thing.

According to his tradition, eighteen-year-old Karl was baptized by pouring rather than immersion. The sacrament of baptism is a big deal in the Mennonite Church, and Gerhard and Susa, whose children were baptized by immersion, were there to show support for her nephew. A thirty-second encounter after the ceremony stuck in Karl's mind. Gerhard and Susa made a beeline to the back of the church to congratulate him. In doing so, they voiced their belief that his baptism was no less holy or meaningful than theirs, and every bit as "legitimate" as an MB baptism.

Other than the chattering and laughter that accompanied any encounter with Gerhard, Karl couldn't recall the details of the conversation. He does remember the feeling they left. The old divisive attitudes were waning, but still smoldering. Gerhard and Susa, his family elders, were telling him they were spiritual equals. They'd made him feel deeply valued. They'd gone out of their way to counter a traditional stereotype that MBs were better than the tradition they'd evolved from.

That's how they lived their life. They knew that one's relationship with God was personal, and not defined by the details of how one worshipped.

Never had any of my grandparents tried to influence me to return to the Church, preached at me for following a lifestyle or beliefs that differed from theirs, or told me I'd end up in hell if I didn't have a major course correction. They understood life wasn't black and white, and living by strict rules wasn't practical. They'd had to make tough decisions in their lives that didn't always align with their religious and cultural group. They trusted me because they knew the energetic DNA and strengths I carried. They knew I'd find my way, even if it took a long time, even if that way differed from theirs.

15

Reminiscent of my motorcycle escort by a friend out of Regina, Saskatchewan, the friends I stayed with near Winnipeg accompanied me out of Manitoba and into Ontario. They rode with me for the day, extending an enjoyable visit that much more. Near Fort Frances, we parted ways. They continued a giant loop that would take them home while I stayed with other motorcycling friends in Fort Frances, Ontario, before continuing to Kingsville, in southwestern Ontario.

East of Winnipeg, the terrain makes an abrupt transition from flat prairie to rocky Canadian Shield. Just as I wasn't prepared for the mild claustrophobia I'd felt in the mountains, I didn't expect the feeling of familiarity when granite and trees appeared. The fertile farmland I'd grown up on was distinctly different than the rugged environment of rocks, forests, and lakes I now moved through, yet I felt at ease there. Perhaps the physical landscape was pure coincidence. Perhaps I was feeling more at home with myself.

As the trains carrying my ancestors had chugged east, I wondered if they'd experienced that same sense that they'd finally found home. After so many years of uncertainty and ping-ponging thousands of miles across Western Canada, they'd hoped Ontario would be their forever home.

Johann never made it past the Beaverlodge frontier, but as my blood grandfather, it was he who continued with Liese on the motorcycle. Besides, he'd become quite close to Gerhard and Susa and the four were having a grand time.

In 1931, when Gerhard and Susa landed in Kingsville, Ontario, most of Susa's family was there. Best of all, Susa lived near her twin sister, Anna, and husband Johann (John) Dueckman and sons Henry, Rudy, and Helmut. Except for their brief stay in Manitoba, Susa and Anna hadn't seen each other since 1924.

When I arrived in September by motorcycle, Susa's nephew, ninety-four-year-old Henry Dueckman, his daughter, Linda, and her husband Roger Epp, took me on a historic tour. Roger chauffeured, Linda navigated, and I sat in the back with Henry, an expert guide and narrator. My four grandparents, of course, took up no space. Liese and Johann had never been here, but they'd heard all about it from Gerhard and Susa.

I'd met Henry once or twice decades ago, and possibly Linda, who is my age, at the same time. But they were not strangers now in spite of the length of time since I'd last seen them. It was soul-quenching to re-establish our connection. They'd scouted the route a week earlier in preparation for my visit, a gesture I found touching. I was also grateful that Henry was still here to relay the family histories and stories, some of which Linda and Roger were hearing for the first time. Like the fact that his great-grandfather, Linda's and my great-great-grandfather, at age eight-seven, took on childcare duties. Daycare or gender-limited roles didn't exist in 1931, when everyone had to pitch in and work outside the home to make ends meet. Every day, Anna would walk her three children the mile to her father's place so her grandfather could care for them while she worked as a housekeeper, then walk back to bring her children home.

KINGSVILLE IS A PRETTY TOWN, with tall trees shading the Victorian two-storey homes lining the main street. Nestled on the shores of Lake Erie, it's surrounded by prime agricultural land. These farms, and those who farmed them, nourished my family.

Life in Kingsville was joyous, but still lowly. At least Susa had her brothers, sisters, father, and grandfather here. Her children had cousins, aunts, uncles, grandparents, and their great-grandfather. Except for two sisters in Winnipeg, her dream of the Koops being together had come true.

Family is important to me, too, especially since I live alone and have no children. The closest any of my six siblings and ninety-one-year-old parents live is almost two hours away— close enough to be called in an emergency, but too far away to drop over for a casual visit. Two nieces live in Alberta and Germany; another niece and five nephews are dispersed around Ontario. Lives get busy and people are drawn in different directions, but when we get together for special occasions, we have fun. I'd love to be able to do it more often. It's one of the reasons why connecting with extended kin through this quest had been so good for my heart.

Gerhard found work in Kingsville as a teamster (he worked the team of horses to manage the farm) for a German farmer named Scratch. A cleared-out woodshed attached to the Scratch house became home. Susa worked too, as a housekeeper for the Miner family, founders of the Jack Miner Migratory Bird Sanctuary. Only two miles separated Anna and Susa. The others were further, but the sisters were within walking distance.

Henry's custom tour started where his grandfather, Susa's father, Heinrich, and family had lived in a red, converted tobacco kiln behind what was known as the Coatsworth house. A field of cash crops and a road were the only things separating them from Lake Erie. The home and kiln with million-dollar views no longer stood, but the trees that had surrounded them did. So did an unpainted wooden barn. It was so easy to imagine Heinrich here, surrounded by the children and grandchildren he loved so much. He'd gotten his family to this land intact.

Although it was only three miles to her father's place from Scratch's farm, it was too far for Susa to walk their children there while she, too, worked as a housekeeper. She had to mind them herself. Little Margaret (Mom), age five, began kindergarten, where she was cared for three days a week. On the off-kindergarten days, Susa would take Margaret, son Ernie, age three, and infant daughter Gertrude along to her job at Jack Miner's home. It was the first time they'd seen indoor plumbing.

Susa and the children began to learn English from the Scratches and from Mom bringing it home from school. By nature, Gerhard was more gregarious than his wife, and he also had more opportunity to interact with "the English" and so picked up the language quicker than Susa. Knowing the value of retaining the connection to one's roots yet wanting to adapt to the culture they now lived in, he insisted German be spoken at home, while English was spoken outside.

As Henry, Linda, Roger, and I sat at the roadside looking out the car windows at what was once the Scratch's property, we tried to imagine life here in the early '30s. One day, when the cupboards were bare, Susa didn't know how they would feed their family supper. Unannounced, her Uncle Dietrich Koop, a Mennonite Bishop, stopped by with a loaf of bread. That got them through until the next day when Susa would earn twenty-five cents and be able to buy three pounds of hamburger meat.

Jack Miner Bird Sanctuary and the Miner homestead were over a mile away and our next roadside stop. In the 1930s, most of the traffic here was tractors and farm equipment, and a physically slight but eminently strong, determined woman wearing a print dress, her long hair pinned in her signature *Schups*. She'd be pushing a pram and leading one or two children down the road. Susa, who never did dishes until she was eighteen, had become the domestic help her family had hired in Russia.

Kingsville had been a good place to recover somewhat after the harshness of their experience in the West. They'd been able to find comfort and replenish their reserves by living close to their family and a larger spiritual community. Likewise, reconnecting with extended kin since my crash, and particularly on the Ancestor Trail, had taken me back to my roots and shown me who I am.

Gerhard and Susa remained in Kingsville for two years before moving to the Niagara area of Ontario where I grew up. Liese and Peter and their four children arrived in 1937.

My ancestors had strong physical, emotional, and spiritual survival skills. No book existed to tell them what to do or how to solve their problems. The years on the prairie had cultivated those inherent strengths. They'd had to devise new ways of being by letting go of old ways of operating that no longer worked and adapting to a completely different life. They'd learned to take life less seriously and with humor. I'd learned to do the same thing. No book told me how to get through my post-crash time or navigate the internal journey it took me on.

They'd started their families, fed, and clothed them, accepted handouts, lived in homes that were little more than hovels, and worked in positions of servitude. Throughout it all, they were steadfast in their gratitude for their freedom and the lifestyle they had. My situation was nowhere near as desperate, but it had still brought me to my knees, and called on inner strength that had been buried for years.

LIESE HADN'T LET poverty or a role as an uneducated, immigrant woman who spoke with an accent define her. She'd stand up for herself and her family to anyone. Yet she couldn't help when Peter refused to let Benny, an excellent student, go to secondary school. Peter did not value education and didn't want any of his children to go to school. He made Benny stay away from school to work often enough to attract the frequent attention of the truant officer.

Mr. Cook, the principal of the third school Benny attended during eighth grade, took kindly to the young boy, who excelled as a student. Mr. Cook tried his best, but even he couldn't convince Peter to let Benny continue in school. Benny cried his eyes out when all his friends went to high school. This was even worse than when he'd sat on the sidelines and watched his friends play hockey on Eagle Lake in Namaka.

It was curious that Benny, my dad, who had been so traumatized by not being able to continue his schooling, would underwrite my post-secondary education only if I went to Bible School. I was angry and in disbelief at the time. Maybe he thought I needed religious edification. In any case, I know he was coming from a place of love and his number one priority was saving my soul.

Benny was at his job as a fire-welder on May 28th, 1945, when he got word that Peter had been killed in a car accident, one sideroad from home. Liese was on her own again, this time with four children besides Benny, ranging in age from two to fifteen. Benny, who'd been supporting the family for years, now had the full responsibility for them. As if the tragedy wasn't enough, Peter had left them in significant debt, over and above a loan for the down payment on the farm, all of which would have to be repaid.

For the rest of Liese's life, Benny supported her, and also his siblings until they could support themselves. He'd inherited

Liese's perseverance, tenacity, and sense of duty, which he passed on to me.

Ben (he'd dropped the diminutive when he married) was upset when Liese, at age seventy, got a full-time job as a housekeeper in the Mennonite long-term care residence beside her apartment and church. His mother didn't need to work! But Liese was in her heyday, holding the job for six years. She had regular contact with her community, didn't have to depend on others for rides to church, and was fully supporting herself for the first time in her life.

For a long time, I'd thought Liese was not a strong woman because she was so poor and dependent on Dad for most of her life. I was so wrong. She did have a temper and got frustrated when things didn't go her way. She also laughed a lot. Few could endure what she'd gone through and maintain that kind of vigor.

During her last decade, Liese wanted nothing more than to go home to Heaven. Physically, she'd had enough of this life. Spiritually, she was more than ready. Finally, on September 18th, 1994, at age ninety-three, she went Home, after a full life. With her last breath, she raised her arms, as if to greet whoever had come to go with her. I have a feeling it was Johann.

Gerhard became the choir director in the Vineland MB Church in 1935. During his twelve years with the choir, he was in his glory, but English was creeping into the church. It was a necessity for integrating into the culture, but that didn't make being comfortable with English, his fourth language, easier. The hymns he loved were best expressed in German, and, for him, they lost their meaning when he had to translate them in his head and grasp the context. He couldn't express himself and felt disconnected from his culture.

In fact, for him, the change in language was the biggest adjustment by far, because with English came a different culture. German had been part of the Mennonite heritage forever. German songs expressed nature better and had songs for the seasons; he felt closer to God. However, new times brought different protocols, rules of etiquette, and customs, including what he saw as relaxed morals and diminished reverence for God.

He had his opinions, but he was always tolerant and respectful of the opinions of others. "Going to church doesn't make you holy. Your relationship with God does," he'd told the Brock University researcher.

Gerhard died on Friday, May 8th, 1981, the day before my birthday. He was buried on May 11th, his birthday. At the May 10th Sunday service at the Vineland MB church he and Susa had attended for so many years, he received the highest accolade the church could award. The minister asked the congregation to stand in honor of Gerhard and sing one of his favorite hymns, a song of praise and gratitude. They all rose and, in German, sang *Grosser Gott, wir loben dich* (Holy God We Praise Thy Name). It was how he'd want to be remembered. I know he was singing along.

Susa lived another five years, passing away on March 26th, 1986. Gerhard's death had left her bereft. Six of eleven siblings who had survived to adulthood preceded her, including her twin sister, Anna, who had died six months earlier. She'd been so happy when her family had been reunited on earth. I can only imagine her joy at joining them again in the afterlife.

OVER THE PAST SIX WEEKS, my grandparents had been with me while we traced their paths and visited the homes and farms they'd established during very different times. A train had carried them most of the way. We'd done it by motorcycle, which they considered far more fun and adventuresome. They'd known all along where their home was. From before I was born, I was the beneficiary of their wisdom, strengths, and unconditional love.

We still had one more stop to make; one that would complete the quest I'd begun in 2013. No way were my grandparents going to miss this one, either.

AFTER TRAVELING APPROXIMATELY 6,500 MILES, the last week would be at a retreat center in the Catskill Mountains in New York State. There I'd take the final course to complete my Energy Medicine Practitioner training. Three years and three months after that first course in Utah had started me on the quest for an energetic connection with my ancestors, this section of road neared an end.

I hadn't learned many new facts about my grandparents' lives, but by visiting the places they'd lived and putting myself in their positions as best I could, I'd gotten to know them at a much deeper spirit level. I'd also gotten to know and understand myself much better. My grandparents had had a blast visiting their old haunts and sharing stories.

Ever since that first Energy Medicine course, I was driven to find out who I was before I'd been *told* who I was. I'd needed to find the answer to the question, "Why am I here?" As I turned sixty, I knew that more road lay behind me than ahead of me. I did not want to go through life without having lived it fully, and understanding the answer was essential to gaining that clarity. Staring down death, as I had with my crash, helps you see it as an ally and teacher, and motivates you to rearrange your priorities.

It was as if I'd traveled light years since then, yet I was closer than ever to where I started life on earth. At the heart of my story was me—my soul, my unique gifts, and ancestors, embodied in a little girl named Elizabeth Ann Jansen. I *was* different than anyone else! We all are. My grandparents hadn't tried to change who they were because of what other people thought of them. They embraced and celebrated their uniqueness.

THE AIR CHANGES when you approach the Menla Mountain Retreat Center; perhaps because it's set atop the oldest known meteor impact crater on earth. It's crisp, clear, and energizing, almost magical. People come here for courses, events, and getaways that combine Western integrative medicine with elements of Eastern medicine and other holistic traditions. It's ideal for introspection.

Gerhard and Susa had been to my first class, but for Liese and Johann, this was their first experience in this kind of setting. On the ride down, Gerhard and Susa had filled them in on what to expect. In their day, they were exposed to only one belief system, based on a literal interpretation of the Christian Bible and 2,000 years of mutation since Christ's original teachings.

Yet they lived beyond that. Belief systems can distort over time, especially during times of rapid change or prolonged crises. In spite of adhering to the status quo of a tightly controlled community, especially when threatened with survival, they had the integrity not to agree blindly with what everyone else did, or to make assumptions. They respected the needs and beliefs of others but were motivated by their own powerful and personal connection to God.

My grandparents had been informed by ancestors who'd been informed by their ancestors. Throughout time, they all had done the best they could with what they had. Their courage and stalwartness allowed me to live in a land of peace and freedom.

It gave me the wherewithal to take the journey in answer to my soul's calling.

In their time, they, too, were on their soul's journey. They were ordinary humans, like me, with their own foibles and shortcomings. They subscribed to a much more literal belief system. Inherently, they knew that changing the stories we tell ourselves changes our lives. It doesn't change the reality, but it alters how we look at events of the past and how we move forward. Through their experiences, they'd left a legacy that gave me the tools and insights to deepen my soul's journey.

Through this quest, I came to understand my parents so much more. They'd been conduits, imbibing my grandparents' experiences, filtering them through their own perspectives, and infusing them into me. They, too, had done the best they could with the teachings and experiences they'd learned.

Dad was kind and generous, with a strong commitment to his role as the head of the family. He could be a strict disciplinarian. As he told me stories from his childhood, and others Liese had passed on, I realized he had never had a strong father figure to mentor him. Johann had died when Dad was two. The only uncle he had in Canada was Liese's brother Jacob, a wonderful man devoted to Liese, but separated by distance during Dad's formative years. Peter, who adopted Dad when he married Liese, had worked hard, but finances were always strained and he hadn't let Dad continue his education past eighth grade. Even as a youth, Dad had to work to support the family, becoming the primary breadwinner when Peter died.

Mom also worked hard her entire life, paying for her education and contributing to the family coffers until she married. Then she raised six children, filled an essential role on the farm, and still pursued her passion of nursing.

Both my parents were born into the immediate aftermath of the Russian Civil War, when their parents' wounds were still raw, and life was tenuous. It was not easy to transition out of survival mode, especially when they lived so close to the edge. For decades, I avoided being alone with Dad, afraid he would corner me and try and convert me. Unease tinged family gatherings. He'd make use of the audience to try and bring us back into the fold. It saddens me to think of how much time went by where his mission blockaded close relationships.

I always knew my parents loved me, but I can see now what I couldn't see growing up. I hadn't realized how terrified they must have felt in their belief that they could lose me, or any of my siblings, because we didn't believe. It was a tremendous burden for them to carry.

Just as their parents had not been emotionally demonstrative to them, my parents' love for us was not expressed through physical affection or by saying, "I love you." We didn't talk about feelings. Our family didn't hug—not until after my divorce, when I began hugging them. That's also when my relationship with my parents started to grow closer. Throughout my life, they'd expressed their love by showing me how to stand up for myself and how to work hard. That's how they'd learned it.

The past few years, delving into our ancestral history together forged an even tighter relationship between us, especially at the heart level. Both of them, now age ninety-one, have had medical challenges requiring their children to pitch in and help out. It's an honor to give back to parents who have given me so much. Just as I gained a deeper understanding of my grandparents through this quest, so, too, it has deepened my appreciation for my parents and their lives.

I recognized they, too, are on a journey. Being more open with them, which began when I rocked their world with my career change and divorce, had already changed our relationship for the better. More recently, I've realized that I am a part of their journey, as much as they are part of mine. Part of honoring who I am means being authentic with them, not trying to cover up to avoid hurting their feelings. Honesty is the utmost way to honor them. How they respond is up to them.

They saw that I own a spirituality, a sacred connection to something much larger than me, without following an organized Christian religion, which even if they didn't understand, they accepted. They saw my transformation, watched me come alive and blossom. It's the life they'd always wished for me, even if the path deviated from where they thought it should go.

No longer am I ashamed of my culture. That disappeared more than a decade ago and has been replaced by profound admiration and respect. Extended kin have supported me and eagerly contributed stories and filled in missing pieces as I've unearthed my family and cultural history. As I've become more knowledgeable about my heritage, they've been curious about their direct ancestors. My blood connection is a priceless treasure. It doesn't mean I need to follow the particulars of their religious beliefs. I have found the way to be true to my heart and my blood. I happened to be born into a Mennonite community, but my lessons have been universal.

I've simultaneously reconciled with my Mennonite heritage and come to terms with the role of healer I've evolved into, a role I was born into. It's at the root of everything I do. I've come full circle from my start in nursing. The gifts, or medicines, that I use for healing are my motorcycle, words in books, articles, stories, blogs, and presentations, and my training, wisdom, and experience in counseling others. Now I'm integrating Energy Medicine practices into that medicine bag.

I've hesitated to use the term "healer" because the voices in my head tell me it sounds too gimmicky. Or they ask, "Who do you think you are to call yourself a healer?" Or, "People will think you're a flake." So be it. I make a difference through my medicines. What's that called, if not a healer? That's what has heart and meaning for me and always has. Like each of us, my gifts are too valuable and too needed to keep them to myself. They are for sharing.

In the end, it all comes together in me—the experiences of my ancestors, my thoughts and beliefs, and my relationship with Spirit. It's my lineage.

AFTER FIVE DAYS of intensive Energy Medicine classes, the closing fire is an extra special ceremony of awe and reverence. This time it held even more significance because I'd reached the end of my training and was now certified to practice.

That didn't compare to the four figures with me around the fire—Gerhard, Susa, Liese, and Johann. They were there to honor God and express their gratitude for his presence during their lifetime, and their opportunity to join me on my quest. With their love, guidance, and wisdom, I've found my way home.

I was here the whole time.

16

Four months after my Ancestor Trail visit to Beaverlodge, aided by the Alberta Genealogical Society, I opened a copy of the probate file for Johann's estate. Dad hadn't known it existed. The file specified the location of six quarter-sections Johann and Liese farmed along with three other families in an arrangement with the ancestors of the local woman I spoke with. My intuition had guided me to the right locations. Although I didn't know exactly where their log house and barns had stood, I'd been on that land, including the cemetery placed on a corner of one of those quarter-sections.

Walking the land of my ancestors had opened such a strong connection to my roots, and to my self. I knew it would be extraordinary for Dad, too, especially now that we had exact coordinates. He'd grown up on those lands.

Dad was ninety-one and frail, but his determination to be independent overshadowed all that. Seven months before I left on the Ancestor Trail, when he was eighty-nine, he'd fallen and broken his hip. In the aftermath, he'd lost his driver's license. His fierce determination to get behind the wheel again fueled his drive to regain strength and mobility.

His recovery was slow, but steady. He could no longer care for Mom in their apartment and had worn himself down trying. Their apartment was in a complex owned and operated by the Mennonite Church, which included independent units and long-term care rooms. Gerhard, Susa, and Liese lived their last years at the same place. Fortunately, a long-term care room soon became available for Mom, within an easy indoor walk for Dad once he'd regained his mobility.

I'd often call him to ask questions about our history. He'd enjoyed unearthing family stories and getting together with *Freundschaft* to help me with my research. Through regular phone calls during my time on the Ancestor Trail, he'd followed every mile while I rode my motorcycle around the country.

"Would you like me to take you to Beaverlodge this summer?" I asked.

I'd been home for nine months, assimilating the reconnection to my roots and writing this book. Beaverlodge and two hand-made wooden valises were his only connection to Johann, his father. Dad walked with a cane, sometimes a walker, but his health issues were now stable. This window of opportunity would be unlikely to open again. He and Mom had been back in 2000, but now we had more facts and history. They'd traveled a lot in their day, to Europe, South and Central America, North America. This would fuel him with stories and memories to last at least through the winter.

"How would we go?" he asked, pondering the idea. He thought I was thinking of putting him on the back of my motorcycle. I laughed.

"We'll fly and rent cars out there," I said. "You cover the travel expenses. I'll look after you." I'd checked with my siblings to make sure they were comfortable with this arrangement.

"In fact, if you want to go to Namaka too, we can extend the trip to a week. It will be tiring, but you'll have lots of time to rest when we get back."

It would be strenuous for both of us, me more from worry that he'd lose his balance, fall, and injure himself, especially when he was alone in his hotel room. Knowing how fatigue made him more vulnerable, I would be afraid to let him out of my sight, but I'd have to, just as he had had to let me be independent. I knew it would be extraordinary.

"I can make it. You can bury me when we get home."

And so began the adventure of a lifetime for both of us. We began planning where we'd go, and whom he wanted to visit. He asked to stay out there one more day.

He was all packed and ready to go when I arrived at 4:00 a.m. on Saturday, August 5th to pick him up for our four-hour flight from Hamilton, Ontario, to Edmonton, Alberta. There, we'd have a four-hour layover before catching a smaller plane to Grande Prairie, twenty-five miles east of Beaverlodge. His movements were slow and getting anywhere took much longer than when I was alone. Plus, I had to manage his luggage and walker, but it was an honor to do that for him. I was also doing it for me.

The flight to his infancy brought out his inner child.

"I wonder what it would be like to land on those clouds," he said, as we flew high above a field of cotton balls. It was a voice I'd rarely heard, one of pure delight.

"How many fish do you think are in those rivers?" he asked, taking in the wilderness between Edmonton and Beaverlodge from 30,000 feet. It was the same terrain I'd ridden on my motorcycle the summer before. The same wilderness Johann had viewed from the train window ninety-one years ago.

Dad loved to fish. For as long as he could, long after it was safe, he'd go on annual fishing trips with "the guys." Otherwise, he'd trailer his sixteen-foot aluminum boat with the fifty-horse-power outboard motor to nearby Lake Ontario or Lake Erie and head five miles out on the water for the best fishing. He loved it when he could take his grandson Fraser along. Only once did he have to call the Coast Guard to his fishing spot because he couldn't start the boat. The gas line had come off and it was an easy fix.

We'd be staying in our hotel for three nights and using it as our base to explore the area. By the time we got there, we'd been traveling fourteen hours and still needed to go out for dinner. He was up for it, no problem. Unbeknownst to us, strangers who'd sat at the table behind us paid our tab on their way out. What an incredible welcome, and confirmation this trip was meant to be. No obstacles or delays had been thrown at us, not even at the airport!

First thing after breakfast the next morning, we headed to the overgrown cemetery where Johann's remains lay. This time I knew to cross the culvert and follow the rutted path to the back of the grove. Towards the end of his life, Dad had become sentimental and emotional, and missed his father more than ever. Making his memories come alive through my research and questions contributed to these overwhelming feelings. It took my powers of persuasion to convince him not to climb amongst the trees, looking for a grave marker. We both knew it was futile, but that didn't get through to his heart.

Lunch was a traditional Mennonite meal with Lydia Wiens and her granddaughter at her home in Grande Prairie. Lydia's parents had been part of the original Beaverlodge Mennonites. Well-done roast beef, boiled potatoes, and vegetables filled the menu—the same one we'd enjoyed every Sunday on Mom's good china. Lydia had more photos and could fill in sketchy details of Johann, Liese, and Dad's time in Beaverlodge. Dad was in his glory, reveling in the stories as the afternoon wore on.

He had no memories of his home, but his affinity for the land was unmistakable. We could piece his life here together from the probate file. Carol, daughter of the man who'd sold Johann the farm, expected us Monday morning and offered to take us on a guided tour. This was part of her history too, one we could help her bring to life.

Johann and three other families had shared an interest in six quarter-sections, only three of which were next to each other. Thank goodness we had a car that was adept at driving across fields. The first surprise was that the cemetery was larger than I realized. I'd thought the road construction had taken off its western boundary, but the road had bisected the unmarked graveyard. That meant the trees on the west side of the road were part of the cemetery.

I'd deduced from archive entries that Johann's remains lay in the northwest quadrant, so learning that the cemetery extended further west meant his gravesite also lay further west. The municipal airport owned that land, but when we explained our story, they gave us permission to drive across the grounds to the cemetery. This side was just as overgrown as the other, but it was comforting to know we'd narrowed down Johann's resting spot. While Carol tramped through the tangle of vines, shrubs, and tree foliage, searching for any sign of a burial site, I stayed with Dad at the periphery.

I pulled the sacred tobacco from my pocket, unsure of what he'd think of the gratitude tradition I'd adopted, but I'd moved well beyond worrying about his judgment. It was more important to be me.

"It's a gift of gratitude and reverence to God. Your prayer can be silent, or you can blow it into the tobacco and then scatter it or lay it on the ground."

He held out his hand. We'd last shared communion forty-five years ago, in an MB church. It didn't even rank compared to the sacredness we shared under the sky at a derelict cemetery.

A cross-country tour of the six quarter-sections followed.

Carol would ask permission of the landowner, whom she'd know, and they'd allow us in. We used the equipment access trails or, if the harvest was in, drove across the field. Many of the fence lines were gone, the fields consolidated into one, but remnants of evidence often remained. The land doesn't forget her history. Carol showed us where the log house and barns had stood between two quarter-sections, now the middle of a canola field. It's likely the families started life in Canada in a single dwelling, then moved into their own as they could get them built. Shelter for farm animals and implements got first priority. That's how they survived.

We walked on each field, absorbing more of the energy of the land that already lived in us. Later, we had lunch with Carol in downtown Beaverlodge and visited her father in long-term care in Grande Prairie. He and Dad were close in age and may have met as children.

We flew to Calgary, and had lunch with Dad's oldest grand-child, my niece Amanda, who helps manage a chic uptown restaurant. With me following and prepared to catch him, he climbed the flight of stairs to the dining area. He clung to his independence, fueled by pride and joy in seeing his grand-daughter.

There was never time for a *Mittagsschlaf*. We had tracked down an old friend he'd worked with in Ontario and hadn't seen in thirty years. I saw Dad to his friend's condo, then left the men to their friendship. Their heartfelt and emotional parting embrace brought me close to tears. They knew they'd never see each other again on earth.

Dinner was with Charlotte Williams, the woman who'd taken me in after my crash. It was such a joy to introduce these people who'd played significant roles in my quest, but so much emotion was tiring. I returned to the hotel exhausted.

Our next day's 150-mile route, to visit mom's cousin Elvira in

Coaldale, took us right past Fort MacLeod. I wanted to thank Quinton in person for his support, and introduce Dad to this man, a stranger from another culture, who'd taken an interest in my quest.

Quinton asked me how I'd made out and I told him my attempts to engage an Elder had been futile.

"The timing mustn't have been right," I said.

"I just saw an Elder from Siksika walk by. Would you like to speak with him?"

"What do you mean, saw?" I asked. Maybe he'd had a vision or was talking in metaphors. How could this be?

"Standing right over there. Would you like me to see if he'll speak with you?"

"Yes! But I have no more tobacco." I'd given it to Quinton. It didn't matter.

I could not believe it. I had stopped on a whim and an Elder from the Siksika Nation, the exact community where I'd gone to the Pow-wow to seek advice from an Elder, stood there, also visiting. No way in a million years could I have orchestrated everything that had come together in this moment.

Quinton led him over and introduced us to Reverend Sidney (Black), a Blackfoot Elder and Anglican Archdeacon. More shock. Evidently, he'd reconciled the teachings of his culture and Christianity.

I didn't know what to say. I didn't want to ruin this opportunity. I prayed for the right words.

I'd convinced Dad to sit down, while I remained standing. It was a hot day and I was afraid his legs would give out from fatigue. My mind went into overdrive, trying to listen, wondering how I'd remember everything because I couldn't take notes or record it, wanting to say the right words, wanting to be respectful, and not blow this one chance. I'd thought when I'd had the "aha" moment about staying rooted to my own culture that the Indigenous lesson was over.

As succinctly as I could, I explained my quest, about wanting to understand the energy of the land and how it had shaped me, and wanting to address the huge gap in my religious upbringing that had separated me from God, from who I was.

Another shock! I'd never said anything like that in front of Dad. I'd be afraid of his reaction, or hurting his feelings, and the repercussions later, but this was my chance to speak with an Elder. Best be open with him.

Dad sat there agog, rooted to his seat, listening to Reverend Sidney's every word.

Something transformative, unexplainable, happened at that meeting. I remember little of it, other than how kind and compassionate Reverend Sidney was. The strength and assurance of 1,000 warriors emanated through his smooth voice and calm, peaceful demeanor. He told stories from his life, most notably about his calling to the ministry in the Anglican Church. He emanated Presence.

"I could have listened to him all day," said Dad.

Dazed, I thanked Reverend Sidney, and Dad and I got on our way. Elvira expected us for dinner in Coaldale. In the olden days, that car ride, where Dad had a captive audience, would have been prime occasion for a "come to Jesus" talk. It never came up. In fact, I couldn't remember the last time he'd cornered me, years ago in a different life. Since I'd been transparent with him and Mom and had accepted myself, so had they.

As Oriah had said, "You put down the rope. The tug of war was over."

Dinner was as I'd dreamt—*Borscht* with *Zwieback*. Soul food. The visit wouldn't have been complete without Elvira driving us to visit her sons on their farm, where Dad reveled in the agrarian activity. The next morning was another good-bye, likely the last.

Erika Meyer met us in Beisker at the Bauer homestead. Dad was four years old when he left, but he remembered the house and yard. We sat in the parlor he'd once played in and probably gotten underfoot in, listening as he told Erika stories she'd never known about her grandparents. From somewhere in the recesses of his mind, he recited a Bible poem in German that Erika's grandfather had taught him. She didn't understand German either, but that didn't diminish the heart gift Dad delivered.

From Beiseker, Liese and Dad had moved to Namaka when Liese married Peter Jansen. We followed their trail. He dozed in the car and became animated when we got out at the land.

I saw unending fields of grain; he saw the vibrant community that existed here in his time. Each quarter-section farm had had a log house, barns, and granaries, all long since razed. There'd be pigs fattening up to be eaten and cows for milking. A variety of horses used to work the land and pull the wagons, or ridden for transport, would have hung around the barnyard. The schoolhouse where he learned English was down the road just south of the railway tracks, gone except for the poplars that shaded it.

Families visited with each other, children got together to play, and everyone attended regular church services. It took Dad's family seven years to concede they couldn't survive on the proceeds of 160 acres, even without drought and dust storms.

The prairie years set the stage for the rest of his life. Out of necessity, he learned to be frugal and stoic. It's how he cared for his mother and younger siblings, and later raised his own family and successfully managed his fruit farm. Those qualities pervaded his life—how he responded to hardship, handled his finances, and eked out his emotions. They were physical, emotional, and spiritual survival techniques he learned from his parents and passed on to his children.

He didn't blink when I offered him tobacco. He looked forward to it and knew what to do.

Friday evening, we'd been invited to Bill and Laura Cormier's home. I'd last seen them a year earlier during my Ancestor Trail trip when Karen and Richard Reynolds and I had dinner at their home. Bill had lived in the area his whole life but didn't know some of the Namaka stories Dad shared. When Bill picked a stranger from Ontario out of the ditch, he had no idea it would lead to a first-hand account of little-known local history

Saturday, our last day before flying home, had a more casual pace. We were going to the Siksika Nation Fair and Pow-wow. Dad had grown up beside the reserve but had never been to a pow-wow. I didn't recognize any faces from when I'd been there the year before, but I recognized the kindness and the welcome to strangers. Dad insisted he was stronger than he was, and I didn't trust his judgment in that respect enough to leave him alone. He was liable to get up and walk somewhere. Half the time I had to remind him to bring his cane. Two security people saw us trying to figure out how to get him and his walker across the parking field and into the arbor and offered us a VIP lift in their golf cart.

Children in full regalia captivated Dad. He smiled and engaged them and their parents in conversation. It was a side of him I hadn't seen. He stood with the crowd during the entrance parade, watching the sea of color flash and twirl, caught up in the frenetic energy. Something in the air touched him as he stood there, and his eyes welled with tears. I left him alone with his thoughts.

The direct route between Siksika and our hotel on the TCH omitted two powerful landmarks. I wanted to share the energy of my crash site, seven miles southwest of Siksika with Dad. It marked a death of old ways, the ending of a gestation period. At the same time, it signified the birth of the reconnection to my lineage, and a deeper connection to self and to Spirit. This time he stayed in the car while I got out, laid tobacco, and stood there. The ground was uneven, and I didn't want to have to haul him out of that ditch. One of us with a history there was enough.

We made our way back across the countryside on Township Road 205. Once at the hamlet of Arrowwood, I turned north. On this side of the 547 Bridge spanning the now languid Bow River, I parked the car on the shoulder and got out. The blue steel girders matched the sky. Weathered and worn plank flooring invited travelers to cross. Between the car and the bridge, high up on a hydro pole, a raucous osprey defended her nest, calling in her partner for reinforcement. He squawked from the treetops. They didn't want me there. A Blackfoot man in a dark blue pickup who'd crossed from the other side stopped to warn me. "They'll attack you. Be careful."

The bridge was missing a huge section the first time I was here, minutes before my crash. Even now, the ospreys, symbolic of the voices that attempted to keep me in old patterns and beliefs, tried to prevent me from crossing. Now I knew better. The bridge was repaired. I could cross.

After dinner, I left Dad in his room and ventured back alone. I crossed the bridge both times, in each direction. It's easy when it's whole.

A MONTH AFTER RETURNING HOME, I called Dad before leaving for a Horizons Unlimited event three hours north of my home. Living two hours away, I tried to keep in touch with regular phone calls throughout the week. I'd be away for four days and wanted to check in on him before leaving. We'd talked for a while before he revealed he felt sick. He'd had chronic sinus and inner ear problems, but this sounded worse than usual. His doctor was in the next day and he promised to go.

Sunday morning as I packed up my tent, my brother Robert called to let me know he'd called paramedics who'd taken Dad to the hospital via ambulance. He had a serious infection that required treatment with intravenous antibiotics. Dad responded well at first, and they said he'd be able to go home after two or three days. But massive infections take an extraordinary toll on ninety-one-year-old bodies. Sometime over the next few days he suffered a stroke, which affected his balance and ability to swallow. But he was determined to get better. He had to, so he could live on his own and drive again.

He worked diligently at learning to swallow without choking and taking his first tentative steps with a walker. It was the same tenacity he'd used to get his mobility back after breaking his hip less than two years ago. He told his caregivers about our trip, filling in the backstory of the pictures on his bulletin board.

At some point, perhaps when he realized he wouldn't likely recuperate to the point where he'd be able to continue living on his own, his fight for independence took a different tack. He'd been clear. He wasn't going to a long-term care facility.

Dad focused on wrapping up his life. Other than as an infant, for the first time in his life, his role had switched from caregiver to care-receiver. He drifted in and out of lucidity, pulled out his PICC lines, intravenous lines, and catheter repeatedly. He told us he was going to a celebration. He wouldn't need them there. As a family, we wrestled with hard decisions, but his actions amplified his wishes.

For more than two weeks, he danced between worlds, seeing and conversing with beings on the other side. He saw and communicated with his mother, father, and sister Hilda, who'd passed away in 1968, sometimes in *Plautdietsch*.

"Dad, when it's your time to go, I think your father will come and meet you."

"I think so, too," he said.

He had time to say individual good-byes to his family. He was affectionate with my brothers in ways they hadn't seen since early childhood. We had extraordinary moments in which to tell him how much we loved him and appreciated all he'd done for us. His smile came from his heart and lit up his whole countenance. Nursing staff commented on his smile and his glow. There was no fear. There was no death-bed attempt to convert his children. He had transcended fear and knew God.

We had not brought Mom in to see him. In her mind, she was her younger self and often didn't identify with Dad as an elderly man. We didn't want to upset either one of them, but after much debate, we realized they both needed the visit.

As our immediate family stood around the bedside, a mother we hadn't known emerged: the nurse. She was so loving, tender, and comforting. She reassured Dad, held his hand, stroked his arm. To us, she had always shown her love in less demonstrative ways.

Unintentional humor, delivered in all seriousness, dispelled the solemnity. "I need you Ben. I can't drive myself." We all laughed through our tears.

She led our family prayer for healing. If healing meant he wasn't going to get better, then it was time to surrender and let God take him.

"I'm happy, and I'm thankful," said Dad, a whisper in a silent room.

During a quiet afternoon, two days later, while I sat at his bedside, he roused from sleep. "I trust," he said to no one, his voice barely audible, yet stronger than ever.

As heartbreaking as those last days were, they were also days of peace, filled with grace and light. Our family took turns sitting with him. Susan, who lives in Winnipeg, was the only sibling missing. She'd visited three weeks earlier and spent most of her four-day-visit, including nights, with him. John had spent the morning with him on what would be Dad's final day. Dad and I were alone together in the afternoon. The hospital coordinator of spiritual care joined me, each of us on one side of an unresponsive Dad, his breathing regular, but rapid and shallow. We talked about our trip and how the energy of the land had been so healing, how Dad looked forward to seeing Johann again.

Not long after John left, Mary and my niece Andrea, Mark's daughter, came in. Robert arrived as Mary left and stayed as Andrea and I stepped out of the room for a few minutes to use the restroom. On the way out, I brushed Dad's leg with my hand and told him we'd be back in a few minutes. When we returned, he'd passed away, with Robert holding his hand, into the light of the Harvest Moon, fitting for a man who loved the land. He'd finished his earth journey.

Trudy waited in the parking lot until I was ready to leave. We rode through the countryside, the evening air balmy and peaceful. Soft breezes carried the aromatic scent from the grape harvest. The energy of this land, and my ancestors had shaped me into who I'd become. And then they'd shown me who I was.

The road stretched out in front of me.

ACKNOWLEDGMENTS

My deepest gratitude is to Spirit. Thank you for my life, and the ancestors and lands that have informed and shaped me.

Thank you to my parents, Bernhard Klassen Jansen and Margaret Reimer Jansen for joining me on this journey with unconditional love, even before I knew I was preparing for a quest. Thank you for sharing your stories and the stories of our ancestors.

My hunger for stories of my ancestors began a decade ago. Thank you to the aunts and uncles who fed that appetite; those who are still with us: Gertrude Janzen and Cathy Tempest; and those who have passed: Walter (Peewee) Reimer, Ernie Reimer, and Irma Crozier.

To my *Freundschaft*, extended kin, who filled in details and offered hospitality on the Ancestor Trail: Elvira Dueck, Hedy Reimer, Martha Neufeld, Lena Goertzen, Cornelius Klassen, Walter Dueckman, Karl Koop, and the late Henry Dueckman.

Much gratitude to my cousin/sister Judy Willems for helping revive and relive memories from our early days.

Thanks to Barbara Wynd for deciphering and translating

from German, the language of my grandparents' hearts, recordings and letters and journals written in *Sütterlin-Schrift*.

Deepest heartfelt gratitude to Oriah Mountain Dreamer for your guidance, mentorship, and teachings. Your wisdom and inspiration helped illuminate my path of rediscovery.

Thank you to Quinton Crow Shoe, member of the Northern Piikani Blackfoot for your support, advice, and belief in my quest. Thank you to Leon Crane Bear, of the Siksika Nation, for reviewing my final draft.

Gratitude to my teachers at The Four Winds, in particular: Alberto Villoldo, Marcela Lobos, and Chris Prietto. Thank you for passing along ancient teachings and showing me how to dream courageously.

Special thanks to John Colyer, Beryl Colyer, Jim Cote, Gail Grabo, Julie Gorman, Paul Gorman, Graham Amy, Mary Jean Amy, Judy Carrell, Tina Pierson, Pat Cooney, Gilbert Schultz, Alvin Schultz, Ila Sisson, and the late Peter Cole.

I offer deep appreciation to Gordon Berdahl, Research Volunteer with the Alberta Genealogical Society. Your diligence uncovered a time and place that would otherwise have remained buried with my grandfather, Johann Klassen, in Beaverlodge.

Thanks to Peter Letkemann for reading an early edition and offering insights into Mennonite cultural and social history.

Thank you to the Beta Readers who reviewed early drafts and offered astute suggestions: J.R. Alcyone, Alison Argue, Lauranne Bailey, Judy Fachko, Nancy Fithian, Bridget Greer, and Sue Knight.

Thank you to editors Joan Dempsey for helping me see what my heart was asking me to write, Dawna Kemper for refining and tempering my prose, and Diana Fitzgerald Bryden for scrutinizing the final copy. Deep gratitude to Paul H. Smith for the cover design.

ABOUT THE AUTHOR

Niagara native Liz Jansen was born into a German Mennonite culture, the granddaughter of Russian refugees. Since she began riding a motorcycle at age sixteen, she's logged hundreds of thousands of miles of mostly solo riding across Canada and the United States. While Liz enjoys the rugged beauty of Ontario's northern wilderness, she has a particular fondness for the open expanses of the Canadian prairies and Midwestern plains. Liz is a member of the Writers' Union of Canada, the Non-Fiction Authors Association, the Alliance of Independent Authors, and the Independent Book Publishers Association. *Crash Landing* is her third book. She lives in Ontario with her cat, Measha, and Trudy, her Triumph Tiger motorcycle. Find her online at www.lizjansen.com.

ALSO BY LIZ JANSEN

WOMEN, MOTORCYCLES AND THE ROAD TO EMPOWERMENT

LIFE LESSONS FROM MOTORCYCLES

Visit www.lizjansen.com

Blog

Resources

Articles

Newsletter

And more....

Email: mail@lizjansen.com

CPSIA information can be obtained
at www.ICGtesting.com
Printed in the USA
LVHW110303230519
618804LV00003B/3/P

9 781987 853087